A Volume in
Research in Social Issues in Management

Theoretical and Cultural Perspectives on Organizational Justice

THEORETICAL AND CULTURAL PERSPECTIVES ON ORGANIZATIONAL JUSTICE

Edited by
Stephen Gilliland, Dirk Steiner,
and
Daniel Skarlicki

INFORMATION AGE
PUBLISHING

80 Mason Street
Greenwich, Connecticut 06830

Copyright © 2001 Information Age Publishing Inc.

All rights reserved. No part of this publication may be reproduced, stored in a retrieval system, or transmitted, in any form or by any means, electronic, mechanical, photocopying, microfilming, recording or otherwise, without written permission from the publisher.

Printed in the United States of America

CONTENTS

Introduction
Stephen Gilliland, Dirk Steiner, and Daniel Skarlicki   vii

Preface
Stephen Gilliland, Dirk Steiner, and Daniel Skarlicki   ix

Part I.   Psychological Models of Organizational Justice

1. Fairness as Deonance
   Robert Folger   3

2. How Do I Know That's Fair? A Categorization Approach to Fairness Judgments
   Maureen L. Ambrose and Carol T. Kulik   35

3. Fairness Heuristic Theory: Assessing the Information to Which People are Reacting Has a Pivotal Role in Understanding Organizational Justice
   Kees van den Bos   63

4. Are Interactional Justice and Procedural Justice Different? Framing the Debate
   D. Ramona Bobocel and Camilla M. Holmvall   85

Part II.   Understanding Diversity Through Organizational Justice

5. Cultural Influences on Perceptions of Distributive and Procedural Justice
   Dirk D. Steiner   111

6. An Organizational Justice Analysis of Diversity Training
   Stephen W. Gilliland and Cindi Kaufman Gilliland   139

7. Justice in the Culturally Diverse Workplace: The Problems of
   Over and Under Emphasis of Cultural Differences
   Kwok Leung, Steven K. Su, and Michael W. Morris   *161*

8. Intervening "Fairly" in Disputes Among Nationally-Different
   Employees: Is this Possible?
   Debra L. Shapiro and Catherine H. Tinsley   *187*

Part III.   Commentary

9. Doing Justice to Organizational Justice: Forming and
   Applying Fairness Judgments
   Jason A. Colquitt and Jerald Greenberg   *217*

10. Information On Contributing Authors   *243*

INTRODUCTION TO *RESEARCH IN SOCIAL ISSUES IN MANAGEMENT*

Stephen Gilliland, Dirk Steiner, and Daniel Skarlicki

Individuals and organizations are confronted with a great variety of problems beyond questions of productivity and profitability. These problems stem from the realities of the organizational environment at the beginning of this new millennium. For example, downsizing continues to be a readily adopted management tool. Thus, organizational change is the norm for modern organizations, and it often results in perceptions of unfairness and breach of one's psychological contract. Further, discrimination and other employment lawsuits are on the rise. Diversity in the workforce is increasing not only in terms of gender and race, but also in age and generational values. And with a record low unemployment and a strong economy, organizations are struggling to attract and retain the best employees. At the heart of these management trends is a growing realization that effective management requires attention to these social issues in management.

Based on a merging of psychology, sociology, and law into management research, scholars are examining new approaches to effective people management, employee responses to organizational change and decision-making, diversity management, privacy in the workplace, work and family issues, and cross-cultural management. A number of theories have been developed to address these issues, including organizational justice, social exchange, relational demography, and agency theory. Research findings and theories have been applied to many areas of management, such as human resource management, labor relations, service management, and business ethics. Specific applications include employee selection, performance evaluation, compensation, dispute resolution, and layoff implementation.

Until now, research on these issues and theories has been spread across a wide variety of journals and edited books. *Research in Social Issues in Management* provides an integrated source for research and critical thinking on social issues on a managerial level—with people management being the primary focus.

Each volume is thematic in nature and is divided into sections on theory development and applications. *Research in Social Issues in Management* will provide a valuable reference for scholars in management, organizational behavior, and applied psychology. Individual volumes may be adopted for graduate classes in human resource management, organizational behavior, organizational psychology, and social psychology. In addition these topics should be of interest to researchers in other areas of business (e.g., behavioral decision making, marketing and management information systems), law, and the social sciences (e.g., sociology, philosophy, and criminology).

Contributing authors of *Research in Social Issues in Management* represent a mixture of leading scholars and rising new experts, as we believe that innovation in theory and research can come from any level of scholar. We also strive for global representation and in each volume attempt to include authors from academic communities outside North America. Manuscripts are both solicited and unsolicited and all papers are peer reviewed. Authors interested in submitting a paper for editorial consideration are encouraged to contact one of the editors. We believe that this series will serve as a quality resource for the fast-growing community of social scientists who study social issues in management. We wish you a warm welcome to this new series!

Stephen W. Gilliland
Dirk D. Steiner
Daniel P. Skarlicki
Series Editors

PREFACE

Stephen Gilliland, Dirk Steiner, and Daniel Skarlicki

At the 1998 annual conference of the Society for Industrial and Organizational Psychology, we organized a roundtable discussion session titled "Innovating organizational justice: Cultural, value, and stakeholders' perspectives." We were impressed by the high level of discussion that this session generated and decided to try to continue the discussion in a conference devoted to these issues. In the summer of 1999, approximately 20 scholars from seven nations met for two days in Nice, France. The theme of the "International Roundtable" on organizational justice was "Innovating research on organizational justice." The format of the meeting allowed for extensive discussion of each of the papers that were presented.

A strong feeling that emerged from this meeting was that organizational justice research has much to contribute to our understanding of people at work. Further, our current research on organizational justice and the application of justice to managerial issues has in some ways been limited by the confines of our academic journals. The papers presented and discussed at the Nice roundtable clearly extended scholarly thinking in new and exciting directions. We invited a subset of the authors who presented their research at this meeting to submit their papers for review for the first volume of our newly developed series *Research in Social Issues in Management*. All papers were reviewed independently by organizational justice scholars.

In keeping with our mission in this series to develop both theories and application we have divided the chapters into two sections. The first section addresses theories of organizational justice and specifically focuses on psychological models of organizational justice. Research in organizational justice has pursued a number of constructs, including distributive, procedural, and interactional justice. In addition to debating the number and labels for these constructs, scholars have related perceptions of organizational justice to a variety of attitudinal and behavioral outcomes. Additionally, justice constructs have been applied to a variety of issues in human resource management including personnel selection, performance appraisal, compensation, dispute resolution, and downsizing. Unfortunately, relatively less attention has been devoted to developing theories of organizational justice. The theories that are discussed in organizational justice research often seem to be subordinate to discussion of constructs and relationships.

In an effort to bring new ideas and enthusiasm to theory development in organizational justice, we have included four chapters that take steps toward developing theories of organizational justice. All four chapters approach theory development from a psychological perspective. Each chapter takes the current state of organizational justice research and theory development in new and innovative directions.

The first chapter in the theory section is written by Rob Folger and is titled "Fairness as Deonance." In this chapter, Folger suggests that organizational justice researchers have become too preoccupied with self-interest-based motives of fairness and have lost sight of how fairness relates to morality. Using a unique and powerful approach to theory development, Folger proposes a hypothetical theory called "*Deonance Theory.*" Doenance is based on the Greek root, *deon*, and refers to obligations or duties. By using the thought experiment of a hypothetical theory, the chapter explores questions regarding what a theory of fairness should attempt to accomplish. Issues addressed include the discussion of a pluralistic set of motives that underlie fairness, and how different "types" of organizational justice have a number of commonalities when considered from the perspective of these underlying motives.

Upon reading this chapter, it is clear, that without actually proposing a complete theory, Folger has outlined the core elements of a theory of justice. This chapter is interesting both in what it is proposing for organizational justice theory and in the new approach it demonstrates for theory development in general. We can envision the use of "hypothetical" or "mythical" theories becoming an accepted process for theory development in management literature.

In the second chapter, Maureen Ambrose and Carol Kulik address the little-researched topic of how people as information processors make judgments about the fairness or unfairness of procedures. They pose three essential questions that underscore the importance of cognitive processing in justice judgments. First, they ask whether some procedural rules or aspects of procedures are more central than others to determining whether a procedure is viewed as fair or unfair. Second, they explore whether the particular domain to which the procedure is applied moderates the importance of these different rules or aspects of procedures. That is, the aspects of a procedure that make us conclude that a selection practice is fair may not be the same as the aspects of a performance appraisal system that lead to it being perceived as fair. And finally, Ambrose and Kulik wonder about the possibility that various individual differences will also moderate the importance of the different procedural rules in making judgments of procedural fairness/unfairness.

The chapter by Ambrose and Kulik then analyzes these three questions by applying cognitive categorization theory. In effect, they propose that we have categories with prototypes concerning what fair procedures are in different contexts. Some elements of the categories are more important than others for determining fairness judgments. Furthermore, categories are organized hierarchically, and our attention can be directed at different times to more superordinate or subordinate levels in the hierarchy. Finally, Ambrose and Kulik propose that the novice versus expert distinction may be an important individual difference variable which could be responsible for differences in the way individuals make judgments about the fairness of procedures. Ambrose and Kulik give clear suggestions for how cognitive categorization can be applied to the process of making fairness judgments. We think that this chapter has great potential to further our understanding of cognitive processing in fairness judgments.

In the third chapter, Kees van den Bos also addresses cognitive processing issues by pointing out clearly that judgments of fairness depend greatly on the information available to us at the time when we make such judgments. He summarizes research from four experiments that show explicitly that less relevant information will influence our judgments if more relevant information is not at our disposition. His results illustrate the necessity of analyzing the information at hand for understanding why people make the judgments they do. These results have important theoretical implications for understanding cognitive processing of justice-related information. They may also have important practical applications—they point out what additional information we may need to provide to people so that they can make appropriate judgments of fairness. For example, frequently, social comparison information is not available to people although it is frequently the most important. In addition, the rigor of Van den Bos' experimental approach to addressing these issues is valuable because of the precise answers it brings to important questions of fairness judgments. We hope that other researchers will be inspired to apply similar levels of rigor and use the experimental approach to clarify questions of causality in organizational justice research.

In the final chapter on theory development, Ramona Bobocel and Camille Holmvall address an issue that is of growing importance to organizational justice research: Is interactional justice better conceptualized as a sub-component of procedural justice, or is it more meaningful for researchers to distinguish between procedural and interactional justice and treat them as separate constructs. They argue that this issue is critical because it can potentially hinder the advancement of the field. The authors explore this debate by asking four basic questions regarding construct validity in organizational behavior (Schwab, 1980): (a) Is there a basis for clear theoretical definition separating the two constructs? (b) Can the two forms of justice be meaningfully distinct at the operational level? (c) Do the two forms of justice differentially explain variance in their consequences? and (d) Do they have different antecedents? The authors review the existing literature on organizational justice in search of answers to each of these four questions. Although Bobocel and Holmvall conclude that the evidence is mixed, they offer several suggestions for future research directions that could contribute to resolving this debate.

The second section of this volume addresses applied issues related to social issues in management and specifically examines issues of diversity. In this section, labeled "Understanding Diversity through Organizational Justice," four chapter address different aspects of managing culturally diverse workplaces. Cultural diversity and multinational workforces have become the norm in many organizations. Managing employees with different backgrounds, values, and communication patterns has presented widespread management challenges. The authors of the chapters in this section all suggest that organizational justice concepts provide a valuable tool for understanding cultural diversity.

In the first chapter, Dirk Steiner presents a model of cultural influence on perceptions of distributive and procedural justice. Why do individuals of different cultures view similar situations differently? Steiner suggests that our expectations play a major role in determining how we perceive situations to be fair or unfair. Further, cultural values and attitudes shape and determine our expectations. Steiner expands upon most cross-cultural research in this area by considering 13 dimensions of culture that are relevant for understanding perceptions of fairness. He discusses how each of these dimensions of culture can influence expectations regarding distributive and procedural justice. Beyond the valuable research suggestions summarized in Steiner's model, this chapter provides a contribution for any research studying cross-cultural issues in the expanded model of cultural dimensions.

The second chapter in this section addresses the practical issue of training people to be more sensitive to differences in values and communication styles that result from diversity in the workplace. Stephen and Cindi Gilliland provide an overview of diversity training and show that the negative reactions it frequently produces can be understood through organizational justice concepts. They propose a number of interesting, testable research propositions, first for applications of organizational justice to training in general and then to the context of diversity training more specifically. Beyond the utility of these propositions to researchers in the field of organizational training, their analysis provides a number of ideas that will be useful to individuals who currently design and conduct diversity training programs. Considerations of justice should allow training practitioners to avoid a number of the potential pitfalls inherent in this type of training.

Kwok Leung, Steven Su, and Michael Morris highlight an important dilemma for scholars and managers regarding the challenges that diversity brings to justice in the workplace. On the one hand, fair treatment could be defined in terms of treating everyone the same despite the presence of different cultures among employees (universalist approach). On the other hand, justice might be better served by emphasizing and acknowledging the many ways that culture can explain differences in employees' attitudes and behavior (particularist approach). The first approach advocates the formulation of organizational policies without regard to race, whereas the second approach calls for an explicit consideration of culture in formal personnel procedures. Leung et al. argue that the merits of debating which approach is right is misguided, and they explore potential problems of each of these extremes. Specifically, the authors consider the relevance of these two approaches with regard to (a) understanding other people's behavior, (b) resource allocation decisions, and (c) career management. In addition to providing a well-articulated discussion of the issues, the authors argue for a contingency approach to reap the benefits and minimize the potential costs of diversity, and they provide some important suggestions for future research and managerial practice.

In the final chapter on understanding diversity through organizational justice, Debra Shapiro and Catherine Tinsley highlight that procedural justice can be defined differently for people from different nations. Given that a large amount of a manager's time is spent intervening in disputes among organizational members, an important question is how might a third party intervene in a way that enhances the likelihood that procedural justice will be maintained? Research on this issue has often studied U.S. participants, and consisted of third-parties who were authority-figures. The American workforce, however, is no longer all-American, and dispute resolution has become the responsibility of members of self-managed work teams (i.e., peers).

Shapiro and Tinsley provide a review of the research literature regarding the extent to which non-U.S. as well as U.S. disputants perceive procedural justice as fair. Specifically, they examine cases where: (a) the dispute resolution procedure gives the disputants outcome control in addition to process control; (b) the third-party is a peer rather than an authority-figure; (c) the third-party shares nationality with only one of the disputants; and (d) all parties involved in the dispute resolution procedure— each disputant and the third party—are from different nations. The authors provide several reasons to explain that national differences between disputants and third parties can impede a universal experience of procedural justice. They offer several possible remedies for intervening "fairly" for all disputants in these situations.

As mentioned earlier, our aim with *Research in Social Issues in Management* is to present collections of papers that address common themes associated with theory development or applications. In order to help identify and reinforce these themes in this and future volumes, we will invite scholars to prepare a commentary chapter that reexamines the issues discussed in the prior chapters. For the current volume, Jason Colquitt and Jerry Greenberg have prepared a chapter titled "Doing Justice to Organizational Justice: Forming and Applying Fairness Judgments." In this chapter, they offer an integration of the first five chapters into one model that captures why and how people form justice evaluations. This integration provides a unique perspective on the complimentary nature of these chapters. Colquitt and Greenberg then apply this integrative model to the final three chapters that examine practical issues associated with managing diversity. Specifically, Colquitt and Greenberg address whether the integrative model offers unique insights and understanding for these issues of diversity. They conclude their chapter with a discussion of the tradeoffs between complexity and parsimony in theories of organizational justice.

We believe the chapters in this volume represent real innovation in the development of theories of organizational justice and the application of organizational justice theories to understanding cultural diversity. We hope you agree.

As with any effort of this nature, there are many contributors behind the scenes responsible for its success and to whom we owe a debt of gratitude. In particular, the format and organization of the conference that took place in Nice in 1999 resulted from input and exchanges with Jean-Léon Beauvois and Russell Cropanzano. The conference also received financial aid from a number of sponsors, and we acknowledge the collaboration of Hélène Masson-Maret for her help in identifying some of these sources. Thus, we owe profound thanks to the Faculté des Lettres, Arts, et Sciences Humaines and the Laboratoire de Psychologie Expérimentale et Quantitative of the Université de Nice-Sophia Antipolis, the Eller College of Business and Public Administration of the University of Arizona, the City of Nice, and the Conseil Général des Alpes-Maritimes for their financial participation. Finally, we thank Sylvie Guirard, Sandra Maheux, and Isabelle Milhabet for their help in coordinating the activities during the conference.

Stephen W. Gilliland
Dirk D. Steiner
Daniel P. Skarlicki
Series Editors

PART I

PSYCHOLOGICAL MODELS OF ORGANIZATIONAL JUSTICE

CHAPTER 1

FAIRNESS AS DEONANCE

Robert Folger

ABSTRACT

If fairness is more than self-interested rationalization, and moral injunctions indeed imply obligations as suggested by the Greek root, *deon*, then the study of organizational justice should look for evidence of moral commitments to fairness that rise above mere self-interest. I argue that we will be prepared to know where to look for such evidence if we were to have a "deontic" theory of fairness, and I try to outline what such a theory would look like. Specifically, I discuss the need to understand fairness based on a pluralistic set of motives (not just self-interest or altruism). From this perspective, I then discuss the following issues that have received considerable attention in organizational justice: (a) the differences between satisfaction and fairness, (b) the interaction between processes and outcomes, and (c) the similarities and differences between distributive, procedural, and interactional justice. Although deonance is not yet a theory of organizational justice, the concepts and issues discussed in this chapter provide a foundation upon which such a theory may be developed.

INTRODUCTION

In a recent *Social Justice Research* editorial, Leo Montada (1998) criticized rational choice theory and its assumption of self-interest as the underlying motive for all behavior. As Montada argued, "the scientific community devoted to research on justice issues . . . needs a reassurance about the prescriptive nature of justice" (1998, p. 79). "Justice is an ought," Montada added, "an end in itself, not merely a means to maximize personal utilities" (p. 79).

This chapter expands Montada's theme. I believe that addressing justice as a prescriptive ought has advantages beyond combating the dangers of rational choice theory, although that goal is also quite important. Along with Montada, I think that the study of justice has not paid enough attention to what Heider (1958) called the "ought force" of motivation involving moral concerns.

Somewhere along the road of theory and research, those of us who study fairness made a wrong turn: We've continued the search for phenomena related to fairness, but we've lost sight of how fairness relates to morality. We're not yet hopelessly lost, but it's going to take us longer to get where we want to go if we continue on some of the paths we've taken so far. I don't have a road map or compass guaranteed to alleviate this problem, but I will offer some preliminary observations about this state of affairs.

I'll couch these remarks in the context of a hypothetical (or at least not-yet fully developed) theory of fairness-related morality called *deonance*. The theory of deonance should be reminiscent of reactance and cognitive dissonance if explained in the intended manner. All three concepts have the same basic type of orientation, for example, and they share many features in common.

"Deonance theory" would purport to explain a category of phenomena called *deontic reactions*. These are morally based reactions such as the experience of righteous indignation sometimes said to accompany perceptions of injustice. The etymological root common to the theory term and the phenomena's term is the Greek *deon*, referring to obligation or duty. In essence, deontic phenomena stem from moral grounds for regulating interpersonal conduct, which leads to negative social sanctions for interpersonal transgressions. In that regard, deontic phenomena include reactions to perceived unfairness. A theory of deonance would explain (a) why people care about fairness, (b) when and why they perceive something to be unfair; and (c) how, when, and why people react to perceived unfairness in particular ways.

If we have lost our way and need to get reoriented, we should consider the destinations we might hope to reach by following a different path. The hypothetical theory of deonance whose outlines I will sketch serves as a placeholder version of theories that might lead us to those destinations. They represent conclusions we might be able to justify if we had a theory that provided a sufficient rationale for such conclusions. For that reason, I begin by listing a set of such conclusions briefly. I explore them further after outlining the nature of deonance.

First, however, let me indicate how this approach contrasts with the directions we've taken previously. A theory of deonance should aim to be both parsimonious and integrative, even though those two requirements sometimes tend to pull in opposite directions. Parsimonious theories do not use more concepts than necessary, meaning that they use as few concepts as possible. Integrative theories explain as many phenomena as possible. The more phenomena to be explained, of course, the harder it is not to include additional concepts in the full set of explanations. The theory of cognitive dissonance appealed to a very minimal set of core concepts, however, and yet it explained a vast array of observations—while also predicting previously unobserved phenomena whose existence was subsequently confirmed. The study of fairness would progress by leaps and bounds if it aspired to develop such theories.

Goals for a Theory of Fairness

What should a theory of fairness try to accomplish? Below is my list. As I said, the items on the following list are described at this point only briefly. I list them in advance of discussing deonance, however, because the deonance coverage of them cannot proceed in a point-by-point or linear manner. Take this as a preview of coming attractions.

1. A deontic approach to fairness should differ from an egoistic one that reduces all behavior to self-interest (what ethicists and philosophers call egoistic explanations). In particular, deontic explanations account for human behaviors in terms of motives whose aims include a reference to the states or conditions of other people or objects (e.g., the collective welfare of a nation, of the human race, or even of the earth as a biosphere). Egoistic explanations acknowledge only the motivational force of aims that refer to the self and to states or conditions of the self. A deontic approach acknowledges a pluralistic range of motives and stipulates that aims can include references regarding end states or conditions of both the self and others. In fact, fairness becomes an aspect of morality beyond mere self-interest only when the interests and welfare of others are taken into account along with one's own interests and welfare.

2. Once a clear-cut distinction differentiates deontic motives from those governed purely by self-interest, the same type of explanatory approach helps clarify questions about differences between satisfaction and fairness.

3. Because deontic motives transcend those aims having only to do with states of the self, they provide a basis for extending the scope of fairness beyond kith and kin. They also transcend good will evoked only by expectations of mutual reciprocity over time. For that reason, deontic motivation helps account for fairness concerns shown among strangers engaged in one-shot encounters, as well as fairness responses displayed by neutral, third-party spectators who have no direct stake in a given instance of injustice.

4. Deontic motives include others' welfare in the aims pursued. Distributive, procedural, and interactional justice reflect three different ways

of thinking about others' welfare. Despite their differences, these aspects of welfare also share this common feature (viz., of referring to states or conditions of welfare). For that reason, deonance theory provides a new way of conceptualizing how distributive, procedural, and interactional justice are alike in one important sense. That perspective allows for greater integration across these otherwise disparate categories.

5. To the extent that distributive, procedural, and interactional justice share a common reference to others' states or conditions of being (welfare), that same commonality makes problematic the prospects for those three forms of justice to interact with one another. Deonance theory, therefore, looks to another source of explanation in accounting for such moderator effects—a source somewhat orthogonal to the traditional interaction of Process x Outcome involving measures or manipulations of those variables in such terms as procedural and distributive justice.[1] This source is moral accountability, which involves attributions about intentions.

DEONANCE: AN INTRODUCTION

It is hard to define the central term in a theory not yet conceptualized, so I won't give a formal definition of deonance per se. To parallel the theories of reactance and dissonance, however, implies (a) a set of motivational consequences likely to follow from (b) an experienced psychological state. Reactance theory, for example, outlined a set of motivational consequences expected when "behavioral freedoms" were threatened or lost. In parallel fashion, deonance theory might describe the motivational consequences instigated when people react to others who violate or attempt to violate, willingly and with presumed impunity, the moral norms of interpersonal conduct that observers feel should not be violated. Presumably the motivational state of deonance influences reactions such as by creating a desire to ensure that the violator or attempted violator does not "get away with it Scot free"—that is, a desire to see that people are held accountable for actions potentially jeopardizing the well-being of others, showing disregard for moral injunctions commonly held sacred, and so on (cf. Folger & Cropanzano, 1998; in press, on "fairness theory" in relation to accountability).

Similarly, the nature of the threatened or violated code of conduct might be clarified by reference to such concepts as *injunctive norms*, which "specify what people approve and disapprove within the culture and motivate action by promising social sanctions for normative or counternormative conduct" (Reno, Cialdini, & Kallgren, 1993, p. 104). For that matter, reactance theory described behavioral freedoms as "acts that are realistically possible" (Brehm, 1966, p. 3)—about which an individual has come to believe "by experience, by general custom, or by formal agreement, that he may engage in them" (p. 4). A theory of deonance, which concerns threatened or violated norms regarding perceived moral duties and obligations about interpersonal conduct, might thus be viewed as addressing actions a person believes that others should *not* feel free to undertake. Deonance theory, therefore, would have implications concerning motivationally instigated impulses of *retributive justice* (fairness of punishment; cf. Hogan & Emler, 1981; Miller & Vidmar, 1981) directed toward those who seemingly feel free to undertake such actions, despite society's having tried to inculcate a sense of obligation not to exercise that freedom. Just as reactance involves desires to reinstate or restore lost or threatened freedoms, deonance would involve desires to re-affirm—in a variety of ways (e.g., by imposing punitive as well as compensatory damages on a wrongdoer)—the validity of moral norms considered appropriate for governing interpersonal conduct.

Rather than a formal definition of deonance, let me instead illustrate it in terms borrowed heavily from Heider's (1958) discussion of *ought* as the apposite concept. Note first that Heider introduced this concept by writing that "people . . . are accountable according to certain standards (*ought*)" (p. 17). Elsewhere he identified these as "standards independent of the individual's wishes" (p. 219). Deonance refers to an experience aroused when motivated by moral considerations. Morality refers to ethical standards that are independent of, and hence capable of existing alongside, pure self-interest alone ("the individual's wishes"). Deonance theory assumes that people try to govern their own interpersonal conduct, and that of others, on grounds of moral accountability. People hold one another mutually accountable for fair conduct.

The role of moral accountability has sometimes been missing from discussions of justice, especially when a concern for fairness has been portrayed as reducible to some form of self-interest or when justice is said to be merely self-interest in disguise (as a useful aspect to impression management). In regarding moral accountability as a motive in competition with motives that relate only to pure self-interest, deonance theory addresses questions concerning "how we come to feel that another person ought to do something, and what effects this feeling has" (Heider, 1958, p. 19). What Heider called "a situation in which we feel that something 'ought to happen'" (p. 218) is one that involves "experiencing the tension of an ought" (p. 219). It is in this sense of motivational tension that deonance theory shares a tension-reduction character with the theories of reactance and dissonance.

Other Heiderian phrases round out the description of this tension state. Here I simply list a few such phrases, as follows, to capture the flavor of Heider's message: "the experience of should," "acting in accordance with . . . [an] implicit injunction," "acting in a manner . . . identified with the right," "ought requiredness" (p. 219). Heider also quoted a passage from Asch's social psychology textbook about how people feel when "action was called for in a given case" (Asch, 1952, p. 357). In such situations, "our apprehension of the facts and their relations, or of the need of the situation, laid a claim on us to improve or to remedy it, to act in a manner fitting to it" (1952, p. 357). The force of that ought-requiredness claim provides the motivational tension experienced when human actions do not fit moral codes of interpersonal conduct.

Heider also described ought in terms of several properties, including one I will call *transcendence*. As Heider put it, "In the case of ought . . . it is not a particular somebody that is felt to . . . command people to do x, but some suprapersonal objective order" (p. 219). In other words, principles of morality regarding interpersonal conduct transcend the self-interest of any given individual. This transcendent, suprapersonal quality implies that "oughts are impersonal," as if "established by objective requirements" (p. 219). When people have the conviction that they ought to take a certain type of action, or that someone else ought to do so, they feel as if they have recognized a feature of the world. They respond as if it were "a requirement on the part of some suprapersonal order" and had "the validity of objective existence" (p. 219). This transcendent feature helps explain such effects as fairness to strangers in one-shot encounters.

Conceptions of fairness grounded in deonance as a motive would improve descriptions, predictions, and explanations of behavior. Let me begin my account, therefore, with an example of data that I think existing theories of fairness do not explain very well. Because deonance is thus far a fictional theory that merely alludes to a sense of moral requiredness or obligation, at least the following example will reveal the types of data such a theory would attempt to explain.

An Illustrative Deontic Effect (Kahneman, Knetsch, & Thaler, 1986)

Kahneman et al. tested whether people would willingly sacrifice a modest amount ($1) for the sake of fairness. In the first part of that study, students indicated a choice of how to divide $20 with an anonymous classmate who could not change the decision. The decision maker's only options were to designate (a) $18 for himself or herself and $2 for the classmate, or (b) $10 for both of them. (They knew that because of limited funds, only a randomly selected 10% of all such student-pairs would actually be paid as designated by the chosen option.) The following describes one of several closely related versions of the second part of this study:

> After completing the first part of the study, the same students were given another question. They were told they would be matched with two students who had not been selected to be paid in the first part of the experiment. One of these students had taken the $18 (called U for uneven) while the other had taken $10 (E). A subject was then asked to choose between the following.

He could take $6 for himself and give $6 to U, or he could take $5 for himself and give $5 to E. Thus the question came down to whether subjects would be willing to pay a dollar to split money with a stranger who had been generous, rather than split with a stranger who had been greedy. A clear majority, 74%, elected to take the smaller reward in order to split with E. (Thaler, 1992, p. 25)

Other versions included one in which the study's first part was not actually conducted, but students thought that it had already taken place in another class. All versions gave similar results.

Explaining Deontic Effects: Selvishness and Bounded Autonomy

Later I will return to the Kahneman et al. study by reporting follow-up data collected with a colleague (Turillo & Folger, in press). For now let me simply mention that we have found the basic effect to be quite robust under conditions in which the student participants can act confidently with assurance of total anonymity. We collect names only on consent sheets that these students pass back to us before receiving the materials for the study itself. Those materials have double-stubbed lottery tickets with them; half of each numbered ticket stays stapled to the pages of material, and the participants keep a correspondingly numbered stub as their basis for receiving payment later. We even reassure students that they can give the stub to a trusted friend who collects the money, so that they need not appear in person (in case they think they might be identified by sight). Their willingness to sacrifice money for punishing unfairness and rewarding fairness, therefore, earns them no social recognition for doing the right thing—just as a failure to do so carries no threat of negative sanction. Such evidence suggests that a concern for fairness acts as an end in itself, rather than as a means to some other end involving an enhancement of self-interest.

Accounting for such effects in terms of an independent motive concerned about fairness as its aim, of course, says very little about the motive itself. To round out the picture of that motive, let me introduce two concepts related to deonance: *selvishness* and *bounded autonomy*.[2]

Selvishness

Deontic phenomena differ from hedonic or egoistic phenomena. Trying to understand fairness in terms of egoistic or hedonic reactions is one of the wrong turns that we who study justice have sometimes made. If we want to avoid some of the dead-ends and cul-de-sacs to which hedonistic and egoistic explanations lead, we can begin by learning some valuable lessons from a recent book on altruism (Sober & Wilson, 1998), called *Unto*

Others. Essentially that book articulates a compelling case for a pluralistic approach to motives rather than a monistic one. Egoism and hedonism (a special case of egoism; cf. Folger, 1998; Sober & Wilson, 1998) are examples of monistic approaches.

Egoistic explanations account for behavior by positing the pursuit of egoistic ends as the only motivational drive in human beings. A person who pursues nothing but egoistic ends has only those motives whose aims refer to a state or condition of that person (e.g., a desire to maximize his/her personal welfare; a desire to be the first astronaut landing on Mars). Deontic explanations, in contrast, are not monistic in the sense of claims about only one possible type of motive; rather, such explanations conform to the possibility of multiple motives (of varying strengths) both within each person and across humans as a species.

Deontic explanations have to be pluralistic by their very nature, because the sense of duty or obligation to which they refer is one involving a counterweight to egoism. A deontic motive involves a desire for a type of end state juxtaposed with an end state referring to another person. An altruistic motive is a type of deontic motive, for example, and an altruistic motive refers to an end state desired for some person or persons other than you. Deonance theory claims that fairness concerns are like altruism in that they refer not only to desired conditions for oneself but also to conditions desired for another person or persons.

How, then, does fairness differ from altruism? If egoism says "me first and only," and altruism says "you first and only," then a deontically based motive for fairness would say "neither me nor you only—and sometimes you first, but sometimes me first (it depends on what's fair)." Among such motives, only pure altruism omits any reference to the self in its aims. Egoistic aims refer only to the self, and the deontic aim of fairness *includes* both self and other(s). In principle, a person could feel the competing tugs of egoistic aims and deontic aims of altruism simultaneously—or could feel such tugs to varying degrees under different sets of circumstances, sometimes in more-or-less equal competition with one another and sometimes with one motive clearly dominating all others.

I call this pluralistic version of motives an account of *selvishness* as opposed to selfishness. Pure selfishness involves aims that refer only to end states or conditions of the self and are considered worthy to pursue even at the expense of others, whereas deontic aims (e.g., of fairness or altruism) include or refer to interests and welfare beyond the self. Nonetheless, all such motives—whether purely selfish or deontically toned—involve the self as the one possessing the motive. The purely selfish person has no regard for others at all. In the extreme, such a person is also known as a sociopath. The "selvish" person, in contrast, has some concern for others along with the degree of self-concern that even those others would think it reasonable for him or her to have. In other words, people possess multiple desires, motives, and concerns, as if different "selves" would be more (or less) satisfied depending on which of those aims were more fully realized. Extending this figure of speech, we could say that sometimes a "committee of the mind" must decide on tradeoffs among interests in a fashion not unlike a political process.

Bounded Autonomy

The selvishness of multiple and potentially competing motives is not unlike a political process in another respect, namely that the "governance" of these interests (ruling among them) requires that one of them cannot hold absolute sway. Rather than complete freedom, the autonomy of each is "bounded" by the demands and legitimate claims of the other motives as competing aims. To have one's autonomy bounded, as when constrained by self-restraint and by social obligation and pressure, is to believe that a system of checks-and-balances should govern one's conduct—rather than feeling free to pursue whimsical aims in an arbitrary and capricious fashion. Indeed, to conceive of autonomy as something legitimate to bind (such as by self-imposed limits set by socially accepted codes of interpersonal conduct) is part and parcel of the very notion that behavior should be normatively governed, directed, and regulated (including on the basis of self-regulation). Recognizing the appropriateness of having your autonomy limited is implied by accepting moral obligations as legitimate grounds for being held accountable regarding your conduct toward others. Our autonomy can also be bound or limited on other grounds (e.g., we cannot fly by flapping our arms), but deontic norms—obligations about interpersonal conduct—constitute a significant source of limits to personal freedom.

This concept of *bounded autonomy* obviously mimics Simon's (1957) related concept of bounded rationality. Whereas bounded rationality refers to limitations based on human fallibility, however, bounded autonomy refers not only to inevitable limitations but also to non-inevitable restrictions that can be accepted (or at least tolerated) to varying degrees. For example, no one finds obeying the voice of conscience an inevitability. Instead, applying self-restraint rather than yielding to an egoistic impulse—bounding the autonomy of egoism with an offsetting attention to fairness, for example—often requires considerable willpower.

We all know that such willpower—indeed, sometimes any willpower at all—can be difficult to muster. I suspect that for that very reason, the commitment to fairness requires a considerable amount of shoring up. In particular, the prospect of negative social sanctions for misconduct—sanctions administered impersonally or "suprapersonally" by the moral community on a collective basis—helps maintain a stronger commitment to fairness. Sometimes we need the added force of outside pressure to help protect us from ourselves (and our baser motives), much like Ulysses needed to have his crew tie him to the mast lest he yield to the Sirens' charms. The concept of bounded autonomy, therefore, views fairness not only as an endorsement of what's right but also as a recognition of social responsibility for correcting others about what's wrong. Commitment to the social compact instills in each of us a certain antipathy toward unfairness, and the emotional capacity to experience moral outrage and righteous indignation, even when the specific act of wrongdoing has no direct implications inimical to our personal welfare. For similar reasons, we are appalled at the very thought of genocide, even when the race threatened with genocide is not our own. Such reactions rise above self-interest in ways that current theories of fairness do a poor job of accommodating.

IMPLICATIONS OF FAIRNESS AS DEONANCE

As I promised earlier, I now want to illustrate fairness-as-deonance further by outlining a research agenda. In each of the following sections, I refer to certain ideas as if their validity were already known—that is, as if deducing them from deontic assumptions were trivial as a means of generating hypotheses, and as if empirical support for them already existed. This, too, is fiction. First, as I've said, no theory of deonance yet exists. Second, it is not clear that the following implications would necessarily flow from such a theory in a deductively logical fashion. Third, as should be obvious by now, research has not been designed for the express purpose of testing such hypotheses. Rather, the following sections represent something like a vision for the future. Like an exercise in which people imagine living 10 years in the future and reflecting back on what had happened over the (imagined) past 10 years, these sections reflect thoughts about what I hope fairness theory and research will some day achieve.

Distinguishing Dissatisfaction from Perceived Unfairness

If fairness does not reduce to self-interest, then satisfaction must differ from fairness—but how? Some have raised this question particularly in light of reviews that collapse that distinction, such as the review of the Process x Outcome interaction by Brockner and Wiesenfeld (1996). Those authors suggested that essentially the same interaction (see note 1) exists whether between procedural justice and distributive justice, for example, or between procedural justice and outcome satisfaction. At first blush, there might seem to be some inconsistency between the following two statements: (a) It is perfectly reasonable to combine the outcome side of that interaction (e.g., unfair outcome vs. dissatisfying outcome) and (b) an important distinction exists between unjust outcomes and dissatisfying outcomes. Let me try to reconcile those apparently contradictory statements in light of a deonance-theory approach to fairness.

Events can produce experienced dissatisfaction in many ways. Some events are relativistic and highly subjective in their evaluative implications for the perceiver, like "beauty in the eye of the beholder." A financial gain of $20 million hardly seems "dissatisfying" on objective grounds, for example, or even on relative grounds when compared to a status-quo position of no gain—yet the directors of huge international conglomerates might be extremely dissatisfied with annual gains of $20 million if those fall far short of market projections, or competitors' gains, or any other yardstick that would cause financial analysts to call for downgrading the conglomerate's stock. Other sources of dissatisfaction are far less relativistic and subjective, of course, such as the experience of pain produced when a person's hand touches a hot burner. The latter example also illustrates that dissatisfaction need not differ from unfairness in terms of severity or intensity of emotional reaction. After all, an intensely emotional reaction to severe pain might accompany a form of punishment (e.g., having a hand removed by a sword) even when the punished person fully accepts the punishment as fair (e.g., when the offender is a member of a religious order stipulating such a punishment for the crime, and the offender fully recognizes and admits his or her guilt).

Let us refer to any of the various forms of dissatisfaction as personally experienced pain, ignoring differences among experiences that obviously do matter and that, in fact, often lead to phenomenologically distinct experiences (and possibly to qualitatively distinct emotions otherwise worth labeling with separate terms). How would unfairness differ from any such pain?

A deonance perspective suggests one simple answer: If the pain is the person's own fault, then the only potential question of fairness would involve mismatches between the degree of suffering and the degree of wrongfulness associated with being at fault. The punishment should fit the crime, in other words, meaning that even a guilty person can receive too much punishment and thereby suffer pain that is not only dissatisfying but also unfair. That same amount of punishment (and thus an equally dissatisfying degree of pain), however, could be totally fair so long as the suffering matched the wrongdoing in fair measure.

Having to suffer the consequences of one's own actions does not seem unfair, therefore, unless the suffering grossly exceeds the imprudence of the action. This way of distinguishing between dissatisfaction (pain) and unfairness has already begun to involve issues regarding the moral accountability of conduct—in other words, conduct subject to evaluation in light of moral standards, including those concerning interpersonal duties and obligations or injunctions (i.e., deontic norms). Such standards of conduct imply needing to be responsible for what happens as a result of one's actions. Similarly, they imply accepting as "deserved" and fair those results that flow as a natural consequence foreseeable at least in principle by reasonably prudent people. "You should reap what you sew," then, is a primitive deontic principle, as is "first, do no harm."

The same principle suggests other forms or sources of unfairness (i.e., types of unfairness other than the mismatch between a guilty party's suffering and the extent of that party's guilt). For example, what about instances in which the person who suffers is not at fault? It seems somehow unfair "when bad things happen to good people," which relates both to the popular book by that title and to Lerner's (1980) just-world hypothesis. Despite Lerner's work and other evidence on victim derogation, and despite some tendencies for victims to blame themselves, a deontic approach points to the potential existence of a moral wrong when the pain suffered is not the sufferer's fault. In such cases, however, it behooves us to distinguish between (a) undeserved outcomes at the hands of fate (e.g., a "freak accident") and (b) undeserved outcomes that stem from the actions of another person or persons. The latter is the focus of deontic explanations, which focus on the social regulation of interpersonal conduct in accord with moral standards.

A deontic approach, therefore, unpacks the logic used implicitly when Brockner and Wiesenfeld (1996) ignored the dissatisfaction-unfairness distinction. A Process x Outcome interaction indicates that one type of information (e.g., process-related) moderates the impact of the other (e.g., outcome-related). When the outcome-related category of information pertains to dissatisfaction absent unfairness, the conditions experienced by the victim still constitute a basis for suffering. How does process-related information moderate the further ramifications of that suffering? Deonance theory suggests that issues of moral accountability play a central role in determining the nature of such reactions. In particular, the processes that govern outcome distributions often provide cues for making attributions of responsibility about fault and blame. When such cues help reduce uncertainty and lead in the direction of confident attributions about another person's moral responsibility for the pain endured, then what started as mere dissatisfaction about that pain turns into a sense of unfairness about it.

Why, then, does the same type of moderating effect also occur when the pain seems unfair at the outset (i.e., the case of a procedural X distributive interaction, involving the moderated impact of distributively unfair outcomes)? If it is so important to distinguish between dissatisfaction and unfairness from a moral point of view, why does process-related information interact with unfavorable outcomes in the same fashion regardless of whether the unfavorability is mere dissatisfaction or genuine unfairness? The answer lies again in the deontic logic of moral accountability. The deontic approach emphasizes adherence to codes of conduct that ought to govern the nature of interpersonal relations. Whether a given person, p, has suffered unfavorably in terms of mere dissatisfaction alone or additionally on grounds of unfairness, the result is still a negative experience. That is, the impact on p's welfare is negative rather than positive. If people have moral responsibilities regarding the welfare of others, then someone accountable for the negative welfare of p (another person, o) becomes an object of judgment potentially subject to negative social sanctions (e.g., criticism). Moral reactions concerning this person, o, tend to moderate the harshness of reactions about the suffering experience as an outcome.

Suppose, for example, that o is a police officer whom the law holds accountable for the manner in which suspects are interrogated, and that p is one such suspect. P might suffer unfavorably when the police officer (o) gets that suspect to confess. If o used excessive physical force to coerce the confession, some might believe the officer violated the suspect's civil rights. If such an illegally obtained confession led to the suspect's conviction, and (even more so) if such events led to the suspect's being imprisoned despite being innocent, then the outcome would be not only unfavorable to the suspect but also unfair (on both procedural and distributive grounds, in the case of an innocent-but-imprisoned suspect).

Let me now restate my point and also illustrate it another way. I'm suggesting that reactions toward outcomes are colored by reactions toward o when o seems morally accountable for those outcomes. O's moral accountability (e.g., the public's belief that certain norms are legitimate for governing police officers' conduct) moderates reactions toward outcomes, therefore, whether those outcomes are negative merely in a dissatisfying sense or also in a distributively unfair sense. Depending on the validity of this deontic hypothesis, we should expect to find the strongest evidence for Outcome x Process interactions on measures of reactions *toward perpetrators*. To the extent that moderated effects also occur for measures of reactions toward outcomes themselves, such effects might be somewhat attenuated relative to the effects on measures of attitudes toward perpetrators—simply because the former constitute an emotional spillover from the latter. Indeed, we might expect to find some statistical indications that reactions toward perpetrators mediate reactions toward outcomes.

That comment leads to a further example. Consider a case in which we start with outcome dissatisfaction and procedural injustice as predictors, taking some measure of (ideally, subsequent) outcome unfairness as a criterion measure. In other words, we expect an interaction such that the highest ratings of outcome unfairness occur when dissatisfying outcomes stem from unfair procedures. I argue that respondents do not always provide high ratings of outcome unfairness—because they realize that calling an outcome unfair reflects badly on the person responsible for that outcome. Sometimes they believe that the responsible party (o) acted reasonably despite an unfair procedure and unfair outcomes (for p). People might be reluctant to call an outcome unfair when it has resulted from o's acting in good faith (without malice), or if use of the unfair procedure is somehow forgiveable (e.g., its use was inadvertent, unavoidable, or otherwise justifiable—such as the "lesser of two evils"). When it seems unkind or unreasonable to blame someone for using an unfair procedure, people might be reluctant to call attention to the fairness of outcomes because such criticism might seem like an unwarranted condemnation of the decision maker.

The Commonality Among Distributive, Procedural, and Interactional Injustice

I have just argued that although the deontic perspective insists on distinguishing between dissatisfaction and unfairness, it also specifies why they act in a similar fashion when moderated by process-related variables (viz., measures/manipulations of procedural or interactional justice). Now I want to claim that a related point holds for distributive, procedural, and interactional injustice. On the one hand, a deontic perspective helps establish important reasons for distinguishing among these terms. On the other hand, the same perspective also stipulates a fundamental commonality among them.

In brief, that commonality involves the notion of pain or suffering already mentioned—negative conditions experienced by someone (i.e., a state of affairs with negative implications for p's welfare). The distribution of material resources constitutes a category of such conditions normally gathered together under the umbrella term of *outcomes*. Negative material conditions, as I've indicated, can be merely dissatisfying or can be both dissatisfying and unfair. The same statement, however, applies to the more psychologically symbolic (less material) impact of being subjected to improprieties of the mechanisms governing the conduct of deliberations such as decision making (procedural injustice) or being subjected to negative interpersonal treatment (interactional injustice). We shy away from calling all three experiences "outcomes," despite the rather compelling arguments along those lines offered by Cropanzano and Ambrose (in press). Our literature has garnered notable accomplishments based on keeping those categories separate from one another. Nonetheless, it strikes me as illogical and misguided to deny their fundamental similarity in one important respect—namely their similarity as negative experiences.

Experiencing an unjust procedure, for example, seems very much in principle like a deprivation of the right to a fair procedure as a deserved "outcome." To grasp that sense of outcome deprivation, imagine playing a game in which players take turns rolling dice, and the numbers from the rolls determine spaces moved on a board. Suppose someone else's duplicitous tactics wrongfully deprive you of your turn, although the outcome of that turn is moot because you are too far behind and have no hope of winning. You still feel deprived. You've missed some of the enjoyment that goes along with merely participating in a competitive activity, plus other sources of pleasure in taking one's turn. Perhaps you had looked forward to a sense of exhilaration from initially not knowing what number the dice would show, followed by the resolution of that uncertainty—and maybe at least a slight thrill from defeating chance, if the throw were successful. Although the duplicity did not deprive you of any outcomes from your chance to win (which was already gone), it did deprive you of these other outcomes associated with the process of taking your turn. For such reasons, subjection to unfair procedures constitutes a negative experience akin to pain and suffering—hence, conceptually in the same generic category as the outcomes to which the label of distributive justice applies.

Similarly, consider instances of interactional injustice of the type that constitute interpersonally insensitive treatment—such as being unjustly insulted, demeaned, regarded without respect for your dignity, and so on (see Bies & Tripp, in press). Children hear "sticks and stones will break my bones, but words will never hurt me" precisely because insults do hurt. We'd like to believe that we can take some of the sting out of them by denying their negative impact, and parents might want to socialize kids accordingly as a means to prevent conflict escalation. Nonetheless, insults cause pain and suffering; if they didn't offer that prospect, no one would ever bother to insult anyone else. Classified as experiences of pain and suffering, therefore, insults fall into the same generic "outcome" category as the deprivation of material benefits from some unfair distribution. In sum, an outcome-like state of experience exists as the same core feature shared in common by distributive, procedural, and interactional justice, despite sound reasons for continuing to treat them as conceptually distinct on other grounds.

If these three ways of talking about unfairness all constitute a negative experience based on a transgression, then why distinguish among them conceptually? Moreover, what are we to make of empirical evidence supporting their separability of impact? Skarlicki and Folger (1997; see also Skarlicki, Folger, & Tesluk, 1999), for example, found a Distributive x Procedural x Interactional justice interaction when examining the combined impact of those predictors on a criterion measure of organizational retaliatory behavior (ORB). The ORB measure captured hostile impulses directed outwardly, against the organization and its members, by employees who felt unfairly treated. Described in simplified terms, the three-way interaction indicated the most intense hostility when reports of injustice revealed perceived violations in all three categories.

Again, a deontic perspective helps make sense of such findings. Because that perspective this time refers to differentiating the three concepts rather than emphasizing their commonality, however, I address that issue as a separate topic in the next major section. This section also leads to several sub-themes that help round out an overall portrayal of the deontic perspective.

DISTRIBUTIVE, PROCEDURAL, AND INTERACTIONAL DIFFERENCES

In addressing several sub-themes under this major heading, I will return periodically to the example of playing a game in which dice rolls determine players' movements around a game board. The situation is not uncommon, not hard to grasp, and not riddled with numerous details of a technical or esoteric nature—in contrast with certain types of issues concerning procedural justice as they might arise in a court of law, where adequately understanding the rules of evidence and related matters might require a comprehensive study of jurisprudence. Essentially this example appeals to the metaphor of procedures as rules, like the rules of game (e.g., rules for turn-taking and for determining spaces moved by outcomes from dice thrown). The simplicity of the metaphor and the example is deceptive, however, in that a few moments' reflection can uncover subtle nuances needing clarification. I will use some of the nuances of this situation to examine the multiplicity of aspects otherwise remaining hidden by the singular-sounding (conceptually unitary) terms of distributive, procedural, and interactional justice.

Procedural Justice and Identity-Based Explanations of Noninstrumental Effects

Consider some of the complexities associated with procedural justice. As indicated in an earlier section, this term can be reconceptualized as possessing outcome-like features (e.g., rights as deserved outcomes and, therefore, rights deprivation as outcome deprivation). One reason for distinguishing procedural justice from distributive justice, however, is that a deprivation of material outcomes (distributive injustice) might not have the same sting as a deprivation of rights (procedural injustice). Lind and Tyler (1988) present a twofold case in that regard. First they noted that a deprivation of procedural rights can have broad-ranging implications because of the instrumental (means-ends) conjunction between procedures and (a) a variety of outcomes across different classes (e.g., salaries; benefits; promotion opportunities), (b) outcomes across persons (e.g., affecting more than one employee or categories of employees), and (c) outcomes over time (i.e., long-term consequences).

Second, Lind and Tyler noted that a deprivation of procedural rights also has noninstrumental implications. In their words, "process control or voice enhances perceived fairness for reasons quite apart from any value it might have in affecting outcomes" (1988, p. 229), just as you might feel angry about being cheated out of your turn during a game even though that turn would do you no good because you have no hope of winning the game. The game example about rule violation, therefore, fits with this noninstrumental perspective and with the further comment by Lind and Tyler that "it is difficult to see how such effects could be accounted for by explanations that suppose that people view procedures solely as instruments for generating either favorable or equitable rewards" (1988, p. 229).

Once this point about noninstrumental considerations arises, however, the subtleties begin. In particular, we should not take the existence of noninstrumental effects as definitive evidence for any particular type of explanation for such effects, including the identity-based reasoning articulated in various writings on the group-value model of procedural justice (Lind & Tyler, 1988) and the relational model of authority (Tyler & Lind, 1992). Logic dictates otherwise: The presence of an effect does not guarantee a given, hypothesized antecedent as its cause, as logical fallacies with names like "affirming the consequent" and "post hoc, ergo propter hoc" remind us. For example, suppose someone argues that either the sun will rise tomorrow in the west if the sun is a luminous chariot driven by a god, or it will rise in the east if the sun is a brilliantly shining rat chasing a moon made of green cheese. When the sun rises in the east tomorrow, we do not take that as evidence for the rat theory. Similarly, if we have evidence that instrumental regard for outcomes does not have as much impact as noninstrumental regard for procedures, we do not have to assume that this evidence supports identity-based theories as the only plausible source of an explanation.

Moreover, an identify-based explanation is actually a variant of self-interest—and for that reason, I urge us to think about other possible explanations. The identity-based explanation claims that people see violations of their procedural rights by authorities as evidence of disrespect for them as members in the same group as the authority. Essentially this disrespect acts as a threat to self-esteem made stronger the more the person bases important aspects of his or her self-identity on being a well-regarded member of the group. But group membership is a type of outcome, or is conceptualizable as standing for the long-term expected value of numerous classes of outcomes made available through group membership. For that matter, self-esteem is a type of symbolic or psychic outcome. Moreover, appealing to identity-based concerns amounts to using an egoistic form of explanation—those that specify motivational aims whose content refers exclusively to the self and conditions experienced by the self (Sober & Wilson, 1998). If we capitulate to egoistic explanations without pursuing deontic alternatives, the shadow of rational choice theory looms in our path. If that does not sound ominous enough, consider that it augurs the prospect of reducing organizational psychology to economics. And if that doesn't scare you, recall (if you're old enough) what psychology was like when dominated by Skinnerian behaviorism, the conceptual twin of economics as based on rational choice theory.

A Deontic Approach to Non-Instrumental Concerns about Procedures

Now consider the game example for two purposes: (a) to yield thought-experiment variations casting doubt on identity-based explanations, and (b) to illustrate the flavor of deontic explanations as alternatives. First consider the following thought experiment and variations. Suppose you've been playing the dice-controlled board game with people whom you do not consider a membership group on which you base your self-identity. These could be casual acquaintances or even total strangers. Does the composition of this group, or potential associations between your self-identity and membership in such a group, affect whether or not you view cheating as an unfair procedure for noninstrumental reasons independent of outcomes from having your turn rather than losing it to duplicity? Is the composition of the group and its implications for self-identity really central to what's unfair procedurally and how you feel about cheating? True, this is an imaginary role-playing exercise, but I suspect that for most of us it suggests grounds for suspicion about identity-based concerns as explanations for the noninstrumental effects of procedures. For those unconvinced by this thought-experiment approach, rest assured that I'll return to examples based on empirical data later on, when I discuss studies following up on the research by Kahneman et al. (1986).

For those whose suspicions about identity-based explanations have been aroused by the game example (or who already had doubts), the next step consists in considering deontic alternatives. First, a deontic approach would apply equally well to strangers as to kith and kin. It would explain why we detest cheating even by those who are not members of groups on which we based our self-identities. It would be consistent with aversions to other morally repugnant classes of events and experience, such as genocide. Like such events, their repulsiveness would not depend on their implications for direct, first-hand experience (e.g., we can be appalled by the thought of genocide even when it threatens some group otherwise considered our enemies, or when it is portrayed in works of fiction such as books or movies). Our reactions would not depend on some long-range projection about future prospects for harm to ourselves, or about long-term prospects for reciprocated benefits.

In short, it would have the characteristics I mentioned earlier when referring to Heider's (1958) description of *ought*. Without pursuing theoretical refinement of such deontic concepts, let me simply refer to the game example in suggesting how we might flesh them out in long-term programs of theorizing and research. In the game example, the episode of cheating might bring to mind such categories as transgressor and transgressed (e.g., you as the player whose rights the cheater violates) or offender and offended party. Such categorizing, however, overlooks two other important ways of classifying features of this situation: (a) an audience category, and (b) a superordinate category referring to such features of the situation as the moral status of the rules of the game themselves.

I mention the audience not because we literally expect games to require audiences, but because audience is an important conceptual category for deontic approaches to fairness. These have a long and distinguished history in moral philosophy, with antecedents such as Adam Smith's "moral spectator." Here space permits only a few brief remarks about this category.

For example, such a category has some useful precedent in the term *scrutineer* used by Walster, Berscheid, and Walster (1973) as indicating either a participant in an exchange or an observer of that exchange. My point is simply that even when the observer is not a participant, and actually has nothing at stake, reactions of outrage to moral transgressions are not uncommon.

I think we can make sense of such reactions from a deontic perspective if we also consider the category of situation features that includes rules for interpersonal conduct within a given class of situations. Most games, for example, exist as games precisely because they require play according to rules. A game without rules would hardly be a game. Violating a game's rules, however, is not merely a matter of jeopardizing a semantic category. We will not understand the fully nuanced complexity of fairness until we stop treating such transgressions as if they were in the same category as logical inconsistencies. This was one of equity theory's problems, for example, in using as a fairness metaphor the "rationalized" (ratio-analyzed, as O/I ratios) set of terms that make an equation unbalanced (mathematically nonequivalent). As Bies (1987) once noted, conceptualizing fairness in that fashion can mistakenly seem to imply that there would be little difference between an addition error and a moral transgression. Surely, however, we react quite differently to genocide than we do to someone's mistake in claiming that $2 + 2 = 5$.

Adams (1965) was not alone in perpetuating this misleading orientation. For example, Aristotle referred to fairness as treating like cases alike and different cases according to the nature of their difference. Described that way, however, unfairness is merely logical inconsistency—the type of logical fallacy that philosophers call a category error. Again, if a transgression were merely a logical error, why would people ever become so emotionally upset about it? No one urges capital punishment for scientists who commit post hoc, ergo propter hoc fallacies, yet some people call for putting other people to death when certain types of moral transgressions occur. Surely this happens because moral transgressions have deontic qualities such as requirements that transcend logical or mathematical consistency.

Let me return to the game metaphor to illustrate this point. Simply put, cheaters not only threaten harm—and, in effect, sometimes threaten something akin to pain and suffering for the cheated—but also make the rules themselves a target of attack. The harm done is not just to other players. Cheaters violate rules and the principles from which rules derive, and such actions constitute a source for moral outrage independent of actual suffering and pain. The ethical values and precepts themselves come under fire when violated—their validity comes into question, their sacredness is profaned. These consequences, too, are "outcomes" that matter, and they matter greatly. They matter as ends in themselves, as aims whose content does not refer exclusively to the self, if Heider's insights about *ought* are correct.

At this point, then, the game metaphor for procedural justice (as rules) helps recall some of the remarks apposite to deonance made by Montada and Heider. Note that I began by mentioning Montada's statement that we need reassurance about the prescriptive nature of justice. Heider's language about ought illustrated what such prescriptiveness or ought-requiredness implies as a force of deontic motivation. In particular, recall that Heider referred to a "suprapersonal objective order" (1958, p. 219) that transcends the self-interest of any given individual—that "oughts are impersonal," as if "established by objective requirements" (p. 219). Even when games are relatively trivial pursuits that people enjoy for fun during their leisure (with little if anything of substance at stake, including self-esteem or a sense of personal identity), their rules exhibit that suprapersonal objective order writ small. When play involves the game of life, those rules are writ large.

The unwritten rules for governing interpersonal conduct matter greatly, and people respond to their violation in numerous ways that show how much it matters to them. When people have the conviction that they ought to take a certain type of action, or that someone else ought to do so, they feel as if they have recognized a feature of the world. To repeat Heider's words once more, I argue that perceived unfairness such as transgressions against the "procedural" rules for public conduct can cause people to respond as if the violation threatened "a requirement on the part of some suprapersonal order" possessing "the validity of objective existence" (p. 219). But this type of threat to our beliefs about objective existence does not produce an experience similar to what we feel when we encounter a perceptual illusion like a reversible staircase or an Escher drawing. We have no desire to punish Escher because he has called into question the validity of our understanding about physical reality. When people transgress the Human Covenant, on the other hand, they can make themselves liable for some of the severest forms of punishment known. Again, I argue (along with Montada and Heider) that the special prescriptive and injunctive character of the claims of the transcendent upon us needs further theoretical and empirical work. Its special character demands that it not be treated reductionistically by conceiving it as a mere means to some other end, selfishly egoistic or otherwise. It is not, for example, the same as the claim upon us that altruism sometimes makes (e.g., to help others in need). Obeying the rules of a game, obviously, is not a matter of altruism.

A Deontic Differentiation of Distributive, Procedural, and Interactional Justice

If I'm somewhere close to being on target about the importance and independence of deontic motives, then their prescriptive qualities can further help us make a variety of additional differentiations among distributive, procedural, and interactional justice. Consider once again the game metaphor. Norms for distributive justice can apply when evaluating the scores achieved in the game and any differences among the rewards or prizes associated with different scores (e.g., evaluated according to equity-like principles such as outcome/input considerations). Norms for procedural justice can apply when evaluating the rules of the game and the extent of adherence to those rules. Norms for interactional justice can apply in regard to such matters as the courtesy and civility with which players treat one another, and in regard to matters such as whether decisions receive sincere, adequate explanations when the decision maker is questioned.

A violation of any of the three types of norms is also like making the rules of the game a target of attack. All three types of transgressions, therefore, deprive people of deserved "outcomes." Nonetheless, the violation or nonviolation of one norm can moderate the impact from the violation or nonviolation of another. A deontic approach brings a special understanding to such moderation effects in terms of moral accountability, a concept independent of the usual grounds for describing those interactions (e.g., as a Distributive x Procedural interaction).

A deontic approach treats such interactions as antecedent-consequent (means-ends) relations, but by referring to attributions of moral responsibility (e.g., inferred motives and intentions) rather than attributions about the physical mechanisms of causality. Simply put, a deontic approach distinguishes between something like two temporal *directions* involved in a moral transgression: (a) pointing forward toward future implications for victims (and perhaps others); and (b) pointing backward toward the moral culprit as a source of those implications, to be held accountable for them. Let me clarify. The conception of "outcome" I've been proposing refers to an effect (state or condition) experienced as negative. A person's welfare might be jeopardized by unfairness as a moral transgression, for example, and the moral values being violated also stand in jeopardy (their validity is under attack). Either the person or the values or both, therefore, receive the impact of the transgression. The transgression has present and future implications for such targets as the recipients of the transgression's impact. As a result, any of the three types of justice can supply the "outcome" variable of a Process x Outcome interaction, because all three forms of injustice suggest harmful implications in the present (and perhaps for the future).

Any of the three types of justice might also, in principle, supply the "process" variable for such an interaction—provided that perceptions concerning that violation yielded crucial attributions of moral responsibility. The second half of the interaction, that is, involves inferences such as those made about someone's reasons for committing an apparent violation of a fairness norm—their motives, intentions, and so forth. Thus, the second half of the interaction involves the second temporal direction I just mentioned, the direction that looks backward toward the past and the origins of the transgression (e.g., the transgressor's motives). From what source did the transgression arise? Was it the result of conduct initiated by someone else, or traceable to that person because of ways in which they contributed to the final result?

We know far too little about attributions of moral responsibility for unfairness transgressions, so speculation will have to do for now. Let me offer one working hypothesis. I suggest that attributions of the other's accountability for unfairness tend to grow stronger (e.g., swiftness or confidence of inference) in an ascending order from distributive to procedural to interactional justice. I can illustrate the intuitions behind that speculation most easily by starting with interactional injustices as the strongest grounds for moral accountability. Suppose I suddenly insult someone in a demeaning, offensive, interpersonally insensitive manner. Are you likely to believe that it was an accident, or that I didn't know what I was doing? No, you probably feel confident in treating such an incident as inner-directed, a willfully intentional act on my part. You ordinarily have reasonably solid grounds for holding me morally accountable for such actions.

Now let's go to the other end of the continuum. Suppose I'm your supervisor, and you don't like the amount of the raise to your annual salary that I've budgeted on the basis of performance appraisals. You are dissatisfied, and perhaps you ruminate most about referent comparisons that make this dissatisfying increase seem like an unfairly low amount of pay (e.g., comparable others in similar industries get paid much more; annual raises given to the employees of companies in those industries were much larger this year).

That constitutes one element in the Outcome x Process interaction, namely the present and future implications (e.g., how upset you are and might continue to be). The second element of that interaction is the other direction (from or by), as reflected in your attributions of moral accountability. Who's responsible for this low pay? The question is problematic because there are too many possible and plausible answers, too many causal antecedents that contribute in complex ways. Did you get your performance instructions correctly? Did you follow prescribed programs of action, but the results on production still fell short of levels required by customer demand? If some aspects of the performance appraisal required subjective judgment, can you be sure that your subjective judgment has greater validity than your supervisor's? And so on. The multitude of such questions make it difficult to be very certain concerning where fault lies and whom to blame for misfortune, much less to be sure that misfortune also constituted clear-cut wrongdoing.

Procedural injustice, I argue (see also Folger & Cropanzano, 1998), constitutes something of a middle ground in between distributive and interactional injustices. On the one hand, grounds for inferring procedural injustice might often seem more clear-cut than those for distributive injustice. Often, that is, rule violation is transparent and obvious. Like the example of insult that I gave a moment ago, such rule violations might also seem unlikely to have occurred accidentally. On the other hand, tracing the moral accountability for a procedural violation to a single source might be problematic. Suppose, for example, you believe that I didn't conduct the performance appraisal according to legitimate standards for procedural justice. You might at the same time not know whether that choice was mine or had been dictated by company policy. I suspect that such sources of ambiguity about moral accountability are relatively more prevalent regarding procedural matters than regarding instances of interactional injustice, although the difference in degree certainly might be slight to nonexistent in some cases, or even reversed in others.

THE DEONTIC QUESTION: WHEN IS VIRTUE ITS OWN REWARD?

Thus far I've spoken a lot about deonance without saying too much unique to it, as opposed to speaking about its features that overlap considerably with notions about fairness already prevalent in the literature. Because the significance of deontic explanation is its differentiation from egoistic explanations based solely on self-interest, the study of deonance is difficult for the same reason that proponents of altruism always struggle against explanations reducing altruism to self-interest. It is hard to define something other than self-interest as a plausible motive even conceptually, let alone to find evidence for such a motive empirically.

If the study of fairness is not to be taken over by economics, however, we must be up to this challenge. Fortunately, a brilliant analysis by Sober and Wilson (1998) has made a strong case for deontic explanations at the conceptual level. For the sake of empirical meat on those theoretical bones, the following discussion adds research results (Turillo & Folger, in press) from work replicating and extending the Kahneman et al. (1986) findings, which I mentioned earlier in this chapter. Recall that Kahneman et al. found self-sacrificial behavior: A substantial majority of their research participants (roughly 75%) willingly forfeited a dollar to punish a person designated as "U" (for Uneven). Supposedly this "U" had previously tried to take $18 of $20 and leave only $2 for another person, although U's attempt was said to have been unsuccessful (his/her allocation-preference form was not among those drawn for pay). Also recall my having noted earlier (cf. Turillo & Folger, in press) that such results replicate under conditions guaranteeing anonymity. Such privacy assurances rule out impression-management concerns as possible alternative interpretations for the robust findings of self-sacrificial behavior.

The self-sacrificial punishment by our participants (giving up $1 in order to punish an $18/$2-preferring person) thus looks quite genuine, which makes it an ideal candidate for exploring the nature, antecedents, and implications of deonance. Examining this self-sacrificial behavior will illustrate some of the ways to study deonance and some of the possible variations in deonance findings. Turillo and I have conducted studies with those aims in mind (Turillo & Folger, in press), and these are continuing with the help of several colleagues (who include Gee, Grahovac, Lavelle, Noe, and Umphress).[3] Because statistical and methodological details are contained in the Turillo and Folger (in press) article, I will report here only some of the types of results being generated and their implications concerning deonance, self-interest, and the like.

For example, if people give up money to prevent a wrongdoer from getting money, then these deontically behaving people might be motivated by a desire to deter future wrongdoing—either some future wrongdoing by this particular ($18/$2-attempting) person or by anyone else. Our results rule out that explanation, however, because the same levels of self-sacrificial punishment occur even when punishers believe that the "punished" person would never learn of the $0 allocation—and that no one else would ever learn about this act of punishment, either.

Hypothetical examples may help illustrate the nature of that finding and related results we have obtained. Suppose five minutes ago, someone in another country first wrote you a $6 check for your birthday, then had a change of heart and shredded the check without telling you anything. Thus, five minutes ago you were "punished" (allocated $0 instead of $6) in the same fashion that our self-sacrificial participants punished the $18/$2 person. Because you didn't know you were "punished" or deprived, the unrevealed check shredding has no effect on your behavior or anyone else's (other than perhaps the check-shredder's future behavior, of course).

Or consider a hypothetical incident during the era when an apartheid regime in South Africa encouraged Krugerand investments. A wealthy uncle's will gives you two strange inheritance options: (a) a check for $500, or (b) $600 in Krugerands. If you refuse to accept the Krugerands, their sale will simply cover overhead costs associated with your uncle's estate. Suppose you choose the $500 check rather than $600 in Krugerands because you don't want to invest in the currency of a regime you consider unfair, thereby self-sacrificially "punishing" unfairness. If such examples are concocted correctly, even if hypothetical and far-fetched, they reflect what we accomplished in our experimental variations on the Kahneman et al. paradigm: People chose $5 instead of $6 in order to "punish" someone for wrongdoing, even though the "punished" person never experienced the consequences of that action.

Our participants knew that by depriving themselves (choosing $5 instead of $6 and thereby giving nothing to an attempted wrongdoer rather than giving that person $6 and also giving themselves $6), *no other material consequences of substance—present or future—would occur.* They would not be sending the wrongdoer a message (e.g., "don't ever try to be so greedy again"), because no information of any kind would go to that person. Nor would they be posting a warning to the public at large (e.g., "see what happens to greedy people who try to take 90% of the money available to a pair of individuals"), because their own self-sacrificial act of other-punishment would go unheralded. Finally, they could not impress anyone by being identified publicly as punishers of wrongdoing, because no one else—not even the investigators—would ever know which research participants (if any) had chosen to make such a decision.

My colleagues and I have also obtained a related finding that has spawned another line of investigation. Our results stem from having Louisiana college students choose between Option X, with the consequences indicated below, and Option Y, with its associated consequences:

	Results for You	Results for Person A	Results for Person B
Your Option X:	$6	$6	$6*
Your Option Y:	$5	$0	$5

Note first that we changed the asterisked entry from the Kahneman et al. value of $0. Note also that at first blush, every conceivable line of argument—rational self-interest, morality, maximal benefit to both A and B, equal benefit to all (cf. fairness as either equality or equity), and greatest good for the greatest number (cf. Pareto optimality and utilitarian reasoning)—points clearly to Option X as the obvious preference. Talk about a no-brainer decision! On the other hand, presumably it might matter who A is and who B is. Suppose B is an anonymous stranger chosen at random but that "What kind of person is A?" becomes crucial. Option X's advantages seem diminished, for example, if Person A is someone so flagrantly unfair that it makes your blood boil (e.g., a terrorist; someone who delights in torturing innocent children). Once we identify A as someone willing to engage in reprehensibly unfair efforts that elicit your moral outrage and righteous indignation, then the money at stake for you—much less the shape of the Option-X distribution—has declining impact on your choice tendencies. Quite plausibly, for example, a large proportion of U.S. citizens would pick Option Y over Option X if they thought Person A was, say, Saddam Hussein, even if all the numbers were multiplied by factors of 1000 or more!

We have created conditions in which *at least 50% of our research participants choose Option Y over X and thereby deprive themselves of $1.* First note that in so doing, they steer away from a pure equality norm or joint-maximization of mutual value norm (e.g., Pareto optimality). Unlike in the Kahneman et al. study (see the asterisk above), our participants also cannot *reward* B with $5 instead of *nothing*. Option X would be more "rewarding" because it gives B $6, whereas Option Y gives B only $5. Thus, our self-sacrificial participants were actually *depriving* B of a dollar at the same that they were depriving themselves of a dollar. Second, unlike the Kahneman et al. participants who gave $5 to an "E" (fair) person by depriving themselves of $1, ours who gave themselves $5 and B $5 did not select B to receive at least some money because of anything meritorious or "E"-like (fair) about Person B. After all, this particular Person B was simply picked at random out of a B pool, and no one in pool B had any special characteristics (meritorious or not, fair or unfair).

CONCLUSION

No formal theory of deonance exists, so I cannot summarize it. I have deliberately aimed in different directions throughout this chapter, hoping that at least one might provoke further thought. In particular, I have called for a search beyond the traditional list of self-interest motives. I have focused on the Option X-versus-Y paradigm (see table above) because when third-party observers self-sacrificially punish attempts to violate fairness norms, their motives appear to extend beyond ordinary self-interest. I will conclude, therefore, with an Option X-versus-Y result that I think raises questions about existing theories—questions that a deonance approach might be better equipped to address (see also Turillo & Folger, in press).

We wanted our research participants (Louisiana students) to feel both psychologically and physically distanced—as third-party observers—from the A/B roles of the other two people (supposedly drawn at random from the managerial ranks of an unnamed company in Virginia). These managers' paychecks were allegedly augmentable by up to $6 without suspicion (i.e., no A or B would think to associate any change in his or her check, or lack thereof, with research done in Louisiana). In this way we eliminated self-identity inclusion or exclusion implications such as might be derived from Social Identity Theory or related approaches to fairness such as the Group Value Model (Lind & Tyler, 1988) or the relational model of authority (Tyler & Lind, 1992). Moreover, pool A was not an "outgroup" of pool B or vice versa (all were simply at the same company). Why, then, did 50% of the students "punish" an A who would never know that he or she had been "punished," especially if those self-sacrificing students not only cost themselves a dollar but also could not hope to accomplish anything constructive in the process?

This is precisely the central question that a theory of deonance both raises and attempts to answer; in other words, a formal theory of deonance will aim to describe the nature of the motive producing that result and to identify the antecedents and consequences of that deontic motive's arousal. Such a theory would not reduce our students' behavior to a form of self-interest (direct or indirect, short- or long-term driven) but would instead try to conceive of their motives as being consistent with the deontic language of "ought requiredness" (Heider, 1958, p. 219). The Greek root, *deon*, refers to that which seems obligatory or required, so deontic theorizing seems better served by the motive-language of "a requirement on the part of some suprapersonal order" that has "the validity of objective existence" and that, therefore, rises above self-interest because "oughts are impersonal" (p. 219). Most of all, a deontic approach will concentrate on Heider's "experience of should" as an "ought force" with motivating impact (p. 219).[4]

To capture the suprapersonal objectivity described by Heider's ought-requiredness as rising above personal-identity and self-interest concerns, we labeled the column-A person by a quote from someone describing that person. The quote invoked a suprapersonal standard of conduct, in an impersonally objective way, to describe A's behavior as morally outrageous (deontically condemnable). The quote came from interview comments that Bob Bies supplied and identified for us as from an employee morally outraged about a manager who delighted in ridiculing subordinates. Bob had interviewed employees at a Virginia company, which is why we used that location as the alleged source of A and B managers in instructions to our students.

We showed column B payouts to our students as described in the table I displayed earlier (either a $6 or a $5 payout for managers drawn randomly from the unnamed company). Column A amounts (either a $6 or a $0 payout to someone drawn from pool A) entailed punishing ($0) or not punishing ($6) someone whose conduct was deontically outrageous—but unrelated to anything such as a prior $18/$2 split (thereby generalizing beyond attempted greed as a fairness violation). Indeed, Bob Bies gave us the interview quotation about the ridiculing manager to represent what he has called *interactional injustice*. In other words, our results show that a substantial proportion of Louisiana students want to keep a ridiculing manager from getting a $6 pay increment. They ensure that by paying $5 rather than $6 to both themselves and another manager at the same company (drawn at random, unidentifiable, and undescribed).

What makes this result both an object lesson for concluding this chapter and a jumping-off point for further developments of deontic theorizing? Consider the motives that cannot explain such behavior: (1) It is not self-serving in a material, financial way. (2) It is not self-serving in a manner consistent with any concern our students might have had about their exclusion from an important membership group that reflected on their own self-identity. That is, the ridiculing behavior that they punished as interactionally unfair did not threaten to exclude them from the membership group of managers, or subordinates, in an unnamed Virginia company (e.g., it would be impossible for them to estimate the odds of their ever working in that company). (3) Students who chose Option Y could not deter future instances of interactional unfairness by their self-sacrificial act. (4) Such students could not bask in public congratulations for having demonstrated self-sacrificial virtue. Indeed, this is truly an instance in which it can be said that virtue was its own reward, because *nothing good results from Option Y.*

Of course, no such action is immune from descriptions that link it with self-interest. A supporter of self-interest models (e.g., rational choice theory) might simply say that those who chose Option Y knew they would sleep better because of their choice. They could anticipate good feelings about the deontically virtuous choice (self-sacrificial punishment of unfairness), and they could anticipate having bad thoughts about themselves if they chose Option X (e.g., I shouldn't have been so greedy as to be influenced by a mere dollar). It would take another entire chapter to answer such objections adequately, and even then no success is guaranteed when trying to attack the inherent circularity of self-interest accounts. A concluding note in this chapter, however, does owe the reader at least some initial thoughts about why those self-interest accounts fail as obstacles to further theorizing about deonance—and why trying to defeat self-interest explanations is less important than trying to understand human motives that rise above self-interest.

It is time to acknowledge that much of human behavior is not consciously driven by an active consideration of future consequences. True, I sleep more soundly after a virtuous day than when I've been a scoundrel. My belief that I will feel better after choosing Y over X, however, does not necessarily explain why I choose Y. Many people who have committed many noble acts have claimed that they simply acted on impulse, without thought for what they might (or might not) accomplish and without considering how they might (or might not) feel about it later. Perhaps it is time to take such claims seriously. Surely we can all at least find plausible the thought experiment of dashing into a burning building to save the child of someone you don't even know, without having time to make many expected-value calculations about that act.

If self-interest and self-identity explanations capture all the attention devoted to the study of fairness, then we will frame fairness questions in ways that preclude other answers. If we ask why someone might identify with victims of unfair treatment (self-identity determinants of empathy with victims), we invite self-interested considerations (Am I like this victim? Could this happen to me?), neglecting other types of issues (What kind of person is this wrongdoer?). A third-party (deontic) perspective reframes the relevant fairness issues by not collapsing the victim's status and the observer's status (i.e., not asking how observers empathize with victims or anticipate similar harm from the same wrongdoer).

Many hypothetical thought experiments contain recognizable grounds for third-party, deontic outrage about intended mistreatment and interactional unfairness. Such examples go hand-in-hand with studies of self-sacrificial punishment by third parties (e.g., Kahneman et al., 1986; Turillo & Folger, in press), raising new questions about human motives that transcend ordinary self-interest or self-identity concern. If this chapter has only succeeded in raising questions and has failed to provide a concluding summary of suggested answers or particular directions for future research, I hope that readers will at least feel puzzled enough about self-interest to suspect that it is not the only human motive underlying fairness concerns.

NOTES

1. Readers unfamiliar with the "traditional" Process X Outcome interaction should consult standard sources such as Brockner and Wiesenfeld (1996) or Folger and Cropanzano (1998). As Brockner and Wiesenfeld note, the original basis for predicting this interaction is referent cognition theory (e.g., Folger, 1986; Folger, Rosenfield, & Robinson, 1983). Essentially, this interaction indicates that when people perceive their outcomes as having been determined by fair procedures, they will not use the quality of outcomes (e.g., degree of outcome unfavorability) as a basis for reactions directed toward those in charge of determining outcomes. When unfair procedures determine the level of outcomes, however, the harshness of reactions against outcome administrators increases with the unfavorability of the outcomes.

2. For less-abbreviated treatments of bounded autonomy, see Folger (1998); Folger and Skarlicki (1998). For related work on fairness and moral accountability, also see Folger & Cropanzano (1998; in press). On self-interest, see Wilbur (1997) and Sober and Wilson (1998).

3. It is possible that some of these people might also appear as coauthors of the journal article cited in this chapter as Turillo and Folger (in press)—another reason for listing them.

4. Concepts and terminology seemingly related to, or at least consistent with, a deontic approach have appeared in many discussions besides those already mentioned in this chapter (e.g., Kim & Mauborgne, 1998; Skitka, 2000), and even that parenthetical listing undoubtedly omits many important contributors. The "experience of should" has received special attention in other work as well (e.g., Folger, 1984; Folger, 1993; Folger & Cropanzano, 1998, in press; Folger & Skarlicki, 1998; Mark & Folger, 1984). Deontic standards can also be conceptualized as counterfactual referents—that is, an ideal or "ought to be this way" state which, when imagined, stands in contrast to some actual state of affairs, such as an apparently intended act of unfair mistreatment (for related work on counterfactuals as comparison standards, see Folger & Kass, 2000).

REFERENCES

Adams, J.S. (1965). Inequity in social exchange. In L. Berkowitz (Ed.), *Advances in experimental social psychology* (Vol. 2, pp. 267-299). New York: Academic Press.

Asch, S.E. (1952). *Social psychology.* New York: Prentice-Hall.

Bies, R.J. (1987). The predicament of injustice: The management of moral outrage. In L.L. Cummings & B.M. Staw (Eds.), *Research in organizational behavior* (Vol. 9, pp. 289-319). Greenwich, CT: JAI Press.

Bies, R.J., & Tripp, T.M. (in press). A passion for justice: The rationality and morality of revenge. In R. Cropanzano (Ed.), *Justice in the workplace: From theory to practice* (2nd ed.). Mahwah, NJ: Lawrence Erlbaum Associates.

Brehm, J.W. (1966). *A theory of psychological reactance.* New York: Academic Press.

Brockner, J., & Wiesenfeld, B.M. (1996). An integrative framework for explaining reactions to decisions: The interactive effects of outcomes and procedures. *Psychological Bulletin, 120,* 189-208.

Cropanzano, R., & Ambrose, M. (in press). Procedural and distributive justice are more similar than you think: A monistic perspective and a research agenda. In J. Greenberg & R. Cropanzano (Eds.), *Advances in organizational justice.* Stanford, CA: Stanford University Press.

Folger, R. (1984). Perceived injustice, referent cognitions, and the concept of comparison level. *Representative Research in Social Psychology, 14,* 88-108.

Folger, R. (1986). Rethinking equity theory: A referent cognitions model. In H.W. Bierhoff, R.C. Cohen, & J. Greenberg (Eds.), *Justice in social relations* (pp. 145-162). New York: Plenum.

Folger, R. (1993). Reactions to mistreatment at work. In K. Murnighan (Ed.), *Social psychology in organizations: Advances in theory and research* (pp. 161-183). Englewood Cliffs, NJ: Prentice-Hall.

Folger, R. (1998). Fairness as a moral virtue. In M. Schminke (Ed.), *Managerial ethics: Morally managing people and processes* (pp. 13-34). Mahwah, NJ: Lawrence Erlbaum Associates.

Folger, R., & Cropanzano, R. (1998). *Organizational justice and human resource management.* Thousand Oaks, CA: Sage.

Folger, R., & Cropanzano, R. (in press). An accountability model of organizational justice. In J. Greenberg & R. Cropanzano (Eds.), *Advances in organizational justice.* Stanford, CA: Stanford University Press.

Folger, R., & Kass, E. (2000). Social comparison and fairness: A counterfactual simulations perspective. In J. Suls & L. Wheeler (Eds.), *Handbook of social comparison: Theory and research* (pp. 423-441). New York: Plenum.

Folger, R., Rosenfield, D., & Robinson, T. (1983). Relative deprivation and procedural justifications. *Journal of Personality and Social Psychology, 45,* 268-273.

Folger, R., & Skarlicki, D. P. (1998). A popcorn metaphor for workplace violence. In R.W. Griffin, A. O'Leary-Kelly, & J. Collins (Eds.), *Dysfunctional behavior in organizations, Vol. 1: Violent behaviors in organizations* (pp. 43-81). Greenwich, CT: JAI Press.

Heider, F. (1958). *The psychology of interpersonal relations.* New York: Wiley.

Hogan, R., & Emler, N. P. (1981). Retributive justice. In M.J. Lerner & S.C. Lerner (Eds.), *The justice motive in social behavior: Adapting to times of scarcity and change* (pp. 125-143). New York: Plenum.

Kahneman, D., Knetsch, J.L., & Thaler, R.H. (1986). Fairness and the assumptions of economics. *Journal of Business, 59,* S285-S300.

Kim, W.C., & Mauborgne, R. (1998). Procedural justice, strategic decision making, and the knowledge economy. *Strategic Management Journal, 19,* 323-338.

Lerner, M.J. (1980). *The belief in a just world: A fundamental delusion.* New York: Plenum.

Lind, E.A., & Tyler, T. (1988). *The social psychology of procedural justice.* New York: Plenum.

Mark, M.M., & Folger, R. (1984). Responses to relative deprivation: A conceptual framework. *Review of Personality and Social Psychology, 5,* 192-218.

Miller, D.T., & Vidmar, N. (1981). The social psychology of punishment reactions. In M. J. Lerner & S. C. Lerner (Eds.), *The justice motive in social behavior: Adapting to times of scarcity and change* (pp. 145-172). New York: Plenum.

Montada, L. (1998). Justice: Just a rational choice? *Social Justice Research, 12,* 81-101.

Reno, R.R., Cialdini, R.B., & Kallgren, C.A. (1993). The transsituational influence of social norms. *Journal of Personality and Social Psychology, 64,* 104-112.

Simon, H.A. (1957). *Administration behavior: A study of decision-making processes in administrative organization.* New York: McMillan.

Skarlicki, D.P., & Folger, R. (1997). Retaliation in the workplace: The roles of distributive, procedural, and interactional justice. *Journal of Applied Psychology, 82,* 434-443.

Skarlicki, D. P., Folger, R., & Tesluk, P. (1999). Personality as a moderator in the relationship between fairness and retaliation. *Academy of Management Journal, 42,* 100-108.

Skitka, L. J. (2000, September). *The moral mandate hypothesis.* Paper presented in K. van den Bos (Chair) Recent Advances in Social Psychological Theories of Justice, a symposium conducted at the International Society for Justice Research, Rishon LeZion, Israel.

Sober, E., & Wilson, D.S. (1998). *Unto others: The evolution and psychology of unselfish behavior.* Cambridge, MA: Harvard University Press.

Thaler, R.H. (1992). *The winner's curse.* New York: The Free Press.

Turillo, C.J., & Folger, R. (in press). Is virtue its own reward? Self-sacrificial decisions for the sake of fairness. *Organizational Behavior and Human Decision Processes.*

Tyler, T.R., & Lind, E.A. (1992). A relational model of authority in groups. In M.P. Zanna (Ed.), *Advances in experimental social psychology* (Vol. 25, pp. 115-191). New York: Academic Press.

Walster, E., Walster, G.W. & Berscheid, E. (1973). New directions in equity research. *Journal of Personality and Social Psychology, 25,* 151-176.

Wilbur, J. (1997). Self-interest. In *The Blackwell encyclopedia of management* (Vol. 11, pp. 576-577). Oxford: Blackwell.

CHAPTER 2

HOW DO I KNOW THAT'S FAIR?

A Categorization Approach to Fairness Judgments

Maureen L. Ambrose and Carol T. Kulik

ABSTRACT

Procedural justice research has advanced substantially in the last two decades. This research has identified factors that lead to perceptions of procedural justice (e.g., opportunities for voice, consistency) as well as consequences of justice perceptions (e.g., satisfaction, acceptance of authority). However, little empirical research has directly examined the cognitive processes that come into play when people translate information about objective procedures into subjective justice judgments. In this chapter we use a categorization approach to explore three issues that are as yet unanswered in the procedural justice literature: (1) Are some attributes more important to fairness judgments than others? (2) Do employees rely on the same attributes when they consider the fairness of different kinds of procedures (e.g., selection procedures, performance appraisal procedures, grievance procedures)? And (3) Are there shared expectations about fair procedures that transcend differences between individuals in different membership groups (e.g., sex, race, occupation)? We discuss how a categorization approach provides insight to these questions. We outline a research program based on this approach and discuss the implications of categorization for procedural justice research.

INTRODUCTION

We know procedural justice is important. Research demonstrates that procedural justice matters across a broad range of organizational settings and has important organizational consequences. Multiple theoretical approaches (see Konovsky, 2000 for a recent review) have described the components of procedures that people consider when they evaluate whether they have been treated fairly. However, with few exceptions (Hafer, 2000; Steiner, Guirard, & Baccino, 1999; Van den Bos, Lind, Vermont, & Wilke, 1997; Van den Bos, Wilke, Lind, & Vermunt, 1998; Van den Bos, Lind, & Wilke, in press), little empirical research has directly examined the cognitive processes that come into play when people translate information about objective procedures into subjective justice judgments. As a result, we can relate procedural variations (e.g., variations in voice, interpersonally sensitive treatment, consistency) to individual reactions (e.g., satisfaction, turnover), but the process by which the individual interprets those procedural variations and chooses to respond remains an unopened black box.

In a variety of domains (e.g., drug testing, layoffs, pay cuts), researchers have contrasted fair and unfair procedures and examined employee reactions. This research has generated a great deal of practical advice for managers about implementing drug testing procedures, telling employees they are being laid off, and instituting pay cuts in ways that reduce the possibility of negative employee reactions and maintain employee morale. But what about the manager who is not facing major organizational changes or restructuring, and who wants advice about making his or her daily human resource practices (e.g., scheduling, task assignment) as fair as possible? Well, organizational justice research has also addressed fairness in human resource decisions such as selection or performance appraisal. Unfortunately, since so much justice research has focused on particular categories of organizational procedures (e.g., selection *or* performance appraisal *or* layoffs), the manager is faced with a long list of procedural features that seem to make a difference—sometimes. But are the features that make drug testing fair the same features that make selection procedures fair? Are all these features equally important to employees? Do all employees see the same procedures as fair? The manager who sincerely wants to design fair organizational procedures is bewildered by the options, and ultimately does nothing. Without knowing how his or her employees will evaluate the procedures that are implemented, the manager has no blueprint, no guidelines for designing these procedures.

The manager's dilemma echoes concerns that have been voiced by reviewers of the justice literature (Greenberg, 1993a; Konovsky, 2000). Greenberg (1993a) noted that in organizational justice research, the operationalizations of justice change with the specific context (e.g., the determinants of a fair performance appraisal may be different from the determinants of a fair pay raise). As a result, the procedural justice literature is becoming increasingly fragmented; researchers continue to identify new areas to which justice concepts can be fruitfully applied but there is little "integrative, theoretical thinking" (Konovsky, 2000, p. 505) across areas. Both researchers and practitioners would benefit from "universal, general" measures of justice concepts that could be adapted as needed to different situations (Greenberg, 1993a, p. 255).

The question of how individuals evaluate procedures to form fairness judgments is fundamentally a cognitive question. Thus, at this point in the evolution of justice research, it is useful to explicitly consider the cognitive processes that underlie procedural fairness judgments. We believe that a cognitive approach is useful for three reasons. First, explicitly considering the cognitive processes underlying procedural fairness judgments resolves several unresolved justice issues. Second, explicitly considering cognitive processes allows us to be proactive in designing procedures of all kinds that will be evaluated as fair. Third, a cognitive approach identifies new avenues for justice research.

In this chapter, we consider how individuals process fairness information when they evaluate procedures and explore the cognitive processes that underlie judgments of fairness. We begin by describing the foci of most justice research to date. We then identify three questions in the procedural justice literature that have yet to be resolved and review the literature relevant to these questions. Next, we briefly review research on categorization and discuss how a categorization framework provides a method for examining these unresolved justice questions. We conclude with a description of a research program based on this integration of justice and categorization and discuss the implications of categorization for future justice research.

TRADITIONAL FOCI OF PROCEDURAL JUSTICE

In the last fifteen years procedural justice has been a dominant theme in organizational research. This research traditionally addresses one of three questions: (1) What are the antecedents of perceptions of procedural fairness? (2) In what organizational circumstances are perceptions of procedural justice important? And (3) What are the consequences of perceived procedural fairness?

As the field of justice evolved, research examining the first question evolved as well. Early research on procedural justice focused on the impact of voice and other structural attributes of procedures on perceptions of fairness (Leventhal, 1980; Leventhal, Karuza, & Fry, 1980; Thibaut & Walker, 1975). In the late 1980s and early 1990s, researchers began to consider the impact of a broader range of variables, including interpersonal treatment (Bies & Moag, 1986; Lind & Tyler, 1988; Tyler & Lind, 1992) and organizational contexts (Mossholder, Bennett, & Martin, 1998; Schminke, Ambrose, & Cropanzano, 2000; Tyler, Degoey, & Smith, 1996).

The second question—in what organizational circumstance does procedural justice matter—dominated procedural justice research from the mid 1980s to mid 1990s. This research demonstrated that procedural justice perceptions are important across a broad range of procedures including performance appraisal (Greenberg, 1986), drug testing (Konovsky & Cropanzano, 1991, 1993), parking appeals (Conlon, 1993), layoffs (Brockner et al., 1994), selection (Gilliland, 1993, 1994), pay cuts (Schaubroeck, May, & Brown, 1994), strategic decision making (Kim & Mauborgne, 1997,1998), and promotion (McEnrue, 1989).

The third question on which procedural justice research focused was the consequences of justice perceptions. This research demonstrates that perceived procedural fairness is related to a broad range of important organizational outcomes. Perceived procedural justice is positively related to job satisfaction (McFarlin & Sweeney, 1992), organizational commitment (Folger & Konovsky, 1989), organizational citizenship behavior (Moorman, 1991), performance (Konovsky & Cropanzano, 1991), and intention to remain (Greenberg, 1990), and negatively related to theft (Greenberg, 1993) and other dysfunctional behaviors (Skarlicki & Folger, 1997; Skarlicki, Folger, & Tesluk, 1999).

While procedural justice research provides much insight into the antecedents and consequences of procedural justice judgments, there are still several issues central to understanding procedural justice that remain unresolved. Below we focus on three of these questions and review justice literature that is relevant to each.

THREE UNANSWERED PROCEDURAL JUSTICE QUESTIONS

Question 1: Relative Importance of Attributes

The first question focuses on how individuals process information about procedures to determine if they are fair.[1] Specifically, are some attributes more important to fairness judgments than others? Research has identified a fairly comprehensive list of attributes that may contribute to procedural fairness. Could the presentation of one procedural attribute or a few procedural attributes have as much impact on fairness judgments as the comprehensive set?

While there is little empirical research that addresses this question directly, many authors suggest that some features of justice are critical to perceptions of fairness. Kim and Mauborgne (1997, 1998) assert that three features—engagement, explanation, and clarity—"collectively capture the domain of procedural justice" (1998, p. 325). Brockner et al. (1998), citing seminal works in procedural justice (Folger & Greenberg, 1985; Lind & Tyler, 1988; Thibaut & Walker, 1975) argue that voice is a central element of procedural justice. Still other researchers (Barrett-Howard & Tyler, 1986; Greenberg, 1986) suggest that consistency is one of the most important determinants of procedural fairness.[2]

Unfortunately, there is little empirical research that examines the relative impact of different procedural attributes. The research that exists does suggest that attributes may vary in their importance or impact on perceptions of fairness. For example, Singer (1990) examined applicants' reactions to selection processes. He found that consistency and ethicality were rated as the most important procedural attributes, while bias avoidance and choice of selectors were less important. Moorman (1991) and Bies, Martin, and Brockner (1993) found the interpersonal behavior of decision makers was better able to predict subordinate attitudes and behavior than features of formal procedures (e.g., opportunity for voice). Similarly, Farh, Earley, and Lin (1997), in a study of Chinese employees, found that the interpersonal behavior of the supervisor was more important than formal aspects of justice (such as mechanisms for appeal and opportunity to participate) in predicting individuals' organizational citizenship behavior. Korsgaard, Schweiger, and Sapienza (1995) suggest that the extent to which a leader considers subordinate input has a consistent powerful impact on procedural justice judgments regardless of other procedural variations (e.g., the amount of direct control subordinates have over the decision).

Summary

Current justice research provides little conclusive evidence regarding our first question. There is some evidence to suggest attributes such as voice and consistency may be critical to judgments of procedural justice, but there is no systematic approach to evaluating which features are central to justice judgments and which are less important. Current research leaves our first question unresolved.

Question 2: Consistency Across Procedures

Our second question addresses how individuals evaluate the fairness of procedures associated with different organizational activities (selection, performance appraisals, grievances). Organizational members are exposed to a variety of procedures. Research demonstrates that procedural justice is important across a broad range of procedures, but we do not know if individuals use the same guidelines for determining if these different procedures are fair. That is, do employees rely on the same attributes when they consider the fairness of different kinds of procedures?

Theoretical work on procedural justice suggests that procedural attributes will be differentially important in different contexts. Leventhal (1980) identified six procedural rules that guide an individual's thinking about procedural fairness: consistency, bias suppression, accuracy, correctability, representativeness, and ethicality. Leventhal maintains that these rules may be given different weights and the "relative weight of procedural rules may differ from one situation to the next" (p. 46). Similarly, Tyler (1996) suggested that different criteria are "used to judge the fairness of procedures in different circumstances" (p. 324).

Empirical research also suggests that the importance of procedural attributes may vary across situations. For example, beginning with Thibaut and Walker's (1975) seminal work on process control and decision control, procedural justice research has demonstrated that voice is important across a broad range of organizational procedures. The positive effect of voice on perceptions of fairness has been shown for performance appraisal (Greenberg, 1986), grievance procedures (Fryxell & Gordon, 1989), and organizational decision making (Rasinski, 1992). The voice effect has been called the most reliable effect in procedural justice research (Lind, Kanfer, & Earley, 1991). Still, voice is not always a significant predictor of justice perceptions. For example, Daly and Geyer (1994) found no voice effect in relocation procedures. Similarly, Tremblay, Sire, and Pelchat (1998), using a justice framework to examine individuals' reactions to benefit plans, report that choice in selection of benefits did not affect benefits satisfaction.

Justice research reveals other differences across procedures in the attributes that are relevant to individuals' justice judgments. Consider research on social accounts. Some studies demonstrate that social accounts increase perceptions of justice (Bies & Shapiro, 1987; Greenberg, 1990, Weaver, 1995). However, research also finds no effect of social accounts on justice perceptions (Konovsky & Folger, 1991). Additionally, there are differences across situations in the effect of different types of social accounts. For example, Conlon and Murray (1996) found that consumers perceived company responses as more fair when the company provided either an explanation or apology than when it provided an excuse. However, in a study of individuals' responses to mediator behavior in a dispute resolution context, Conlon and Ross (1997) found that only explanations increased the perceived fairness of the procedure. Both apologies and excuses were perceived as less fair. In contrast, Cobb, Folger, and Wooten (1995) suggest that in an organizational change context, apologies can increase the perceived fairness of the change procedure. And, Mishra and Spreitzer (1998) suggest a similarly positive effect of apologies in a downsizing context.

Research on the group value model also suggests that context may affect perceptions of fairness. Tyler and Degoey (1995) report that neutrality and standing received different weights in different contexts. Neutral treatment was the dominant determinant of procedural justice judgments in a community setting. However, standing dominated procedural justice judgments in a family setting.

Summary

Procedural justice research has examined perceptions of fairness across a broad range of settings. However, this research has not systematically examined whether individuals use the same criteria to assess fairness across these varied procedures and has not compared the evaluation of procedural attributes across situations. Existing research suggests that there are both similarities and differences in the attributes used to evaluate fairness. However, there is not a coherent pattern of findings that can guide organizations in their design of specific procedures. Thus, the answer to the second question remains unresolved.

Question 3: Consistency Across People

The third question as yet unanswered by justice research is the consistency of attribute use and importance across people. Furby (1986) suggests that perceptions of justice are most likely to result when expectations are met. These expectations result in part from cultural socialization (see Steiner, this volume) but also personal experiences unique to the individual (Furby, 1986). Organizations consist of members who differ in demographics, values, and experience. It would not be practical for organizations to design procedures tailored to match the expectations of each individual. Thus we ask, "Are there shared expectations about fair procedures that transcend these member differences?"

Research on procedural justice provides some evidence to support the assertion that individuals do share expectations about what constitutes fair procedures. Tyler, Degoey, and Smith (1996) report similar effects of group-value constructs across four diverse settings (family, university employees, university students, and the U.S. Supreme Court). They conclude the similarity of the findings "attest to the robustness of the group-value model" (p. 924).

Research on procedural justice and demographics also suggests individuals may share similar expectations about what constitutes fairness. For example, Kulik, Lind, Ambrose, and MacCoun (1996) found no gender differences in how litigants in arbitration hearings defined procedural justice. Lee and Farh (1999) report that gender did not moderate the relationship between procedural justice and supervisory trust or organizational commitment. Tyler (1988) investigated several personal characteristics (e.g., expectations of fair treatment, education, race, liberalism, sex, age, and income) and found that these variables had no effect on the relative importance of dimensions (e.g., consistency, impartiality, correctablity) in contributing to citizens' perceptions of fairness.

Substantial research has examined the effect of group membership on perceptions of procedural justice (Huo, Smith, Tyler, & Lind, 1996; Huo & Tyler, in press; Smith, Spears, & Oyen, 1994; Smith & Tyler, 1997; Smith, Tyler, Huo, Ortiz, & Lind, 1998). Much of this research focuses on the effect of the match between the subordinate's and supervisor's group membership or individuals' identification with a group, and does not directly inform our discussion. However, some of this research is relevant to our interest in shared expectations. Lind, Huo, and Tyler (1994) found that Asian, Black, Latino, and White college students expressed general agreement about their preferences for procedures to resolve a hypothetical dispute. Huo and Tyler (in press) report that Asian, Black, Latino, and White university employees generally agreed on the factors (e.g., trustworthiness, neutrality) that contributed to perceptions of procedural justice in their interactions with supervisors.

There is also evidence that both participants and observers evaluate the fairness of procedures similarly. Tyler (1990) argues that there is a normative basis for procedural justice judgments and that both observers and participants share expectations about fairness. This theoretical assertion is supported by Skarlicki, Ellard, and Kelln (1998) who found that third-party observers' responses to information about layoff procedures were similar to that of layoff victims and layoff survivors. Additionally, Brockner et al. (1994) report that the interaction between procedural justice and outcome negativity was similar for three different groups exposed to layoffs: victims, survivors (observers), and employees who knew they would soon be laid off.

On the other hand, there is also evidence to suggest that members of different demographic or cultural groups differ in how they evaluate procedural fairness. For example, Giacobbe-Miller (1995) found that procedural justice judgments varied according to the perceiver's affiliation with labor or management. Parker, Baltes, and Christiansen (1997) report that organizational support for affirmative action was more strongly related to perceptions of procedural justice for women and racial minorities than for white males. Sweeney and McFarlin (1996) report that the relationship between procedural justice and positive work outcomes (job satisfaction, intention to remain) was stronger for women than for men. Farh et al. (1997) report a similar relationship between gender, procedural justice and organizational citizenship behavior. White, Tansky, and Baik (1995) found both significant gender and cultural differences for perceptions of procedural fairness for a sample of U.S. and Korean respondents. Leung, Smith, Wang, and Sun (1996) found that interactional justice was not a predictor of job satisfaction for a sample of Chinese hotel employees;

research on U.S. samples consistently reports a positive relation between these two variables (e.g., Brockner & Greenberg, 1990; Moorman, 1991).

Research also suggests that individual difference variables may affect the importance of procedural fairness attributes. For example, Huo et al. (1996) found that employees who identified strongly with their ethnic group (but not with their employing organization) tended to discount procedural variations when they experienced a conflict with a supervisor from a different ethnic group. Farh et al. (1997) found procedural justice was most strongly related to organizational citizenship behavior for Chinese respondents who embraced less traditional values. Schminke, Ambrose, and Noel (1997) found that individuals who were more formalist in their ethical orientation were more sensitive to procedural justice than ethical utilitarians. Brockner et al. (1998) reported that high self-esteem individuals were more affected by voice than low self-esteem individuals. However, they note that Vermunt, Blaaun, van Knippenberg and van Knippenberg (1998) found that low self esteem individuals were more affected by respect and consideration (elements of interactional justice) than high self-esteem individuals.

Summary

While research has examined the effect of individual and cultural differences on procedural justice, this research does not provide a consistent pattern of results. Some research demonstrates no effect of group membership. However, for other procedures group membership does impact procedural justice evaluations. The current research has not systematically examined the general question, "Are there shared expectations about fair procedures?" And the existing research does not provide a clear answer.

PROCEDURAL JUSTICE AND COGNITIVE CATEGORIZATION

The justice research reviewed above suggests a complex relationship between procedural attributes and individuals' responses to those procedures. Although research relevant to each question exists, this research does not provide clear answers to our questions. Much of the research we reviewed was not designed to address the general issues we have identified. Thus, although extant research hints at possible answers, these answers remain incomplete and fragmentary. A framework for understanding these fragments is lacking.

We suggest that categorization theory provides a systematic way of addressing how individuals make justice judgments and allows us to "make sense" of the complex set of results. Below, we review research on categorization and use a categorization framework to explain how procedural justice judgments are formed.

Content and Use of Cognitive Categories

When people interact with the world, they must process an abundance of information about objects, persons, and situations. They must process this information about the environment quickly and efficiently or run the risk of being overwhelmed by these processing demands. Cognitive categories provide a mechanism for facilitating this information processing.

A category is a cognitive structure that represents knowledge about a particular concept or stimulus, including its features and the relations among those features (Fiske & Taylor, 1991). Research suggests that people use cognitive categories to organize information about a wide variety of objects (e.g., vehicles, furniture), people (e.g., athletes, librarians), and situations (e.g., restaurants, parties) (Cantor, Mischel, & Schwartz, 1982; Cohen, 1981; Dahlgren, 1985; Rosch, 1978; Rosch & Mervis, 1975). In organizational settings, research indicates that cognitive categories play a role in influencing reactions to jobs (Kulik, 1989; Jacobs, Kulik, & Fichman, 1993), job applicants (Kulik & Clark, 1994; Perry, 1994), employee performance (Feldman, 1981; Nathan & Lord, 1983), and leaders (Lord, Foti, & DeVader, 1984; Phillips & Lord, 1982).

In addition to allowing individuals to efficiently process information about familiar objects, persons, and situations, categories play an important role in helping people to understand new encounters. When people encounter an unfamiliar object, person, or situation, they must make sense of the target. Individuals access cognitive categories as they decide how to classify the new encounter. Most categories do not have a set of "necessary and sufficient" features that all category members must display. Instead, categories are "fuzzy sets" and contain some borderline members that display only some of the features associated with the category. However, the "best" example of a category is the category prototype—a typical or ideal category member that displays all of the essential features of the category (Fiske & Taylor, 1991). This prototype is used to decide whether the new encounter is "close enough" to be considered a category member. For example, a "robin" might be a prototype of the category "birds" because a robin displays many or all of the features associated with the category—it sings, it has wings, it flies, it eats worms.

An unfamiliar object, person, or situation is categorized through a matching process in which the perceiver compares the features of the new encounter with the features of relevant category prototypes. For example, if a person encounters a new creature that *might* be a bird, the person could retrieve information about a robin (the prototypical "bird") from memory and compare its features with those of the unfamiliar creature. This matching process has been demonstrated to underlie a variety of social and organizational assessments. For example, Cantor, Smith, French, and Mezzich (1980) found that psychiatric diagnosis involved a matching process in which clinicians compared the symptoms displayed by a particular patient with the features comprising psychiatric syndrome prototypes. Niedenthal, Cantor, and Kihlstrom (1985) found that students preferred the type of housing for which their prototype of the tenant of this type of housing most closely matched students' self-descriptions. Lord et al. (1984) demonstrated that managers who exhibited prototypical leader behaviors were more likely to be perceived as leaders than managers who exhibited anti-prototypical behaviors.

We suggest that perceivers also have cognitive categories for common procedural situations (e.g., performance appraisals, legal trials). In other contexts, situational categories have been found to contain information about the typical behavior of people in these situations, as well as descriptions of the physical setting and other situational attributes (Cantor et al., 1980). Therefore, we might expect a procedural category (e.g., a legal trial) to contain information about the physical setting (e.g., wood-paneled courtrooms), the procedural attributes (e.g., formal procedures, voice provided through a structured question-and-answer exchange), and the behavior of people (e.g., lawyers, judges, witnesses) typically observed in examples of that category.

People do not need to have personal experience with procedures to have established category prototypes—prototypes can be developed through television, by hearing about other people's experiences, or through direct encounters. For example, much of the information any individual person has about the fairness of an organization's procedures comes not from personal experiences but instead from the broader collective experience of other people (Lind, Kray, & Thompson, 1998). There is evidence both in a growing body of research on survivors' reactions to layoffs (e.g., Brockner & Greenberg, 1990; Brockner et al., 1994) and in the literature on the perception of crime (e.g., Tyler, 1980), that people incorporate the experiences of others into their own judgments of situations. As a result, people are likely to have cognitive categories (and associated prototypes) for those procedures with which they are familiar (e.g., procedures for assigning chores to family members) and those with which they may have little experience (e.g., U.S. Supreme Court proceedings).

Little justice research has been directed toward identifying the content of these procedural categories, but there is evidence that supports the idea of a categorization approach. For example, Tyler (1988, p. 131) concluded that citizens used "positively interrelated clusters of procedural criteria" to decide whether they had been treated fairly by police or court authorities. More recently, Tyler (1996, p. 324) described these interrelated criteria as a "template." If procedures are associated with features that tend to co-occur, perceivers can readily develop categorization schemes to organize their observations and experiences. Then, people can evaluate the fairness of a particular procedure by comparing the elements of that procedure to their template of fairness.

Category membership has implications for the perceiver's evaluative or emotional response to objects, persons, or situations. Each of the features associated with a category has attached to it an "affective tag" that indicates its evaluative value. If a perceiver is highly motivated and not under time pressure, he or she can use these evaluative tags to produce an overall evaluation of new objects, persons, or situations (Fiske & Neuberg, 1990). However, the category label also has an affective tag that can substitute for the evaluations of all the individual attributes associated with the category. If a target provides a sufficient match to the category prototype, the target can simply "take on" the affective tag associated with the category. For example, Kulik (1989) found that perceivers evaluated a job description more positively when the job description contained features associated with a more positively-tagged job prototype (e.g., "manager") than when the job contained features associated with a less positively-tagged prototype (e.g., "supervisor")—even though the features themselves were evaluatively neutral. Perceivers evaluate new people more positively when the people display attributes associated with the perceiver's "old flame" category prototype (Fiske, 1982). And decision makers evaluate job applicants more positively when they are described as having traits and attributes consistent with the incumbent prototype (Kulik & Clark, 1994; Perry, 1994).

In some domains, research suggests that people have positively-tagged and negatively-tagged versions of the same category. For example, Feldman (1981) suggested that performance appraisal ratings may result from the rater's categorization of the ratee as either a "good performer" or "poor performer." If a manager considers one of his or her employees to be a good performer, a request to evaluate that employee may elicit from the manager's memory traits and behaviors typically characteristic of good performers that may or may not describe the target employee. Once the good performer category has been accessed, judgments about the employee may be based on the category evaluation.

We suggest that people similarly have categories for "fair" and "unfair" versions of procedures. We provide a hypothetical display of fair and unfair performance appraisal procedure prototypes in Figure 1. The prototypes have associated physical settings, procedural attributes, and behaviors. It is important to remember that these are prototypes—they represent "pure types" of procedures. The actual performance appraisal procedure an employee encounters in his or her work life may contain a mix of "good" and "bad" features. The employee's evaluation of that particular performance appraisal procedure depends on whether the particular procedure provides a better match to the "fair" or "unfair" prototype.

The idea that people use procedural categories to evaluate particular procedures has important implications for procedural justice research, and we will discuss it in more detail in our implications section. However, first we consider how a categorization approach informs our thinking for each of our "unanswered" questions.

FAIR PERFORMANCE APPRAISALS	UNFAIR PERFORMANCE APPRAISALS
Subordinate office	Boss is rude
Opportunity for input	Long overdue
Reasonable standards	Boss' office
Boss is polite	Unrealistic standards
Narrative justification	Numerical rating
	Boss does all the talking

Figure 1. Hypothetical prototypes associated with fair and unfair performance appraisal procedures.

CATEGORIZATION AND THE THREE UNANSWERED QUESTIONS

Central and Peripheral Elements of Cognitive Categories

Our first question addressed the criticality and potency of certain procedural attributes. Specifically, we considered whether some attributes are more important than others in determining perceptions of procedural fairness. A categorization approach provides a clear framework for evaluating this question.

Category features are not all equally important in determining category membership. Research suggests that category features can be identified as central or peripheral (Perry, 1994; Perry & Bourhis, 1996; Smith, Shoben, & Rips, 1974). Central features are more typical of the category and are weighted more heavily than other features in defining category membership (Smith et al., 1974). A feature may be central because it is characteristic of many category members or because it is relatively more defining of the target category compared to alternative categories (Perry, 1994). For example, "wings" may be a central feature of the category "birds" because all or most birds *do* have wings, and the characteristic of wings helps to distinguish birds from other kinds of animals. Peripheral features are less typical of the category and consequently are weighted less heavily than other features in defining category membership. A feature may be peripheral because it is characteristic of relatively fewer category members, or because it is not more defining of the target category compared to alternative categories. For example, "flies" may be a peripheral feature of the category "birds." There are birds (e.g., penguins) that do *not* fly, and there are other categories (e.g., airplanes) with which "flies" may be more strongly associated.

As perceivers compare the features of a new encounter to a category prototype, they initially consider all the features of the new object or person (Smith et al., 1974). Eventually, however, attention becomes focused on the central features. A target may be identified as a category member even if the target matches the prototype on only a few features—as long as those features are central.

Again, there is little justice research that explicitly addresses this issue. However, research does suggest that some features may be central to perceptions of fairness. The pervasive effect of voice suggests it may be a central feature. Similarly, the consistent effects of the group value attributes—standing, benevolence, and neutrality—make these attributes candidates for central features. In contrast, the qualified effects of apologies and excuses suggest these attributes may be peripheral features, characteristic of fewer category members than their central feature cousins.

However, it is important to note that situational categories (such as the categories we suggest exist for procedures) also include information about people and physical settings. Justice research focuses almost exclusively on procedural attributes. But these attributes are only one component of a "fair procedure" or "unfair procedure" category. Current research provides no information about features of the physical setting and people that may be critical to evaluations of fairness.

Structure and Organization of Cognitive Categories

Our second question concerned whether individuals used the same attributes when evaluating different procedures. Procedural justice research demonstrated that there were both similarities and differences across procedures. Categorization provides a framework for understanding these results.

Research indicates that cognitive categories are hierarchically structured according to their level of abstraction (Rosch, 1975, 1978; Rosch & Mervis, 1975). Superordinate categories are the most abstract and subordinate categories are the least abstract (Rosch, 1978). For example, perceivers may have a superordinate category for "doctor" and a subordinate category for "oncologists I met at Wilshire Memorial." Between these levels of abstraction lie basic level categories (e.g., "oncologist"). Superordinate categories tend to be more inclusive; that is, people associate more members and more features with categories at upper levels of the hierarchy (Fiske & Taylor, 1991). Prototype structures have been identified at different levels of abstraction (Rosch & Mervis, 1975). Prototypes at more abstract levels (i.e., superordinate levels) are likely to contain central features associated with lower level prototypes (Brewer, Dull, & Lui, 1981). For example, the prototype of a superordinate category of "fruit" is likely to contain many of the central features associated with less abstract categories (e.g., "oranges").

Justice research has not investigated the content of procedural categories. However, we can speculate that there are global categories for "fair procedures" and "unfair procedures." At lower levels of abstraction, there may be categories associated with different contexts (e.g., organizational, legal, personal) and procedures within those contexts (e.g., promotion, selection, performance appraisal). The superordinate category level (e.g., fair procedures) is likely to contain those attributes that are common across procedures. However, as categories become more specific, the critical attributes become more differentiated.

Using a categorization framework, the mixed results observed in the justice literature may be explained by people's attention being directed toward different categorization levels. The particular category level (and associated prototype) used as a basis for decisions depends on the person's goals and expertise (Fiske & Taylor, 1991).

Although some research suggests that basic (mid-level) categories are frequently used in decisions, other research suggests that superordinate categories are especially useful when people make higher order judgments (Murphy & Wisniewski, 1989). When employees evaluate a specific procedure such as a benefit plan (Tremblay et al. 1998), a grievance procedure (Fryxell & Gordon, 1989), or a customer complaint procedure (Conlon & Murray, 1996) they are likely to focus on a basic (mid-level) level of categorization that emphasizes the differences between categories and their prototypes. However, when an employee decides whether she has been fairly treated by her employer and needs to consider procedures used across a variety of human resource domains (e.g., selection, pay raises, promotions, and task assignment), a superordinate level of categorization may be more relevant.

Thus, a categorization approach suggests that there are both shared attributes of fair procedures as well as unique procedural attributes. It is the level of categorization that determines the degree of similarity or differentiation between procedures.

Social Construction of Cognitive Categories

Our final question considered whether individuals from different groups based their judgments of procedural fairness on the same attributes. Categorization research addresses this issue as well.

One important element of cognitive categories is that they are socially shared—that is, research generally finds high agreement among people in the attributes they associate with a category prototype. The amount of agreement among people depends in part on the level of the category hierarchy. Lower levels of the category hierarchy tend to involve more idiosyncratic information based on personal experience, while higher levels of the hierarchy are more likely to contain socially-shared and generally accepted information about the category. Because category prototypes are abstracted from a variety of information sources, most people will never encounter the actual prototype (Fiske & Taylor, 1991). However, since people have access to shared sources of information (e.g., television, newspapers, organizational grapevine), the prototypes show remarkable similarity.

In addition, research generally finds little evidence that individual differences such as age, race, sex, or occupation influence the content or use of cognitive categories. For example, Rumiati and Lotto (1996) found no differences between students and bank clerks in the category structure these groups had for "money" and Hess and Bolstad (1998) found that age made no difference in the use of cognitive categories in identifying people as members of occupations.

One important individual difference variable that does influence categorization processes is expertise. Experts tend to have more information than novices and to have more extensive (both laterally and hierarchically) categorization schemes (Isenberg, 1986). When subgroup differences are observed in categorization processes (e.g., between men and women), these differences appear to be a function of familiarity (expertise) with the category domain (e.g., desserts) rather than a function of gender per se (Peracchio & Tybout, 1996).

The categorization research on expertise suggests a possible explanation for the justice research that reports differences across membership groups in reactions to justice attributes. It is possible that some of the differences attributed to group demographics are really a function of members of different groups having different degrees of familiarity with the attributes associated with different procedures. For example, Schminke et al. (1997) speculate that the differences they observed between ethical formalists and ethical utilitarians may have resulted from formalists' greater sensitivity and attention to procedural issues in general. Differences observed among demographic subgroups (e.g., Parker et al., 1997; Sweeney & McFarlin, 1996) may be attributable to these groups acquiring expertise with different aspects of procedures. For example, Gilligan (1977, 1982) suggests that women have been socialized to maximize the interpersonal aspects of their relationships—resulting in women having more experience in evaluating procedural elements. Members of racial minorities may have paid more attention to affirmative action procedures in the past, honing their knowledge of variations in these procedures and developing more elaborate categorization schemes to understand subtle differences. Similarly, some of the cross-cultural effects found in the justice research may be a function of people from some countries being less familiar with procedures that are very common in the United States.

In fact, a closer examination of the justice research indicates that the observed differences among subgroups are in the *relative* weights that each group gives to procedural attributes or the *relative* strength of the relationship between attributes and reactions across groups. Across groups, the same attributes are important to justice judgments. Thus, consistent with the categorization framework, procedural attributes are shared.[3]

CATEGORIZATION IMPLICATIONS FOR PROCEDURAL JUSTICE RESEARCH

Thus far, we have demonstrated that categorization theory has the potential to resolve several unanswered questions in the justice literature. In this section, we consider a research agenda for the categorization approach and consider the implications of this approach for future research on procedural justice.

Research Agenda

Content and Organization of Procedural Categories

The categorization approach provides a framework for synthesizing the complex findings reported in the justice literature. However, our interpretation of these findings and our conclusions are speculative at this point. These questions cannot be directly addressed until we identify the content and organization of procedural categories.

Some indication about the content of procedural categories may be obtained from seminal theory in the justice literature. For example, Thibaut and Walker's (1975) work provides strong evidence that decision and process control (voice) are likely to be important elements in many procedural categories. Leventhal's (1980) taxonomy similarly suggests a series of important dimensions that are likely to be part of many procedural categories. However, it is important to note that these theories were developed to address a particular procedural domain—with Thibaut and Walker being most concerned about legal procedures, and Leventhal being more concerned with resource allocation issues. As a result, these theoretical approaches have only limited overlap in the procedural features they emphasize (Tyler, 1988). Categorization schemes based on these theories may capture some of the basic-level category content but miss the superordinate level. In addition, as we noted above, categorization schemes based on these theories are likely to neglect many features associated with the contexts in which procedures are enacted. Prototypical features of the physical setting and behaviors of people in the situation warrant attention.

Therefore, we recommend that researchers take a more data-driven approach to identifying the content and organization of procedural categories. Rosch's (Rosch 1975, 1978; Rosch & Mervis, 1975) research methods have been successfully applied to a variety of social and organizational domains (e.g., Brewer et al., 1981; Kulik, 1989; Perry, 1994). Justice researchers have used similar methods to identify important procedural dimensions. For example, Greenberg (1991) used categorization methodology when he asked students to sort explanations of performance ratings written by managers at manufacturing plants, and Shapiro (1993) asked students to generate examples of what it meant to have one's views "considered." However, this research was designed to understand the categorization of a particular feature (e.g., explanation, voice) within a particular domain (e.g., performance appraisal, appeal to a third party)—it does not capture the full procedural categorization scheme.

Process data can be difficult to obtain and our suggestions about its usefulness are yet to be assessed. This data-driven approach may produce results that converge with existing theory, but it may also identify additional procedural dimensions that are not represented in existing theoretical models. In fact, in the short run, a cognitive approach may complicate the theoretical picture by adding to the already lengthy list of procedural components that have been associated with subjective justice judgments. However, in the long run, process data obtained through cognitive methodology (e.g., Q-sorts, protocol analysis) may produce justice models that are more accurate descriptions of the underlying cognitive processes that people engage in as they form justice judgments.

Research on the Three Unanswered Questions

If we are successful in identifying a categorization scheme that captures most organizational procedures, we can directly address the three "unanswered questions" discussed in this chapter. First, research should examine which procedural variations represent "central" features that are most critical for procedural categorization. Identifying these central features might enable us to design more powerful and more efficient interventions. For example, emphasizing a central feature would increase the likelihood that a procedure would be evaluated as "fair." Alternatively, if the central feature cannot be changed in the particular organizational context, the category prototype may identify other clusters of procedural characteristics that can be changed as a package—and facilitate a shift to a "fair procedure" category.

Second, research needs to examine the impact of directing individuals' attention toward different levels of the category hierarchy. Two issues are relevant here. Research should examine what influences the level of abstraction that the individual spontaneously uses to evaluate procedures and what are the implications of different levels of abstraction for fairness judgments. For example, unfamiliar procedures (e.g., the introduction of a new drug testing program) are likely to be evaluated at a more abstract level. Thus, certain central features may be most critical in individuals' categorization of the procedure as fair or unfair. However, changes in existing procedures (e.g., a refinement to the promotion system) are likely to activate evaluations at the specific procedure category level. Thus, procedure-specific attributes are more likely to be critical for categorization. Additionally, it would be useful to examine how the "common features" contained in the superordinate categories influence employee reactions to organizational procedures. Superordinate categories may be more predictive of some important dependent variables (e.g., turnover) than the basic level categories (i.e., reactions to specific procedures). Most procedural justice research has focused on these basic level categories.

Third, research should examine the role of expertise in justice judgments. It may be that expertise is a more relevant predictor of subgroup differences than demographic variables. We know of no justice research that has examined individuals' prior experience or familiarity with particular procedures. However, it is clear that individuals do vary in their knowledge about procedures. For example, some employees have had multiple experiences with downsizing and other organizational restructuring — these employees may have much more developed categorization schemes for relevant procedures than employees who have not experienced downsizing. In addition, employees who have moved across organizations over the course of their careers may have a greater sense of the range of procedural options and may have larger, more flexible categories than employees who have worked for one organization for many years.

Implications for Future Justice Research

In addition to addressing our three unanswered questions, categorization theory has implications for justice research in general and can suggest new directions for research. First, the idea that people use procedural categories to evaluate particular procedures has important implications for procedural justice research. As we noted in our general discussion of categories, individuals can evaluate a target by combining the evaluative tags associated with the specific features displayed by the target or by relying on the evaluative tag associated with the category. From a justice perspective, this suggests that positive evaluations of fair procedures can be the result of either the cumulative evaluation of individual features (e.g., advanced warning, opportunity to appeal) or the match of the procedure to the category (e.g., "fair procedure" and the application of the category tag). Thus, as we note above, designing procedures that provide a good fit to positively valent categories streamlines the evaluation process and may result in more positive evaluations, even though fewer positive individual features are present.

This leads to the second implication for justice research. A categorization approach allows us to be more proactive in our design of fair procedures. Categories provide the blueprint for successful procedural design. If we can identify the features that are central to the instantiation of the "fair procedure" category, we can design procedures with a minimum number of features that consistently evoke that category. In fact, some peripheral procedural features, although positively evaluated on their own, may contribute little additional value and can be ignored without any negative impact.

A categorization approach also suggests new directions for procedural justice research. Two intriguing questions come to mind: (1) Can we change perceptions of fairness without changing the procedure itself? (2) Do procedural prototypes contain information about the perceiver's behavior?

Procedural justice research focuses primarily on attributes of the procedure. However, the situational prototypes on which our model is based include not just procedural attributes, but behaviors and physical settings as well, and research suggests that people rely heavily on visual, physical cues during the categorization process (Fiske & Taylor, 1991). The justice literature has begun to pay attention to interpersonal treatment (Bies & Moag, 1986; Lind & Tyler, 1988; Tyler & Lind, 1992) but has completely neglected the physical setting despite the fact that the physical setting has been found to impact organizational behavior in other areas (Oldham & Fried, 1987; Oldham, Kulik, & Stepina, 1991). For example, suppose that a "fair" performance appraisal procedure is one that involves high participation, that uses quantifiable standards, and that is usually conducted in the subordinate's office. Can we change perceptions of fairness by transplanting the identical performance appraisal interaction from the boss's office to the subordinate's office? Some of the dimensions associated with procedural categories are subject to interpretation—is a procedure automatically seen as more participative if it is conducted in the subordinate's office?

Second, do procedural prototypes contain information about the perceiver's behavior? Situational prototypes include typical behaviors of the people in the situation—including the perceiver. Traditional procedural justice research tries to predict behavior *from* procedural attributes (e.g., interpersonal insensitivity is associated with negative reactions). But a categorization approach may permit us to predict behavior by identifying behaviors that are specifically associated with procedural categories. For example, suppose that there exist several subordinate categories associated with firing procedures. All of these categories may be negatively-tagged, but the prototypes (each with a specific cluster of procedural features and supervisor behaviors) are associated with different employee reactions. One cluster may be associated with an emotional outburst ("The only thing

I can do now is cry") while another (with a different cluster of procedural features and supervisor behaviors) may be associated with physical violence ("I'm going to make somebody pay for this"). Understanding the content of the categories—both procedural features and perceiver behavior—would allow us to specify which behavior is likely to occur, based on the category evoked.

CONCLUSION

Justice research flourished in the 1980s and 1990s. However, despite its success in identifying antecedents and consequences of procedural justice, this empirical research provided little understanding of how individuals process information to form justice evaluations. In this chapter, we used a cognitive approach to understand how individuals make fairness judgments. We suggest this approach provides a way for resolving some previously unresolved issues in procedural justice, provides a framework for proactively designing fair procedures, and generates new avenues for future justice research. We believe an explicit consideration of the cognitive processes that underlie procedural justice judgments can be a fruitful path for justice researchers. We see this chapter as the first step along that path.

NOTES

1. There is research on the fairness heuristic (see Van den Bos, this volume) that addresses a slightly different variant of this question. Fairness heuristic research examines the conditions under which individuals rely on procedural information to guide their outcome evaluations (i.e., outcome fairness and outcome satisfaction). Here our interest is in how *information* about procedures is processed to determine if the procedures are fair. However, it is useful to note that research on the fairness heuristic has taken a cognitive approach to examining justice judgments.

2. These procedural attributes are operationalized differently, which can make comparisons across studies difficult. For example, while operationalizations of voice all involve input, they differ both in terms of the kinds of input (e.g., providing factual information, expressing preferences) and the forms of input (e.g., an open-ended request for information, choosing from a defined menu of options.)

3. The one exception to this finding is the research by Leung et al. (1996). Leung et al. found no effect for interactional justice in a sample of Chinese hotel workers. This finding is inconsistent with research on U.S. samples. However, as categories are "socially" shared, culture may affect the development of categories and influence which attributes come to be associated with fairness.

REFERENCES

Barrett-Howard, E., & Tyler, T.R. (1986). Procedural justice as a criterion in allocation decisions. *Journal of Personality and Social Psychology, 50,* 296-304.

Bies, R.J., Martin, C.L., & Brockner, J. (1993). Just laid off, but still a "good citizen"? Only if the process is fair. *Employee Responsibilities and Rights Journal, 6*, 227-238.

Bies, R.J., & Moag, J.S. (1986). The predicament of injustice: The management of moral outrage. In L.L. Cummings & B.M. Staw (Eds.), *Research in organizational behavior* (Vol. 9, pp. 289-319). Greenwich, CT: JAI Press.

Bies, R.J., & Shapiro, D.L. (1987). Interactional fairness judgments: The influence of causal accounts. *Social Justice Research, 1*, 199-218.

Brewer, M.B., Dull, V., & Lui, L. (1981). Perceptions of the elderly: Stereotypes as prototypes. *Journal of Personality and Social Psychology, 41*, 656-670.

Brockner, J., & Greenberg, J. (1990). The impact of layoffs on survivors: An organizational justice perspective. In J. Carroll (Ed.), *Applied social psychology and organizational settings* (pp. 45-75). Hillsdale, NJ: Erlbaum.

Brockner, J., Konovsky, M., Cooper-Schneider, R., Folger, R., Martin, C., & Bies, R.J. (1994). Interactive effects of procedural justice and outcome negativity on victims and survivors of job loss. *Academy of Management Journal, 37*, 397-409.

Brockner, J., Siegel, P.A., Martin, C., Reed, T., Heuer, L., Weisenfeld, B., Grover, S., & Bjorgvinsson, S. (1998). The moderating effect of self-esteem in reactions to voice: Converging evidence from five studies. *Journal of Personality and Social Psychology, 75*, 394-407.

Cantor, N., Mischel, W., & Schwartz, J.C. (1982). A prototype analysis of psychological situations. *Cognitive Psychology, 14*, 45-77.

Cantor, N., Smith, E.E., French, R., & Mezzich, J. (1980). Psychiatric diagnosis as prototype categorization. *Journal of Abnormal Psychology, 89*, 181-193.

Cobb, A.T., Folger, R., & Wooten, K. (1995). The role justice plays in organizational change. *Public Administration Quarterly, 19*, 135-151.

Cohen, C.E. (1981). Person categories and social perception: Testing some boundaries of the processing effects of prior knowledge. *Journal of Personality and Social Psychology, 40*, 441-452.

Conlon, D.E. (1993). Some tests of the self-interest and group-value models of procedural justice: Evidence from an organizational appeal procedure. *Academy of Management Journal, 36*, 1109-1124.

Conlon, D.E., & Murray, N.M. (1996). Customer perceptions of corporate responses to product complaints: The role of explanations. *Academy of Management Journal, 39*, 1040-1056.

Conlon, D.E., & Ross, W.H. (1997). Appearances do count: The effects of outcomes and explanations on disputants fairness judgments and supervisory evaluations. *International Journal of Conflict, 8*, 5-31.

Dahlgren, K. (1985). The cognitive structure of social categories. *Cognitive Science, 9*, 379-398.

Daly, J.P., & Geyer, P.D. (1994). The role of fairness in implementing large-scale change: Employee evaluations of process and outcome in seven facility relocations. *Journal of Organizational Behavior, 15*, 623-638.

Farh, J., Earley, P.C., & Lin, S. (1997). Impetus for action: A cultural analysis of justice and organizational citizenship behavior in Chinese society. *Administrative Science Quarterly, 42*, 421-444.

Feldman, J. M. (1981). Beyond attribution theory: Cognitive processes in performance appraisal. *Journal of Applied Psychology, 66*, 127-148.

Fiske, S.T. (1982). Schema-triggered affect: Applications to social perception. In M.S. Clark & S.T. Fiske (Eds.), *Affect and cognition: The 17th annual Carnegie symposium on cognition* (pp. 55-78). Hillsdale, NJ: Erlbaum.

Fiske, S.T., & Neuberg, S.L. (1990). A continuum of impression formation, from category-based to individuating processes: Influences of information and motivation on attention and interpretation. In L. Berkowitz (Ed.), *Advances in experimental and social psychology* (pp. 1-74). San Diego, CA: Academic.

Fiske, S.T., & Taylor, S.E. (1991). *Social cognition* (2nd ed.). New York: McGraw-Hill.

Folger, R., & Greenberg, J. (1985). Procedural justice: An interpretative analysis of personnel systems. In K.M. Rowland & G.R. Ferris (Eds.), *Research in personnel and human resources management* (Vol. 3, pp. 141-183). Greenwich, CT: JAI Press.

Folger, R., & Konovsky, M. (1989). Effects of procedural and distributive justice on reactions to pay raise decisions. *Academy of Management Journal, 32*, 115-130.

Fryxell, G.E., & Gordon, M.T. (1989). Workplace justice and job satisfaction as predictors of satisfaction with union and management. *Academy of Management Journal, 32*, 851-866.

Furby, L. (1986). Psychology and justice. In R.L. Cohen (Ed.), *Justice: Views from the social sciences* (pp. 153-203). New York: Plenum.

Giacobbe-Miller, J. (1995). A test of the group values and control models of procedural justice from the competing perspectives of labor and management. *Personnel Psychology, 48*, 115-142.

Gilligan, C. (1977). In a different voice: Women's conceptions of the self and morality. *Harvard Educational Review, 47*, 431-446.

Gilligan, C. (1982). *In a different voice: Psychological theory and women's development.* Cambridge, MA: Harvard University Press.

Gilliland, S.W., (1993) The perceived fairness of selection systems: An organizational justice perspective. *Academy of Management Review, 18*, 694-734.

Gilliland, S.W. (1994). Effects of procedural and distributive justice on reactions to a selection system. *Journal of Applied Psychology, 79*, 691-701.

Greenberg, J. (1986). Determinants of perceived fairness of performance evaluations. *Journal of Applied Psychology, 71*, 340-342.

Greenberg, J. (1990). Employee theft as a reaction to underpayment inequity: The hidden cost of pay cuts. *Journal of Applied Psychology, 75*, 561-568.

Greenberg, J. (1991). Using explanations to manage impressions of performance appraisal fairness. *Employee Responsibilities and Rights Journal, 4*, 51-60.

Greenberg, J. (1993a). Justice and organizational citizenship: A commentary on the state of the science. *Employee Responsibilities and Rights Journal, 6*, 249-256.

Greenberg, J. (1993b). Stealing in the name of justice: Informational and interpersonal moderators of theft reactions to underpayment inequity. *Organizational Behavior and Human Decision Processes, 93*, 81-103.

Hafer, C.L. (2000). Do innocent victims threaten the belief in a just world?: Evidence from a modified stroop task. *Journal of Personality and Social Psychology, 79*, 165-173.

Hess, T.M., & Bolstad, C.A. (1998). Category-based versus attribute-based processing in different-aged adults. *Aging, Neuropsychology, and Cognition, 5*, 27-42.

Huo, Y.J., Smith, H.J., Tyler, T.R., & Lind, E.A. (1996). Superordinate identification, subgroup identification, and justice concerns: Is separatism the problem; is assimilation the answer? *Psychological Science, 7*, 40-45.

Huo, Y.J., & Tyler, T.R. (in press). Ethnic diversity and the viability of organizations: The role of procedural justice in bridging differences. In J. Greenberg & R. Cropanzano (Eds.), *Advances in organizational justice*. Stanford, CA: Stanford University Press.

Isenberg, D.J. (1986). The structure and process of understanding: Implications for managerial action. In H.P. Sims Jr., D.A. Gioia & associates (Eds.), *The thinking organization: Dynamics of organizational social cognition* (pp. 238-262). San Francisco: Jossey Bass.

Jacobs, S.L., Kulik, C.T., & Fichman, M. (1993). Category-based and feature-based processes in job impressions. *Journal of Applied Social Psychology, 23*, 1226-1248.

Kim, W.C., & Mauborgne, R. (1997). Fair process: Managing in the knowledge economy. *Harvard Business Review, 75*, 65-75.

Kim, W.C., & Mauborgne, R. (1998). Procedural justice, strategic decision making, and the knowledge economy. *Strategic Management Journal, 19*, 323-338.

Konovsky, M.A. (2000). Understanding procedural justice and its impact on business organizations. *Journal of Management, 26*, 489-511.

Konovsky, M., & Cropanzano, R. (1991). Perceived fairness and employee drug testing as a predictor of employee attitude and job performance. *Journal of Applied Psychology, 76*, 698-707.

Konovosky, M., & Cropanzano, R. (1993). Justice considerations in employee drug testing. In R. Cropanzano (Ed.), *Justice in the workplace*. Hillsdale, NJ: Erlbaum.

Konovsky, M., & Folger, R. (1991). The effects of procedures, social accounts, and benefits level on victims' layoff reactions. *Journal of Applied Social Psychology, 21*, 630-650.

Korsgaard, M.A., Schweiger, D.M., & Sapienza, H.J. (1995). Building commitment, attachment, and trust in strategic decision-making teams: The role of procedural justice. *Academy of Management Journal, 38*, 60-84.

Kulik, C.T. (1989). The effects of job categorization on judgments of the motivating potential of jobs. *Administrative Science Quarterly, 34*, 69-90.

Kulik, C.T., & Clark, S.C. (1994). Category-based and feature-based cognitive processes: The role of unfavorable information. *Journal of Applied Social Psychology, 24*, 1891-1918.

Lee, C., & Farh, J. (1999). The effects of gender in organizational justice perception. *Journal of Organizational Behavior, 20*, 133-143.

Leung, K., Smith, P.B., Wang, Z., & Sun, H. (1996). Job satisfaction in joint venture hotels in China: An organizational justice analysis. *Journal of International Business Studies, 27*, 947-962.

Leventhal, G.S. (1980). What should be done with equity theory? New approaches to the study of fairness in social relationships. In K. Gergen, M. Greenberg, & R. Willis (Eds.), *Social exchange: Advances in theory and research* (pp.27-55). New York: Plenum Press.

Leventhal, G.S., Karuza, J., & Fry, W.R. (1980). Beyond fairness: A theory of allocation preferences. In G. Mikula (Ed.), *Justice and social interaction* (pp.167-213). New York: Springer-Verlag.

Lind, E.A., Kanfer, R.E., & Earley, P.C. (1991). Voice, control, and procedural justice: Instrumental and noninstrumental concerns in fairness judgments. *Journal of Personality and Social Psychology, 59*, 952-959.

Lind, E.A., Kray, L., & Thompson, L. (1998). The social construction of injustice: Fairness judgments in response to own and others' unfair treatment by authorities. *Organizational Behavior and Human Decision Processes, 75*, 1-22.

Lind, E.A., & Tyler T.R. (1988). *The social psychology of procedural justice.* New York: Plenum Press.

Lord, R.G., Foti, R.J., & DeVader, C.L. (1984). A test of leadership categorization theory: Internal structure, information processing, and leadership perception. *Organizational Behavior and Human Performance, 34*, 343-378.

McEnrue, M.P. 1989). The perceived fairness of managerial promotion practices. *Human Relations, 42*, 815-827.

McFarlin, D.B., & Sweeney, P.D. (1992). Distributive and procedural justice as predictors of satisfaction with personal and organizational outcomes. *Academy of Management Journal, 35*, 626-637.

Mishra, A.K., & Spreitzer, G.M. (1998). Explaining how survivors respond to downsizing: The role of trust, empowerment, justice, and work redesign. *Academy of Management Review, 23*, 567-588.

Moorman, R.R. (1991). Relationship between organizational justice and organizational citizenship behaviors: Do fairness perceptions influence employee citizenship? *Journal of Applied Psychology, 76*, 845-855.

Mossholder, K.W., Bennett, N., & Martin, C.L. (1998). A multilevel analysis of procedural justice context. *Journal of Organizational Behavior, 19*, 131-141.

Murphy, G.L., & Wisniewski, E.J. (1989). Categorizing objects in isolation and in scenes: What a superordinate is good for. *Journal of Experimental Psychology: Learning, Memory, and Cognition, 15*, 572-586.

Nathan, B.R., & Lord, R.G. (1983). Cognitive categorization and dimensional schemata: A process approach to the study of halo in performance ratings. *Journal of Applied Psychology, 68*, 102-114.

Niedenthal, P.M., Cantor, N., & Kihlstrom, J.C. (1985). Prototype matching: A strategy for social decision making. *Journal of Personality and Social Psychology, 48*, 575-584.

Oldham, G.R., & Fried, Y. (1987). Employee reactions to workspace characteristics. *Journal of Applied Psychology, 72*, 75-80.

Oldham, G.R., Kulik, C.T., & Stepina, L.P. (1991). Physical environments and employee reactions: Effects of stimulus screening skills and job complexity. *Academy of Management Journal, 43*, 929-938.

Parker, C.P., Baltes, B.B., & Christiansen, N.D. (1997). Support for affirmative action, justice perceptions, and work attitudes: A study of gender and racial-ethnic group differences. *Journal of Applied Psychology, 82*, 376-389.

Peracchio, L.A., & Tybout, A.M. (1996). The moderating role of prior knowledge in schema-based product evaluation. *Journal of Consumer Research, 23*, 177-192.

Perry, E.L. (1994). A prototype matching approach to understanding the role of applicant gender and age in the evaluation of job applicants. *Journal of Applied Social Psychology, 24*, 1433-1473.

Perry, E.L., & Bourhis, A.C. (1998). A closer look at the role of applicant age in selection decisions. *Journal of Applied Social Psychology, 28*, 1670-1697.

Phillips, J.S., & Lord, R.G. (1982). Schematic information processing and perceptions of leadership in problem solving groups. *Journal of Applied Psychology, 67*, 486-492.

Rosch, E. (1975). Cognitive representations of semantic categories. *Journal of Experimental Psychology: General, 104,* 192-233.

Rosch, E. (1978). Principles of categorization. In E. Rosch & B.B. Lloyd (Eds.), *Cognition and categorization* (pp. 27-48). Hillsdale, NJ: Erlbaum.

Rosch, E., & Mervis, C.B. (1975). Family resemblances: Studies in the internal structure of categories. *Cognitive Psychology, 7,* 573-605.

Rumiati, R., & Lotto, L. (1996). Varieties of money: Experts' and non-experts' typicality judgments. *Journal of Economic Psychology, 17,* 403-413.

Schaubroeck, J., May, D.R., & Brown, F.W. (1994). Procedural justice explanations and employee reactions to economic hardship: A field experiment. *Journal of Applied Psychology, 79,* 455-460.

Schminke, M., Ambrose, M.L, & Cropanzano, R. (2000). The effect of organizational structure on perceptions of procedural fairness. *Journal of Applied Psychology, 85,* 294-304.

Schminke, M., Ambrose, M.L., & Noel, T.W. (1997). The effect of ethical frameworks on perceptions of organizational justice. *Academy of Management Journal, 40,* 1190-1207.

Shapiro, D.L. (1993). Reconciling theoretical differences among procedural justice researchers by re-evaluating what it means to have one's views "considered": Implications for third-party managers. In R. Cropanzano (Ed.), *Justice in human resource management* (pp. 51-78). Hillsdale, NJ: Erlbaum.

Singer, M. (1990). Determinants of perceived fairness in selection practices: An organizational justice perspective. *Genetic, Social, and General Psychology Monographs, 116,* 477-494.

Skarlicki, D.P., Ellard, J.H., & Kelln, B.R. (1998). Third-party perceptions of a layoff: Procedural, derogation, and retributive aspects of justice. *Journal of Applied Psychology, 83,* 119-127.

Skarlicki, D.P., & Folger, R. (1997). Retaliation in the workplace: The roles of distributive, procedural, and interactional justice. *Journal of Applied Psychology, 82,* 434-443.

Skarlicki, D.P., Folger, R., & Tesluk, P. (1999). Personality as a moderator in the relationship between fairness and retaliation. *Academy of Management Journal, 42,* 100-108.

Smith, E.E., Shoben, E.J., & Rips, L.J. (1974). Structure and process in semantic memory. *Psychological Review, 81,* 214-241.

Smith, H.J., Spears, R., & Oyen, M. (1994). "People like us": The influence of personal deprivation and group membership salience on justice evaluations. *Journal of Experimental Social Psychology, 30,* 277-299.

Smith, H.J., & Tyler, T.R. (1997). Choosing the right pond: The impact of group membership on self-esteem and group-oriented behavior. *Journal of Experimental Social Psychology, 33,* 146-170.

Smith, H.J., Tyler, T.R., Huo, Y.J., Ortiz, D.J., & Lind, E.A. (1998). The self-relevant implications of the group-value model: Group-membership, self-worth and treatment quality. *Journal of Experimental Social Psychology, 34,* 470-493.

Steiner, D.D., Guirard, S., & Baccino, T. (1999, April). *Cognitive processing of procedural justice information: Application of the oculometer.* Paper presented at the Annual Conference of the Society for Industrial/Organizational Psychology, Atlanta.

Sweeney, P.D., & McFarlin, D.B. (1997). Process and outcome: Gender differences in the assessment of justice. *Journal of Organizational Behavior, 18*, 83-98.

Thibaut, J., & Walker, L. (1975). *Procedural justice: A psychological analysis.* Hillsdale, NJ: Erlbaum.

Tremblay, M., Sire, B., & Pelchat, A. (1998). A study of the determinants and of the impact of flexibility on employee benefit satisfaction. *Human Relations, 51*, 667-688.

Tyler, T.R. (1980). Impact of directly and indirectly experienced events: The origin of crime-related judgments and behaviors. *Journal of Personality and Social Psychology, 39*, 13-28.

Tyler, T.R. (1988). What is procedural justice? Criteria used by citizens to assess the fairness of legal procedures. *Law and Society Review, 22*, 103-135.

Tyler, T.R. (1990). *Why people obey the law.* New Haven, CT: Yale University Press.

Tyler, T.R. (1996). The relationship of outcome and procedural fairness: How does knowing the outcome influence judgments about the procedure? *Social Justice Research, 9*, 311-325.

Tyler, T.R., & Degoey, P. (1995). Community, family, and social good: The psychological dynamics of procedural justice and social identification. *Nebraska Symposium on Motivation, 42*, 53-91.

Tyler, T.R., Degoey, P., & Smith, H. (1996). Understanding why the justice of group procedure matters: A test of the psychological dynamics of the group-value model. *Journal of Personality and Social Psychology, 70*, 913-930.

Tyler, T.R., & Lind, E.A. (1992). A relational model of authority in groups. In M. Zanna (Ed.), *Advances in experimental social psychology* (Vol. 25, pp. 115-191). New York: Academic Press.

van den Bos, K., Lind, E.A., & Wilke, H.A.M. (in press). The psychology of procedural and distributive justice viewed from the perspective of fairness heuristic theory. In R. Cropanzano (Ed.), *Justice in the workplace: Volume 2. From theory to practice.* Hillsdale, NJ: Erlbaum.

van den Bos, K., Lind, E.A., Vermunt, R., & Wilke, H.A.M. (1997). How do I judge my outcome when I do not know the outcome of others? The psychology of the fair process effect. *Journal of Personality and Social Psychology, 72*, 1034-1046.

van den Bos, K., Wilke, H.A.M., Lind, E.A., & Vermunt, R. (1998). Evaluating outcomes by means of the fair process effect: Evidence for different processes in fairness and satisfaction judgments. *Journal of Personality and Social Psychology, 74*, 1493-1503.

Vermunt, R., Blaauw, E., van Knippenberg, B., & van Knippenberg, D. (1998). *The influence of self-esteem on the use of outcome information and procedural information to evaluate the fairness of outcomes.* Unpublished manuscript.

Weaver, G. (1995). Does ethics code design matter? Effects of ethics code rationales and sanctions on recipients' justice perceptions and content recall. *Journal of Business Ethics, 14*, 367-385.

White, M.M, Tansky, J.A., & Baik, K. (1995). Linking culture and perceptions of justice: A comparison of students in Virginia and South Korea. *Psychological Reports, 77*, 1103-1112.

CHAPTER 3

FAIRNESS HEURISTIC THEORY:

Assessing the Information to Which People are Reacting has a Pivotal Role in Understanding Organizational Justice

Kees van den Bos

ABSTRACT

In this chapter, I focus on what I think is one of the most important aspects of fairness heuristic theory: To understand what people judge to be fair we have to carefully assess to what information they are reacting. To illustrate why this is important, a review of four studies is presented. Each one addresses different justice issues. Furthermore, each experiment shows that people look for information that is most relevant to their current situation. Moreover, the studies point out that when the most relevant information is not available, people use other information to assess what is fair and how to react to the situation at hand. In this way, less relevant but available information may be used as a heuristic substitute for more relevant yet missing information. After reviewing these four experiments, a plea is made for the importance of (1) carefully analyzing the information to which people are reacting, and (2) conducting experimental research, which, in my opinion, can substantially further our understanding of organizational behavior in general and organizational justice processes in particular.

INTRODUCTION

This chapter is about organizational justice and organizational behavior. In particular, it is about how people come to label experiences as fair or unfair. I start this chapter from the premise that justice processes play a crucial role in organizations and organizational behavior. This assumption is based on numerous articles, books, and research studies that all have shown that how people are treated in organizations (or other situations for that matter) may greatly affect their beliefs, feelings, attitudes, and behaviors (see, e.g., Cropanzano & Folger, 1989, 1991; Cropanzano & Greenberg, 1997; Folger, this volume; Folger & Konovsky, 1989; Gilliland, 1994; Greenberg, 1990; Steiner & Gilliland, 1996; Sweeney & McFarlin, 1993). Folger (1984) has even noted that "the importance of justice cannot be overstated" (p. ix). Being treated fairly by your organization and the people who work in it typically leads to things like higher commitment to the organization and more extra-role citizenship behavior (Folger & Cropanzano, 1998). People who have been experiencing unfair treatment, on the other hand, are more likely to leave their jobs, show lower levels of commitment, and may even start behaving in anti-normative ways (Greenberg, 1993). Therefore, understanding what people judge to be just and fair is a key issue for understanding organizational behavior (Ambrose & Kulik, this volume; Cropanzano & Folger, 1989, 1991; Cropanzano & Greenberg, 1997; Folger & Konovsky, 1989; Greenberg, 1990, 1993).

But how do people judge something to be fair or unfair? In the current chapter, I would like to answer this important question by focusing on what I think are central aspects of fairness heuristic theory, a framework Allan Lind, Riël Vermunt, Henk Wilke, and I have been working on for the last couple of years. I would especially like to focus on what I think is one of the most important aspects of this theory: To understand what people judge to be fair we have to carefully assess to what information people are reacting. To illustrate why this is important, I will present a review of four studies. Each one addresses different justice issues. Furthermore, each experiment shows that people look for information that is most relevant to their current situation. Moreover, the studies point out that when the most relevant information is not available, people use other information to assess what is fair and how to react to the situation at hand. In this way, less relevant but available information may be used as a heuristic substitute for more relevant yet missing information. In the first three studies, I focus on an important case of the fair process effect: the positive effect perceived procedural fairness typically has on people's judgments of outcomes. In the fourth study, I present data on an important fair outcome effect: the positive effect of perceived outcome fairness on judgments of procedure. After reviewing these four experiments, I make a plea for the importance of (1) carefully analyzing the information to which people are reacting, and (2) conducting experimental research, which, in my opinion, can substantially further our understanding of organizational behavior in general and organizational justice processes in particular.

EQUITY AND THE FAIRNESS HEURISTIC

One of the most widely-accepted answers to the question of what people judge to be fair has been provided by equity theory (e.g., Adams, 1965; Walster, Berscheid, & Walster, 1973; Walster, Walster, & Berscheid, 1978). In essence, equity theory proposes that people judge an outcome as fair when their own outcome-to-input ratio equals some comparative or referent outcome-to-input ratio. This process is often—but not always (see, e.g., Van den Bos, Wilke, Lind, & Vermunt, 1998)—driven by social comparison with other people's outcomes and inputs such that people judge their outcome as fair when the ratio of their own outcomes and inputs equals that of comparison others. Equity theory and other related conceptions of justice—such as relative deprivation theory (Crosby, 1976; Stouffer, Suchman, DeVinney, Star, & Williams, 1949) and the conceptions of Blau (1964), Deutsch (1975, 1985), and Homans (1961)—emphasize the importance of social comparison information in the process of evaluating outcomes. As argued by Messick and Sentis (1983), the comparison of a person's outcome with those of comparison others influences the person's beliefs about the fairness or justice of the person's own outcome, and affects how satisfied he or she is with the outcome.

Equity theory has received wide support in social and organizational studies. In fact, equity theory has been so successful that the 1976 volume of the prestigious *Advances in Experimental Social Psychology* was devoted entirely to this framework. In the volume it was proposed that the theory probably could serve as the general theory social psychology had been waiting for (see Berkowitz & Walster, 1976). Furthermore, some articles that appeared in the volume even went so far as to argue that equity ratings are the most important type of fairness judgments.

Thus, equity theory has been very influential. One of its basic propositions is that, in order to judge whether an outcome is fair, people have to know what outcomes comparison others have received. However, in the first study that I discuss here (Van den Bos, Lind, Vermunt, & Wilke, 1997) we wondered whether people always know the outcomes of others, as important articles on equity theory have suggested (for overviews, see Adams, 1965; Messick & Sentis, 1983; Walster et al., 1973, 1978). We proposed that they frequently do not. For instance, in everyday life we often do not know the salaries of the people with whom we work, and even if we do, we may not have a good idea of their contributions. Thus, we argued that social comparison information about outcomes is often not available. We therefore reasoned that in everyday life the issue of how people form outcome judgments is more complicated than is suggested by important articles on equity theory (for overviews, see Adams, 1965; Messick & Sentis, 1983; Walster et al., 1973, 1978).

Furthermore, we proposed that when information about outcomes of others is not available, people would start using information that is available. But what information is available? We suggested that procedural information is frequently present. Then, in many situations people may turn to the fairness of procedures to determine how to react to their outcome. In other words, people may use procedural fairness as a heuristic substitute to judge the fairness of their outcome. Therefore, in situations where a person only knows his or her own outcome (and is not informed about the outcome of another person), we predicted a fair process effect: People will react more positively toward their outcomes following a fair rather than an unfair procedure.

However, we also argued that when a person does have information about the outcome of a comparable other person, he or she will use this social comparison information as a basis for reactions to their outcome. Therefore, we expected less strong fair process effects in situations where a person knows what outcome the referent other receives. In other words, we predicted that when people had social comparison information about outcomes there would be less need for procedural fairness to serve as a heuristic substitute in the outcome judgment process.

The results of two studies, one a scenario study and one a traditional experimental study, corroborated our line of reasoning. In the present chapter, I will only discuss the second experiment. In it, participants were invited to the laboratory to participate in a study on how people perform tasks. In the first part of the instructions, participants were informed that they would participate in the study with another person, referred to as Other. We explained that after all participants were run, a lottery would be held among all participants with the winner receiving 100 Dutch guilders (approximately 60 U.S. Dollars). Participants were told that a total of 200 lottery tickets would be divided among all participants. It was also communicated to the participants that after the work round the experimenter would divide some lottery tickets between them and the other participant. The task was then explained to the participants. After this, participants practiced the tasks for two minutes and then worked on the tasks for 10 minutes. After the work round, participants were told how many tasks they had completed in the work round, and—to ensure that participants compared themselves to Other—it was communicated to the participants that Other had completed an equivalent number of tasks.

After this, our experimental manipulations were induced. First, the procedure was manipulated. In the voice condition, the experimenter allegedly asked participants to type in their opinions about the percentage of tickets that they should receive relative to Other. Participants in the no-voice condition were informed that they would not be asked to type such an opinion. It was then communicated to the participants that they received three lottery tickets. This was followed by the manipulation of the outcome of the other participant. In the Other better condition, the participant was informed that Other received five tickets. In the Other worse condition, participants were informed that Other received one ticket. In the Other equal condition, participants were told that Other received three tickets. In the Other unknown condition, participants were told nothing about the number of tickets Other received. After this, participants were asked how fair they considered the three lottery tickets that they received, how satisfied they were with the three lottery tickets that they received, how fair they considered the procedure used to assess the number of tickets that they received, and how satisfied they were with the procedure used to assess the number of tickets that they received.

The results of participants' procedure and outcome judgments are presented in Table 1. As expected, *procedural* judgments (procedural fairness and satisfaction) were not affected by the manipulation of outcome (outcome of Other better, worse, equal, or unknown), and only showed main effects of procedure: Participants judged the procedure to be more fair and were more satisfied with it in the presence of a voice opportunity than without it. These results are important because they show that our manipulation of procedure was perceived as intended.

As hypothesized, participants' *outcome* judgments (outcome fairness and satisfaction) showed that participants who did not know the outcome of the other participant judged their outcome to be more fair and were more satisfied with it when they had received an opportunity to voice their opinion than when they had not received such an opportunity. Furthermore, in the conditions in which participants knew the outcome of the other participant, outcome judgments did not differ as a function of whether participants were or were not allowed a voice.

TABLE 1
Mean Procedure and Outcome Judgments in Van den Bos, Lind, Vermunt, and Wilke (1997, Study 2)

Dependent variable	Procedure	Outcome of Other Participant			
		Unknown	Better	Worse	Equal
Procedural fairness	Voice	5.2_a	4.5_a	5.3_a	4.9_a
	No voice	3.4_b	2.9_b	3.4_b	4.0_b
Procedural satisfaction	Voice	5.4_a	5.0_a	5.5_a	5.1_a
	No voice	2.8_b	3.2_b	3.9_b	4.0_b
Outcome fairness	Voice	4.7_b	2.1_d	1.8_d	6.2_a
	No voice	3.4_c	2.4_d	2.0_d	6.1_a
Outcome satisfaction	Voice	$5.1_{b,c}$	2.3_e	$4.4_{c,d}$	6.1_a
	No voice	3.5_d	2.8_e	5.0_c	$6.0_{a,b}$

Note. Entries are means on 7-point Likert-type scales; higher values indicate more positive ratings of the dependent variable in question. For each dependent variable, means with no subscripts in common differ significantly ($p < .05$).

These findings strongly support fairness heuristic theory's line of reasoning: When people do not have information about outcomes of others they indeed use procedural fairness as a heuristic substitute to assess how to react to their outcome (yielding fair process effects on people's outcome judgments), but they rely less on procedure information when they are informed about the outcome of a comparison other (resulting in nonsignificant fair process effects). More generally, the findings point out that it is important to carefully assess what information is available to people when they are trying to form fairness judgments. The findings also suggest that equity theory is not a descriptive theory of what people judge to be fair, but rather a prescriptive theory. That is, the theory dictates what information people need to judge their outcome as fair or unfair, yet it does not deal with the issue of what happens when important information is missing. Thus, the results of Van den Bos, Lind, et al. (1997) suggest that classifying information conditions is an important precondition before we as scientists and practitioners can be certain that the processes proposed by equity theory are operating.

It is important to note here that Skitka (1998) has replicated the Van den Bos, Lind et al. (1997) findings by using different operationalizations than the above-mentioned manipulations. In the Van den Bos, Lind et al. experiments, certainty about outcome fairness was manipulated by giving participants either complete or incomplete information about social comparison-based equity. Skitka has found comparable effects by making a distinction between situations in which people have a very clear a priori sense of what outcomes would be fair and just (a moral mandate) and situations in which they do not have a clear moral mandate. Using the concept of moral mandates as an operationalization of outcome certainty is an important new operationalization, I think, and it is easy to see that moral mandates can be used successfully to explore the intriguing relationship between procedural and distributive justice in general, and the use of heuristics in particular. In fact, moral mandates may turn out to be an operationalization that can be used more easily in survey studies and in organizational settings than social comparison-based equity.

WILL THE FAIR PROCESS EFFECT ATTENUATE IN THE PRESENCE OF ANY SOLID OUTCOME INFORMATION?

The Van den Bos, Lind et al. (1997) paper was the first in a series on what we like to call the heuristic substitutability principle; that is, the proposition that people use less relevant but available information when more relevant information is missing. In the second study that I review here (Van den Bos, Wilke, Lind, & Vermunt, 1998), my coauthors and I decided to try to take this principle one step further.

Although the study by Van den Bos, Lind et al. (1997) supported the substitutability principle, our manipulations in that study were extreme endpoints of an outcome information continuum: Participants either did not have any outcome reference point at all or they had a complete social comparison-based equity reference point. Therefore, our findings provided some evidence for fairness heuristic theory's substitutability proposition, but it can be argued—as we did in the Van den Bos, Lind et al. article—that it is not clear whether these results suggest that fair process effects will attenuate in the presence of any solid outcome reference point. In the Van den Bos, Wilke, Lind, and Vermunt article (1998), we therefore investigated whether people would use procedural fairness information in the outcome evaluation process when a reference point other than social comparisons was present. More specifically, we focused on people's intrapersonal expectations about outcomes as an important reference point for evaluating outcomes (cf. Steiner, this volume).

People's expectations about what outcome they will receive has been an area of special attention in distributive justice research (Van den Bos, Vermunt, & Wilke, 1996). Research has shown expectations to be an important factor in the psychological process of forming outcome judgments (cf. Steiner, this volume). For example, a significant study in the relative deprivation literature is that of deCarufel and Schopler (1979), who reasoned that outcome improvement may be a source of rising expectations, and that when these rising expectations are violated by improvements that fail to rise at the same rate, people may be dissatisfied with their improved outcomes (see also Folger, 1977; Ross, Thibaut, & Evenbeck, 1971). After reviewing the domain of social justice research, Furby (1986) concluded that "the notion that meeting expectations is central in the definition of justice" (p. 183; see also Adams, 1965). This suggests that outcome expectations may serve as a significant reference point in the process of evaluating the outcomes one receives (cf. Folger 1977; Steiner, this volume).

In the Van den Bos, Wilke, Lind, and Vermunt (1998) research, we wanted to explore the psychology of expectation-based versus social comparison-based outcome judgments by examining the strength of procedural fairness effects in the presence of each type of reference point. We compared the strength of procedure effects in the presence of social comparison-based versus expectation-based information. In the second study presented in the article, all participants received three lottery tickets, and this outcome was manipulated to be better than expected (participants had expected to receive one ticket), worse than expected (five tickets had been expected), equal to the outcome of a comparison other (Other received three tickets), better than the outcome of the comparison other (Other received one ticket), or worse than the outcome of the comparison other (Other received five tickets). The second independent variable was the presence or absence of an opportunity to voice an opinion (cf. Van den Bos, Lind et al., 1997). The primary dependent variables were participants' procedural fairness and satisfaction judgments and outcome fairness and satisfaction perceptions.

In the literature on the effects of reference points in judgment and choice (e.g., Boles & Messick, 1995; Loewenstein, Thompson, & Bazerman, 1989; Messick & Sentis, 1985), it is argued, among other things, that an important difference between reference points is whether they are based on social comparisons or expectations. Furthermore, within the social justice domain there is evidence that expectation-based reference points are generally sufficiently weak or ambiguous, thereby allowing fair process effects to occur (cf. Walker, LaTour, Lind, & Thibaut, 1974). After all, as argued by Blau (1964), and demonstrated by the results of Austin, McGinn, and Susmilch (1980), intrapersonal comparisons often provide a weaker basis for evaluations of outcome fairness than social comparison equity information. Similarly, fairness heuristic theory proposes that people need not just any information (such as expectations) but specific fairness information (such as social comparison-based equity information) in order to decide how to behave in the course of social interactions (Lind, 1992, 1998).

On the basis of this, we argued that knowing that your outcome is equal to, better than, or worse than the outcome of a comparison other provides more relevant information and a more diagnostic reference point regarding how to respond to your outcome than when you only know that your outcome is better or worse than expected. Following fairness heuristic theory's substitutability proposition, this implies that people who receive an outcome that is better or worse than expected will use other information—such as procedural information—more than people who receive an outcome that is equal, better, or worse than that of the comparison other. Therefore, we predicted an interaction between procedure and outcome, such that outcome evaluations would show strong effects of procedural fairness when outcomes were better or worse than expected, whereas less strong fair process effects would appear when outcomes were equal to, better than, or worse than the outcome of a comparison other.

The results of the procedure and outcome judgments are presented in Table 2. As expected, we only found main effects for procedure on the *procedure* judgments (both fairness and satisfaction). Participants thought their procedure to be more fair and showed higher levels of satisfaction with it when they were allowed voice as opposed to no voice. Thus, our manipulation of procedure was successful.

On the other hand, participants' *outcome* judgments showed strong interaction effects. In the conditions where participants' outcome was better or worse than expected, strong, significant effects of procedure were found, indicating that participants judged their outcome to be more fair and were more satisfied with it following the voice procedure as opposed to the no-voice procedure. In the conditions where outcomes were equal to, better than, or worse than the outcome of the comparison other,

TABLE 2
Mean Procedure and Outcome Judgments in Van den Bos, Wilke, Lind, and Vermunt (1998, Study 2)

Dependent variable	Procedure	Outcome				
		Better than expected	Worse than expected	Equal to Other	Better than Other	Worse than Other
Procedural fairness	Voice	4.6$_a$	4.8$_a$	4.6$_a$	5.1$_a$	5.0$_a$
	No voice	3.3$_b$	2.4$_b$	3.3$_b$	3.5$_b$	3.1$_b$
Procedural satisfaction	Voice	5.7$_a$	5.4$_a$	5.4$_a$	5.0$_a$	5.1$_a$
	No voice	3.3$_b$	2.3$_b$	3.2$_b$	3.4$_b$	3.1$_b$
Outcome fairness	Voice	5.5$_b$	4.2$_c$	6.4$_a$	1.9$_e$	2.4$_{d,e}$
	No voice	4.2$_c$	3.0$_d$	6.3$_{a,b}$	2.5$_{d,e}$	2.6$_{d,e}$
Outcome satisfaction	Voice	6.1$_a$	3.1$_c$	6.1$_a$	4.7$_b$	2.4$_{c,d}$
	No voice	5.2$_b$	2.1d	6.2$_a$	4.7$_b$	3.1$_c$

Note. Entries are means on 7-point Likert-type scales; higher values indicate more positive ratings of the dependent variable in question. For each dependent variable, means with no subscripts in common differ significantly ($p < .05$).

weaker, nonsignificant procedure effects were found, indicating that participants' outcome judgments were not affected as a function of whether or not they were allowed voice.

These findings are important because they show that when people receive outcomes that are better or worse than expected, they indeed use procedural fairness—as a heuristic substitute—to determine how to react to their outcome (resulting in strong fair process effects), but that they rely less on procedural information when they receive outcomes that are equal to, better than, or worse than those of comparison others (yielding less strong fair process effects).

Van den Bos, Lind et al. (1997) provided some initial data on fairness heuristic theory's notion that in order to explain the fair process effect we have to carefully analyze what information is available to people when forming outcome judgments. However, the Van den Bos, Lind, et al. results might have represented attenuation of the fair process effect in the presence of any solid outcome reference point. The studies by Van den Bos, Wilke, Lind, and Vermunt (1998) revealed that it is not just a question of any reference point (such as expectations), but rather specifically social comparison equity information that matters. If people do not have such an unambiguous, relevant reference point about outcomes they rely on other information—such as procedural information—when assessing how to respond to their outcome.

It is possible, of course, that we found the interaction effects we did because our manipulations of outcome expectations were not strong enough to be informative to our participants. That is, perhaps if we had used stronger expectation manipulations (cf. Van den Bos et al., 1996) our participants would have found little reason to refer to the procedure in evaluating the outcomes. We believe there are several things that argue against this interpretation of the findings. First, we matched the objective magnitude of the social comparison-based and the expectation-based manipulations. This does not guarantee that the two sorts of conditions had similar subjective meaning, but it does suggest that the manipulations were probably similarly potent. Second, a total of 500 participants took part in the two experiments presented in the Van den Bos, Wilke, Lind, & Vermunt (1998) article, thus enhancing the statistical power of our findings. Third, the means in the better than expected and worse than expected conditions in both studies make it clear that our expectation manipulations were potent enough to have substantial impact on outcome evaluations. And fourth, the substantial research literature on the fair process effect contains instances of the effect in the context of very strong variations of outcome expectations (see Lind & Tyler, 1988; Tyler & Lind, 1992). Nonetheless, I would like to emphasize here that the point of the findings presented in Table 2 is that it is people's relative certainty of a judgment that matters. This implies that ordinarily mere expectations might not provide as much certainty about fairness as social comparison information. But perhaps sometimes, at least under some conditions, the certainty could be greater from expectations than from social comparison. Future research may want to further explore the relative importance of social comparison-based and expectation-based reference points.

The findings presented in Table 2 also yielded differential effects on outcome fairness and satisfaction judgments. That is, the difference between the equal to Other condition versus better than Other and worse than Other conditions was greater for judged fairness than for judged satisfaction (for details, see Table 2). This pattern of effects nicely replicated the results reported by Van den Bos, Lind et al. (1997), and suggests that satisfaction judgments are more strongly affected by relative egoism than fairness judgments. Moreover, in accordance with the work by Blau (1964) and Austin et al. (1980), outcome variations relative to social comparisons were more directly related to fairness than outcome variations relative to expectations. These results show that although outcome fairness and favorability are closely related, they are different, and that people may differentially form judgments on these two dimensions of outcome evaluation. This suggests that researchers should not confuse these two types of judgments, and that they should draw an explicit distinction between outcome fairness and favorability; a distinction that has been largely overlooked since the Messick and Sentis (1983) work.

WHEN DO WE NEED PROCEDURAL FAIRNESS?

In the third study that I review here (Van den Bos, Wilke, & Lind, 1998), we used the substitutability principle to try to answer the question of when people start paying attention to fairness in general, and to procedural fairness in particular. Fairness heuristic theory recognizes that in several situations fairness is a salient issue. More specifically, the theory proposes that people especially need fairness judgments when they are concerned about potential problems associated with social interdependence and socially based identity processes. These problems are related to what has been termed "the fundamental social dilemma" (e.g., Lind, 1995). In essence, this dilemma is concerned with the question of whether one can trust others not to exploit or exclude one from important relationships and groups (cf. Huo, Smith, Tyler, & Lind, 1996; Lind & Tyler, 1988; Smith, Tyler, Huo, Ortiz, & Lind, 1998; Tyler & Lind, 1992).

An important subgroup of social relations is authority processes. Based on the work by Tyler and Lind (1992; Tyler & DeGoey, 1996), fairness heuristic theory argues that, because ceding authority to another person raises the possibility of exploitation and exclusion, people frequently feel uneasy about their relationship with authorities and about the outcomes they receive from them. On the basis of this line of reasoning, Van den Bos, Wilke, and Lind (1998) suggested that when people are trying to decide how to react to an outcome they received from an authority, they want to have information about whether they can trust the authority.

These ideas led us to ask: Do people often have direct information about an authority's trustworthiness? We suggested that they frequently do not. Furthermore, we proposed that if people do not have information about the authority's trustworthiness, they still are interested in trying to find out how to judge the outcome they received from the authority. How do they do this? We suggested that in such situations—in which information about the authority's trustworthiness is missing—people refer to the fairness of the authority's procedures to decide how to react to the outcome. In other words, in situations in which definitive trust information is lacking, procedural fairness serves as a heuristic substitute for deciding how to evaluate an outcome one has received from the authority. As a consequence, we expected that when people do not have information about the authority's trustworthiness, they would react more positively toward an outcome they received from the authority when the authority has been employing a fair as opposed to an unfair procedure.

On the other hand, this line of thought also suggested that when people do have direct, explicit information about the authority's trustworthiness, they may be less in need of procedural fairness as a heuristic substitute. We therefore expected that if people do *not* have information about the authority's trustworthiness, recipients would react more positively toward the outcome when the authority has been employing a fair as opposed to an unfair procedure, but that less strong fair process effects would be found if people have received direct information about the authority's trustworthiness.

To test these predictions we manipulated experimentally information that an authority was very trustworthy or untrustworthy (as indicated by persons who previously had interacted with the authority) or no information about the authority's trustworthiness was given. We also varied whether or not participants were allowed an opportunity to voice their opinion. The outcome that participants received was held constant across conditions (all participants received three lottery tickets). The main dependent variables included participants' procedural fairness and satisfaction judgments and outcome fairness and satisfaction perceptions.

The results of the procedure and outcome judgments are presented in Table 3. As expected, only main effects of procedure were found on the *procedure* judgments (both fairness and satisfaction). Participants judged their procedure to be more fair and were more satisfied with it following voice than following no voice. However, as predicted, participants' *outcome* judgments showed strong interaction effects. These effects indicated strong, significant effects of procedure in the conditions where participants did not know whether or not they could trust the authority: Participants judged their outcome to be more fair and were more satisfied with it when they had received voice than when they had not received voice. Weaker, nonsignificant, effects of procedure resulted when participants knew that they could or could not trust the authority, indicating that in these conditions participants' outcome judgments did not differ as a function of voice versus no-voice procedures.

Thus, these results show that people's reactions to an outcome they received from an authority are strongly affected by procedural fairness information when they do *not* know whether the authority can be trusted.

TABLE 3

Mean Procedure and Outcome Judgments in Van den Bos, Wilke, and Lind (1998, Study 2)

		Trust		
Dependent variable	Procedure	Unknown	Positive	Negative
Procedural fairness	Voice	4.8_a	4.8_a	4.7_a
	No voice	2.8_b	3.3_b	2.9_b
Procedural satisfaction	Voice	4.8_a	4.9_a	4.5_a
	No voice	2.7_b	3.2_b	2.7_b
Outcome fairness	Voice	4.7_a	$3.9_{a,b,c}$	$3.3_{b,c}$
	No voice	3.0_c	$4.2_{a,b}$	$3.5_{b,c}$
Outcome satisfaction	Voice	4.9_a	$3.9_{b,c}$	$3.4_{b,c}$
	No voice	3.2_c	$4.2_{a,b}$	$3.5_{b,c}$

Note. Entries are means on 7-point Likert-type scales; higher values indicate more positive ratings of the dependent variable in question. For each dependent variable, means with no subscripts in common differ significantly (p < .05).

This suggests that recipients who do not have information about an authority's trustworthiness are more willing to accept the outcomes the authority gives to them if they are allocated outcomes by fair rather than unfair procedures. However, when people have been informed about the authority's trustworthiness, they are less in need of procedural fairness information, yielding weaker fair process effects on their outcome judgments. The results suggest that people especially need procedural fairness information for deciding how to react to outcomes they received from an authority when they do not know whether the authority can be trusted. In other words, people may start to use fairness judgments as heuristic substitutes for an authority's trustworthiness when direct information about the authority's trustworthiness is missing.

A careful inspection of Table 3 reveals that positive and negative trust did not affect outcome judgments. It is important to note that there is good reason to argue that positive and negative trust should not necessarily affect outcome judgments. Tyler, Boeckmann, Smith, and Huo (1997; Tyler & DeGoey, 1996; Tyler & Lind, 1992), for example, have shown that valenced trust is more important for attitudes and behaviors that have a longer-term horizon (e.g., willingness to comply) than variables such as perceived outcome satisfaction or fairness. Consistent with this argument, the manipulation-check findings that were presented in the Van den Bos, Wilke, and Lind (1998) article reveal that positive and negative trust information did in fact affect trust perceptions as well as voluntary compliance with the authority's decisions. Our positive and negative trust information was therefore perceived as intended and was successful at affecting some well-specified variables. This is important because it shows that positive and negative trust were manipulated successfully. Even more important, the findings summarized in Table 3 reveal that it may be more valuable to focus on the distinction between known versus unknown trust than on positive versus negative trust. Focusing on the former distinction may in fact reveal insights for the psychology of organizational justice and trust that previous research—focusing on the latter distinction—has missed.

In the previously reviewed studies (Van den Bos, Lind et al., 1997; Van den Bos, Wilke, Lind, & Vermunt, 1998), we focused on the content of outcome information and on procedural fairness acting as a heuristic substitute when outcome information is missing or weak. The Van den Bos, Wilke, and Lind (1998) results expanded the line of reasoning from these previous studies to other, more socially-oriented information: trust. It can now be concluded that people especially need procedural fairness information when strong, unambiguous outcome fairness information or information about the authority's trustworthiness is lacking. What is especially interesting about the findings is that they provide strong evidence for one answer to the question of why people care about justice. People care about justice, and especially procedural justice, when they do not have direct, explicit information regarding whether they can trust others not to exploit or exclude them from important relationships and groups.

WHAT ARE WE TALKING ABOUT WHEN WE TALK ABOUT NO-VOICE PROCEDURES?

In contrast to the previous three studies, in the fourth study (Van den Bos, 1999), I focused on the reverse effect: the positive effect of perceived outcome fairness on judgments of the procedure. This instance of the fair outcome effect is the mechanism I used to show that there are important psychological implications of making a distinction between what I called explicit and implicit no-voice conditions.

Following Folger's research (e.g., Folger, 1977; Folger, Rosenfield, Grove, & Corkran, 1979), studies on procedural justice have frequently investigated how people react to being allowed an opportunity to voice their opinion versus not being allowed such an opportunity. In general this is now the most accepted manipulation of procedural justice (e.g., Brockner et al., 1998; Lind, Kanfer, & Earley, 1990; Lind & Tyler, 1988; Tyler, 1987; Tyler & Lind, 1992; Tyler, Rasinski, & Spodick, 1985; Van den Bos, Vermunt, & Wilke, 1996).

An important aim of the Van den Bos (1999) paper was to make a distinction between two types of no-voice procedures that exist in everyday life and which have been used in previous research studies. One type of no-voice procedure has been used in studies by Folger (1977) and Lind et al. (1990). In both these studies, only participants who got voice were informed about a possibility that participants could get an opportunity to voice their opinion about an important decision the experimenter was going to make, and after this they were informed that they got such an opportunity. Participants in the no-voice condition were not informed about a possible voice opportunity and hence implicitly were not allowed a voice. I labeled this as an implicit no-voice procedure. In my own research thus far I have used a different type of no-voice procedure (see Van den Bos, Lind et al., 1997; Van den Bos et al., 1996; Van den Bos, Wilke, & Lind, 1998; Van den Bos, Wilke, Lind, & Vermunt, 1998; see also Brockner et al., 1998, Study 5; Hunton, Hall, & Price, 1998): In both the voice and the no-voice conditions, participants were informed that there was a possibility that participants could get an opportunity to voice their opinion about a decision the experimenter was going to make. Participants in the voice conditions were told that they got voice whereas participants in the no-voice conditions were informed that they did not get an opportunity to voice their opinion. I called this latter procedure an explicit no-voice procedure.

To my knowledge, previous research has not made a distinction between implicit and explicit no voice, and in previous articles (including my own papers!) these two types of no-voice procedures have been treated as if they were one and the same thing. In the Van den Bos (1999) article I tried to show, however, that making this distinction is not only methodologically important but also may help to further our insights into the fair outcome effect. On the basis of the substitutability proposition, I argued that when information about the procedure is not available (as in the case of implicit no-voice procedures), people may find it difficult to decide how they should judge the procedure, and they therefore may use the fairness of their outcome to assess how to respond to the procedure. As a result, the procedural judgments of these people may show strong fair outcome effects. However, persons who are explicitly denied voice have explicit information about procedure and hence have to rely less on outcome information, yielding weaker fair outcome effects on procedural judgments.

The second study in the Van den Bos (1999) article was an experiment that was comparable to those reviewed above. In the voice condition, the experimenter asked participants to type in their opinion about the percentage of tickets that they should receive relative to the other participant. Participants in the explicit no-voice condition were informed that they would not be asked to type their opinion about the percentage of tickets that they should receive relative to the other participant. In the implicit no-voice condition, participants did not receive any information about voice or no voice procedures (and hence implicitly received no voice opportunity). After this, participants received three lottery tickets, and they were told that the other participant received either three tickets (equal to Other condition) or five tickets (worse than Other condition). Main dependent variables were procedural and outcome judgments (fairness and satisfaction).

The results of the procedure and outcome judgments are presented in Table 4. As expected, *outcome* judgments showed only a main effect of outcome: Participants judged their outcome to be more fair and were more satisfied with their outcome when it was equal to as opposed to worse than the other participant's outcome. The outcome manipulation was therefore successfully operationalized.

Also consistent with predictions, *procedure* judgments showed strong interaction effects. There were strong, significant outcome effects in the implicit no-voice condition, revealing that participants judged their procedure to be more fair and were more satisfied with it when their outcome was equal to rather than worse than the outcome of the other participant. In the explicit no-voice and the voice conditions, weaker, nonsignificant effects of outcome were found, indicating that in those conditions procedural judgments (both fairness and satisfaction) did not differ as a function of the other participant's outcome.

These findings show that it is important to make a distinction between implicit and explicit no-voice procedures. When information about proce-

TABLE 4
Mean Procedure and Outcome Judgments in Van den Bos (1999, Study 2)

		Procedure		
Dependent variable	Outcome	Implicit no voice	Explicit no voice	Voice
Procedural fairness	Equal to Other	6.0_a	3.6_c	$5.6_{a,b}$
	Worse than Other	2.3_d	$2.8_{c,d}$	4.9_b
Procedural satisfaction	Equal to Other	5.9_a	3.6_c	$5.3_{a,b}$
	Worse than Other	2.3_d	$2.8_{c,d}$	4.6_b
Outcome fairness	Equal to Other	6.0_a	6.4_a	6.6_a
	Worse than Other	2.4_b	2.5_b	2.1_b
Outcome satisfaction	Equal to Other	5.5_a	5.9_a	5.7_a
	Worse than Other	2.5_b	2.7_b	2.3_b

Note. Entries are means on 7-point Likert-type scales; higher values indicate more positive ratings of the dependent variable in question. For each dependent variable, means with no subscript in common differ significantly ($p < .05$).

dure is not available—as is the case when persons implicitly have not received voice—people may find it difficult to decide how they should judge their procedure. They therefore use the fairness of their outcome, as a heuristic substitute, to determine how to respond to the procedure. As a result, the procedural judgments of these people show strong fair outcome effects. However, individuals who have received procedural information, such as persons who explicitly have been denied voice or those who have received voice, have to rely less on outcome information, yielding weaker fair outcome effects on procedural judgments.

In the studies that I discussed earlier in this chapter, the possible effects of information about a procedure on outcome judgments were explored (see Van den Bos, Lind et al., 1997; Van den Bos, Wilke, & Lind, 1998; Van den Bos, Wilke, Lind, & Vermunt, 1998). In most of these fair process studies, my coauthors and I focused on the contents of outcome information and on the issue of procedural fairness acting as a heuristic substitute when outcome information is missing or weak. The Van den Bos (1999) results have expanded the line of reasoning from these previous studies to the reverse effect: the influence of outcome information on procedural judgments. Collectively, these studies show that procedural and outcome information can each act as a substitute for missing information about outcome and procedure respectively.

Now that it has been identified that important differences within no-voice procedures exist, future research may want to focus on other rules of procedural justice (see Leventhal, 1980, for a list). It is interesting to note here that there is some evidence suggesting that when information about *biased procedures* is absent (as opposed to present) people rely more on outcome information (Daly & Tripp, 1996). In fact, the Daly and Tripp article appears to be the only one thus far that has paid attention to the effects of availability of procedural information (absent vs. present) as a possible moderator of the effects of variations in outcome on perceptions of procedure. What is especially interesting about the Van den Bos (1999) findings is that they make an important distinction between implicit and explicit no-voice procedures. This is a significant distinction because it furthers our understanding of the psychology of important social justice phenomena and because it specifies what we are talking about when we talk about no-voice procedures.

GENERAL DISCUSSION

In this chapter, I hope to have shown that an important aspect of fairness heuristic theory's perspective on the psychology of organizational justice is that it demands that researchers specify what information is known to people and what information is not available or is difficult to interpret. Furthermore, fairness heuristic theory argues that in incomplete or insufficient information conditions, people process information heuristically; for example, they use other information—such as procedural or outcome fairness—to substitute for information that would be most directly relevant but that is actually missing. This suggests that fairness heuristic theory offers a more contextual account of the justice judgment process than do previous theories (such as equity theory). Attending to the nature of justice information that is actually available may greatly enhance our understanding of organizational justice issues. Such analyses should contribute to a better understanding of why people behave the way they do in organizations. Armed with this understanding, it may be possible to supply people with additional information causing them to react differently, and hopefully more positively, toward the organization.

Another interesting aspect of the findings reviewed here is that they show that people may clearly distinguish between judgments of procedures and outcomes (for details, see Tables 1-4). These differential effects on participants' judgments of procedures and outcomes suggest that people make clear distinctions between procedural and distributive justice issues. A similar conclusion can be drawn on the basis of research by Greenberg (1986) and by Sheppard and Lewicki (1987). These authors asked respondents to describe fair and unfair events that had occurred in their lives. The findings of their studies revealed that people distinguish between issues related to procedural and distributive justice. Future research may focus on conceptual and practical problems with this distinction (cf. Folger, 1996; see also Bobocel & Holmvall, this volume), and should explore the conditions under which these two concepts are perceived as different versus similar concepts (cf. Cropanzano & Ambrose, 1996; see also Van den Bos, Lind, & Wilke, in press; Van den Bos, Vermunt, & Wilke,

1997). I think, however, that the distinction between procedural and distributive justice is not merely a conceptual one, invented by theorists, but frequently arises naturally in people's cognitions about justice.

I want to make one final point on the methodology used in the studies reviewed here. The initial studies on procedural justice were laboratory experiments conducted by Thibaut and Walker (1975). Some early critiques (e.g., Hayden & Andersen, 1979) of the Thibaut and Walker work argued that whereas the internal rigor of the studies reduced alternative causal explanations, questions remained about whether the findings were representative of, or generalizable to, particular populations, settings, independent variables, and dependent variables. In other words, these critics argued that the high internal validity achieved by Thibaut and Walker may have been attained at the expense of external validity.

Prompted in part by these criticisms, procedural justice researchers then started using surveys, a methodology that can yield high external validity (Lind, 1994). In fact, nowadays the bulk of procedural justice research employs survey research methods (Tyler & Lind, 1992). However, in survey studies usually all (dependent and independent) variables are measured at the same time, with the consequence that questions about causality cannot be addressed. It can be concluded—as Lind (1994) has—that procedural justice research is founded on a number of untested assumptions about causality.

It seemed useful, therefore, to conduct laboratory experiments in which independent variables were manipulated prior to the measurement of dependent variables. Furthermore, as I tried to show in this chapter, laboratory experiments provide the researcher with a high degree of control in setting up the kinds of situations needed to investigate the issues one is interested in. Therefore, findings of laboratory experiments, with strong internal validity, are presented in this paper. In our studies, we also tried to achieve acceptable levels of external validity. To do this we used stimulus materials based on real situations and that had important consequences for our participants (and debriefing interviews indicated that we were successful in this). Nevertheless, the manipulations may have been extreme. The experiments were therefore very good tests of the fairness heuristic theory predictions, but care must be taken in applying the results directly to real-world settings. Other research methods will be needed to show that the effects reported here occur in real world situations (e.g., quasi-experiments or field experiments), and to provide an indication of the frequency to which these effects occur in everyday life (e.g., by means of surveys). Thus, future research might use other methods to investigate the issues that have been identified in this chapter. However, it is my hope that the current chapter has shown that using experiments as a research method can really help to achieve a better understanding of the exciting issues of organizational justice.

ACKNOWLEDGMENT

Work on this paper was supported by a fellowship of the Royal Netherlands Academy of Arts and Sciences awarded to Kees van den Bos. I thank Rob Folger and Dirk Steiner for their helpful comments on a previous version of this chapter.

REFERENCES

Adams, J.S. (1965). Inequity in social exchange. In L. Berkowitz (Ed.), *Advances in experimental social psychology* (Vol. 2, pp. 267-299). New York: Academic Press.

Austin, W., McGinn, N.C., & Susmilch, C. (1980). Internal standards revisited: Effects of social comparisons and expectancies on judgments of fairness and satisfaction. *Journal of Experimental Social Psychology, 16*, 426-441.

Berkowitz, L., & Walster, E. (Eds.). (1976). *Advances in experimental social psychology, Vol. 9: Equity theory: Toward a general theory of social interaction.* New York: Academic Press.

Blau, P.M. (1964). *Exchange and power in social life.* New York: Wiley.

Boles, T.L., & Messick, D.M. (1995). A reverse outcome bias: The influence of multiple reference points on the evaluation of outcomes and decisions. *Organizational Behavior and Human Decision Processes, 61*, 262-275.

Brockner, J., Heuer, L., Siegel, P.A., Wiesenfeld, B., Martin, C., Grover, S., Reed, T., & Bjorgvinsson, S. (1998). The moderating effect of self-esteem in reaction to voice: Converging evidence from five studies. *Journal of Personality and Social Psychology, 75*, 394-407.

Cropanzano, R., & Ambrose, M.L. (1996, April). *Procedural and distributive justice are more similar than you think: A monistic perspective and a research agenda.* Paper presented at the Annual Meeting of the Society for Industrial and Organizational Psychology, San Diego, CA.

Cropanzano, R., & Folger, R. (1989). Referent cognitions and task decision autonomy: Beyond equity theory. *Journal of Applied Psychology, 74*, 293-299.

Cropanzano, R., & Folger, R. (1991). Procedural justice and worker motivation. In R.M. Steers & L.W. Porter (Eds.), *Motivation and work behavior* (Vol. 5, pp. 131-143). New York: McGraw-Hill.

Cropanzano, R., & Greenberg, J. (1997). Progress in organizational justice: Tunneling through the maze. In C.L. Cooper & I.T. Robertson (Eds.), *International review of industrial and organizational psychology* (pp. 317-372). New York: Wiley.

Crosby, F. (1976). A model of egoistical relative deprivation. *Psychological Review, 83*, 85-112.

Daly, J.P., & Tripp, T.M. (1996). Is outcome fairness used to make procedural fairness judgments when procedural information is inaccessible? *Social Justice Research, 9*, 327-349.

deCarufel, A., & Schopler, J. (1979). Evaluation of outcome improvement resulting from threats and appeals. *Journal of Personality and Social Psychology, 37*, 662-673.

Deutsch, M. (1975). Equity, equality, or need? What determines which value will be used as the basis of distributive justice? *Journal of Social Issues, 31*, 137-149.

Deutsch, M. (1985). *Distributive justice: A social psychological perspective.* New Haven, CT: Yale University Press.

Folger, R. (1977). Distributive and procedural justice: Combined impact of "voice" and improvement of experienced inequity. *Journal of Personality and Social Psychology, 35*, 108-119.

Folger, R. (1984). Preface. In R. Folger (Ed.), *The sense of injustice: Social psychological perspectives* (pp. ix-x). New York: Plenum.

Folger, R. (1996). Distributive and procedural justice: Multi-faceted meanings and interrelations. *Social Justice Research, 9*, 395-416.

Folger, R., & Cropanzano, R. (1998). *Organizational justice and human resource management.* Thousand Oaks, CA: Sage.

Folger, R., & Konovsky, M. (1989). Effects of procedural and distributive justice on reactions to pay raise decisions. *Academy of Management Journal, 32*, 115-130.

Folger, R., Rosenfield, D., Grove, J., & Corkran, L. (1979). Effects of "voice" and peer opinions on responses to inequity. *Journal of Personality and Social Psychology, 37*, 2253-2261.

Furby, L. (1986). Psychology and justice. In R.L. Cohen (Ed.), *Justice: Views from the social sciences* (pp. 153-203). New York: Plenum.

Gilliland, S.W. (1994). Effects of procedural and distributive justice on reactions to a selection system. *Journal of Applied Psychology, 79*, 691-701.

Greenberg, J. (1986). Determinants of perceived fairness of performance evaluations. *Journal of Applied Psychology, 71*, 340-342.

Greenberg, J. (1990). Organizational justice: Yesterday, today, and tomorrow. *Journal of Management, 16*, 399-432.

Greenberg, J. (1993). Stealing in the name of justice: Informational and interpersonal moderators of theft reactions to underpayment inequity. *Organizational Behavior and Human Decision Processes, 54*, 81-103.

Hayden, R.M., & Andersen, J.K. (1979). On the evaluation of procedural systems in laboratory experiments: A critique of Thibaut and Walker. *Law and Human Behavior, 3*, 21-38.

Homans, G.C. (1961). *Social behavior: Its elementary forms.* New York: Harcourt, Brace, & World.

Hunton, J.E., Hall, T.W., & Price, K.H. (1998). The value of voice in participative decision making. *Journal of Applied Psychology, 83*, 788-797.

Huo, Y.J., Smith, H.J., Tyler, T.R., & Lind, E.A. (1996). Superordinate identification, subgroup identification, and justice concerns: Is separatism the problem; is assimilation the answer? *Psychological Science, 7*, 40-45.

Leventhal, G.S. (1980). What should be done with equity theory? New approaches to the study of fairness in social relationships. In K.J. Gergen, M.S. Greenberg, & R.H. Willis (Eds.), *Social exchange: Advances in theory and research* (pp. 27-54). New York: Plenum.

Lind, E.A. (1992, March). *The fairness heuristic: Rationality and "relationality" in procedural evaluations.* Paper presented at the Fourth International Conference of the Society for the Advancement of Socio-Economics, Irvine, CA.

Lind, E.A. (1994). *Experimental studies of procedural justice.* Unpublished manuscript.

Lind, E.A. (1995). *Social conflict and social justice: Lessons from the social psychology of justice judgments.* Inaugural oration, Leiden University, Leiden, The Netherlands.

Lind, E.A. (1998). Procedural justice, disputing, and reactions to legal authorities. In A. Sarat, M. Constable, D. Engel, V. Hans, & S. Lawrence (Eds.), *Everyday practices and problem cases* (pp. 177-198). Evanston, IL: Northwestern University Press.

Lind, E.A., Kanfer, R., & Earley, P.C. (1990). Voice, control, and procedural justice: Instrumental and noninstrumental concerns in fairness judgments. *Journal of Personality and Social Psychology, 59,* 952-959.

Lind, E.A., & Tyler, T.R. (1988). *The social psychology of procedural justice.* New York: Plenum.

Loewenstein, G.F., Thompson, L., & Bazerman, M.H. (1989). Social utility and decision making in interpersonal contexts. *Journal of Personality and Social Psychology, 57,* 426-441.

Messick, D.M., & Sentis, K. (1983). Fairness, preference, and fairness biases. In D.M. Messick & K.S. Cook (Eds.), *Equity theory: Psychological and sociological perspectives* (pp. 61-94). New York: Praeger.

Messick, D.M., & Sentis, K. (1985). Estimating social and nonsocial utility functions from ordinal data. *European Journal of Social Psychology, 15,* 389-399.

Ross, M., Thibaut, J., & Evenbeck, S. (1971). External referents and past outcomes as determinants of social protest. *Journal of Experimental Social Psychology, 7,* 401-418.

Sheppard, B.H., & Lewicki, R.J. (1987). Toward general principles of managerial fairness. *Social Justice Research, 1,* 161-176.

Skitka, L.J. (1998). *Do the means justify the ends, or do the ends justify the means? A test of the moral mandate hypothesis.* Unpublished manuscript.

Smith, H.J., Tyler, T.R., Huo, Y.J., Ortiz, D.J., & Lind, E. A. (1998). The self-relevant implications of the group-value model: Group-membership, self-worth and treatment quality. *Journal of Experimental Social Psychology, 34,* 470-493.

Steiner, D.D., & Gilliland, S.W. (1996). Fairness reactions to personnel selection techniques in France and the United States. *Journal of Applied Psychology, 81,* 134-141.

Stouffer, S.A., Suchman, E.A., DeVinney, L.C., Star, S.A., & Williams, R.M. (1949). *The American soldier: Adjustment during Army life* (Vol. 1). Princeton, NJ: Princeton University Press.

Sweeney, P.D., & McFarlin, D.B. (1993). Workers' evaluations of the "ends" and the "means": An examination of four models of distributive and procedural justice. *Organizational Behavior and Human Decision Processes, 54,* 23-40.

Thibaut, J., & Walker, L. (1975). *Procedural justice: A psychological analysis.* Hillsdale, NJ: Erlbaum.

Tyler, T.R. (1987). Conditions leading to value-expressive effects in judgments of procedural justice: A test of four models. *Journal of Personality and Social Psychology, 52,* 333-344.

Tyler, T.R., Boeckmann, R.J., Smith, H.J., & Huo, Y.J. (1997). *Social justice in a diverse society.* Boulder, CO: Westview.

Tyler, T.R., & DeGoey, P. (1996). Trust in organizational authorities: The influence of motive attributions on willingness to accept decisions. In R. Kramer & T.R. Tyler (Eds.), *Trust in organizations: Frontiers of theory and research* (pp. 331-356). Thousand Oaks, CA: Sage.

Tyler, T.R., & Lind, E.A. (1992). A relational model of authority in groups. In M. Zanna (Ed.), *Advances in experimental social psychology* (Vol. 25, pp. 115-191). San Diego, CA: Academic Press.

Tyler, T.R., Rasinski, K.A., & Spodick, N. (1985). Influence of voice on satisfaction with leaders: Exploring the meaning of process control. *Journal of Personality and Social Psychology, 48,* 72-81.

Van den Bos, K. (1999). What are we talking about when we talk about no-voice procedures? On the psychology of the fair outcome effect. *Journal of Experimental Social Psychology, 35,* 560-577.

Van den Bos, K., Lind, E.A., Vermunt, R., & Wilke, H.A.M. (1997). How do I judge my outcome when I do not know the outcome of others?: The psychology of the fair process effect. *Journal of Personality and Social Psychology, 72,* 1034-1046.

Van den Bos, K., Lind, E.A., & Wilke, H.A.M. (in press). The psychology of procedural and distributive justice viewed from the perspective of fairness heuristic theory. In R. Cropanzano (Ed.), *Justice in the workplace, Volume 2: From theory to practice.* Mahwah, NJ: Erlbaum.

Van den Bos, K., Vermunt, R., & Wilke, H.A.M. (1996). The consistency rule and the voice effect: The influence of expectations on procedural fairness judgements and performance. *European Journal of Social Psychology, 26,* 411-428.

Van den Bos, K., Vermunt, R., & Wilke, H.A.M. (1997). Procedural and distributive justice: What is fair depends more on what comes first than on what comes next. *Journal of Personality and Social Psychology, 72,* 95-104.

Van den Bos, K., Wilke, H.A.M., & Lind, E.A. (1998). When do we need procedural fairness? The role of trust in authority. *Journal of Personality and Social Psychology, 75,* 1449-1458.

Van den Bos, K., Wilke, H.A.M., Lind, E.A., & Vermunt, R. (1998). Evaluating outcomes by means of the fair process effect: Evidence for different processes in fairness and satisfaction judgments. *Journal of Personality and Social Psychology, 74,* 1493-1503.

Walker, L., LaTour, S., Lind, E.A., & Thibaut, J. (1974). Reactions of participants and observers to modes of adjudication. *Journal of Applied Social Psychology, 4,* 295-310.

Walster, E., Berscheid, E., & Walster, G.W. (1973). New directions in equity research. *Journal of Personality and Social Psychology, 25,* 151-176.

Walster, E., Walster, G.W., & Berscheid, E. (1978). *Equity: Theory and research.* Boston: Allyn & Bacon.

CHAPTER 4

ARE INTERACTIONAL JUSTICE AND PROCEDURAL JUSTICE DIFFERENT?
Framing the Debate

D. Ramona Bobocel and Camilla M. Holmvall

ABSTRACT

There is growing uncertainty in the organizational justice literature as to whether it is meaningful to distinguish the concepts of interactional justice and procedural justice. In the present paper, we take stock of the relevant issues. Drawing on Schwab's (1980) article on construct validity in organizational behavior research, we pose four principal questions by which researchers can evaluate whether these two constructs are fundamentally different. In a final section, we summarize our analysis and identify some key areas for future research. By highlighting the central issues, our hope is that the present framework will serve as a foundation from which the literature can build productively toward a resolution.

INTRODUCTION

Social scientists have long recognized that people's attitudes and behaviors in a variety of social contexts are influenced by their perceptions of fairness. Accordingly, scholars have focused on determining what comprises the experience of fairness. Much of the early research on social justice focused on the concept of *distributive justice,* which refers to people's concerns about the fairness of the distribution of valued outcomes such as their pay (e.g., Adams, 1965; Deutsch, 1985; Homans, 1961). One central aim of research on distributive justice was to determine the variables that lead people to perceive a particular outcome as fair, and to understand the reactions (e.g., resentment, dissatisfaction) that follow from perceived violations of distributive justice (for reviews of this research, see Folger & Cropanzano, 1998; Greenberg, 1982).

Since the seminal work of Thibaut and Walker (1975), researchers have embraced the concept of *procedural justice*, which refers to people's concerns about the fairness of the decision-making procedures used to determine outcomes (e.g., Folger & Greenberg, 1985; Lind & Tyler, 1988). Taken as a whole, research on procedural justice over the past 25 years suggests that people's perceptions of the fairness of the process by which an allocation is made contribute over and above their perceptions of distributive justice in determining their overall experience of fairness. In addition, it is argued that the perception of procedural justice plays a particularly strong role (more so than distributive justice perceptions) in the formation of long-term evaluations of institutions and authorities (for reviews, see Cropanzano & Greenberg, 1997; Folger & Cropanzano, 1998; Lind & Tyler, 1988; Tyler, Boeckmann, Smith, & Huo, 1997).

On the basis of the current research literature, then, it seems clear that both distributive justice and procedural justice are important concepts. More recently, Bies and Moag (1986; also see Bies, 1987) introduced a third justice concept—*interactional justice*—to refer to people's concerns about the quality of interpersonal treatment that they receive during the enactment of decision procedures. Whereas there is more consensus in the literature regarding the distinction between distributive justice and procedural justice (cf. Cropanzano & Ambrose, in press), there has been growing uncertainty as to whether it is meaningful to distinguish the concepts of interactional justice and procedural justice. Some researchers subsume interactional justice issues under the rubric of a broader conceptualization of procedural justice (e.g., Blader & Tyler, 2000; Folger & Greenberg, 1985; Lind & Tyler, 1988; Tyler & Bies, 1990; Tyler & Lind, 1992). In contrast, a growing number of researchers have argued that procedural justice is best conceptualized more narrowly to reflect people's perceptions of the fairnes of the "formal structure" of decision-making procedures (i.e., non-social aspects of decision process). For this latter group of researchers, it is meaningful to reserve the concept of interactional justice to refer to more "social" or interpersonal aspects of process.

Since the term interactional justice was introduced, there has been a wave of research showing its relation with important organizational variables. At the present time, most researchers agree that both the structural and social aspects of procedures are important. Where researchers have not yet reached consensus is whether people's concerns about the structural and social aspects of procedures should be conceptualized as independent constructs (procedural justice and interactional justice, respectively) or as part of the same underlying construct (namely, procedural justice). A critical question in the justice literature, then, is whether researchers should conceptualize procedural justice and interactional justice as fundamentally different justice concepts.

Why should justice researchers be concerned with resolving this question? The central reason is described in a classic paper by Schwab (1980) on construct validity in organizational behavior research. On the one hand, the adoption of new concepts can clearly be of scientific value because they might help to explain additional variance in important dependent variables of interest. Thus, if people's concerns about the structural and social aspects of decision process in fact reflect distinct concepts, then by subsuming them under the rubric of a single concept (namely, procedural justice), researchers might fail to discover important insights. Such insights could ultimately deepen our understanding about people's experience of justice and the reasons why they are affected by the perception of justice and injustice. Yet, as Schwab points out, when researchers discard older, more familiar concepts and adopt those that appear to be new, there is a risk of concept redundancy, which in turn threatens parsimony in scientific explanation. Thus, if people's concerns about structural and social aspects of decision process reflect the same fundamental construct, then by labeling them as different (i.e., as procedural justice and interactional justice, respectively), researchers could be studying redundant concepts. If so, this would ultimately undermine the advancement of knowledge. Greenberg (1990) noted a decade ago that there may be redundancy between the concepts of interactional justice and procedural justice, but despite his call for integration, the literature has become more fragmented over the years. There is wide discrepancy and inconsistency in how researchers conceptualize and therefore in how they study people's justice perceptions.

In the present article, we draw on Schwab's (1980) analysis with the aim of framing the debate about the concepts of interactional justice and procedural justice. According to Schwab, researchers can ask at least four broad questions to evaluate whether any two constructs are distinct from each other: First, is there a clear theoretical definition of the purportedly new construct by which we can distinguish it conceptually from existing similar concepts? Relatedly, is there a theory (i.e., nomological net; Cronbach & Meehl, 1955), which specifies why the new construct is distinct and delineates the purported relations between the new construct and other constructs? Second, are there adequate procedures to operationalize the theoretical definition of the new construct? Third, does the new construct produce different consequences or explain additional variance in dependent, criterion, variables that is unexplained by the older construct? Fourth, can researchers identify through empirical procedures unique antecedents, or determinants, of the new construct? To the extent that researchers can provide positive answers to each of these questions, then the utility of distinguishing the new concept as fundamentally different from existing concepts gains support and becomes clearer.

Our central goal in this article is to take stock of the relevant issues concerning the debate about the concepts of interactional justice and procedural justice in a systematic fashion. Thus, the four questions outlined above are addressed here with respect to these two concepts. Accordingly, the paper is divided into four major sections, in which we review the literature pertaining to each of the four questions in turn. In a final section, we summarize our analysis and identify some key areas for future research. Although our intent is not to resolve the debate in this chapter, our hope is to provide a foundation from which the literature can build greater consensus.

QUESTION 1:
CAN RESEARCHERS DISTINGUISH INTERACTIONAL JUSTICE FROM PROCEDURAL JUSTICE AT THE THEORETICAL LEVEL?

To the extent that researchers view interactional justice to be distinct from procedural justice, it is critical that these two concepts be distinguishable at the conceptual level. How has the concept of interactional justice been defined, and is it possible to distinguish it from the definition of procedural justice? Relatedly, why do people care about interactional justice? Are the underlying psychological processes different from those that explain previous procedural justice findings? In this section, we consider both the question of construct definition and the question of underlying mechanism.

Construct Definition

In their seminal chapter, Bies and Moag (1986) argued that, whereas previous models of procedural justice advanced by Thibaut and Walker (1975) and Leventhal (1980) distinguished between the fairness of procedures and the fairness of outcomes (i.e., the means by which decisions are made and the ends of those decisions), they failed to distinguish the fairness of the structure of decision procedures from the *enactment of those procedures*. Bies and Moag argued that allocation decisions are "a sequence of events in which a procedure generates a process of interaction and decision making through which an outcome is allocated to someone" (p. 45). Accordingly, they suggested that decision procedures and their enactment (as well as the outcomes of decisions) can be conceptualized as separate aspects of an allocation sequence; each aspect is potentially subject to fairness considerations. Put simply, they argued that prior research on procedural justice had neglected to adequately consider two aspects: people's concerns about the structure of decision procedures and their concerns about the enactment of those procedures.

Within Bies and Moag's (1986) analysis, then, the concept of procedural justice is confined to people's perceptions of the fairness of the formal structure of decision procedures. Under this view, procedural justice is said to be determined by explicit rules, identified in earlier conceptual models and research (e.g., Leventhal, 1980; Thibaut & Walker, 1975) and discussed fully elsewhere (e.g., Cropanzano & Greenberg, 1997; Folger & Cropanzano, 1998; Lind & Tyler, 1988). For example, procedures are said to be structured fairly when they ensure that (a) all people are treated consistently, (b) accurate information is used to make decisions, (c) personal biases of decision makers are suppressed, (d) those affected are represented, or have voice into the decision process, (e) there are appeal mechanisms by which recipients can correct a wrong decision, and (f) ethical norms are not violated. Bies and Moag recognized that certain of these criteria are "fuzzy" in that they may encompass aspects of both structure and enactment, although the problem of specifying the boundaries of the procedural and interactional justice concepts within their framework has not been fully resolved. This has posed some difficulty for the measurement of these concepts, as we will discuss later.

In contrast to procedural justice, interactional justice was said to refer to people's concerns about the "quality of interpersonal treatment that [recipients] receive during the enactment of organizational allocation procedures" (p. 44). In particular, Bies and Moag (1986) focused on the fairness of the communication aspect of interpersonal treatment, and they identified four "criteria people use to judge the fairness in communication during the allocation of resources" (p. 46). These four criteria for fair communication were truthfulness, respect, propriety of questions, and justification. The criteria were derived from content analyses of the descriptions of fair and unfair corporate recruiting experiences provided by MBA students. Subsequently, the four criteria have been summarized by most researchers into two broader classes. In brief, interactional justice has typically been said to comprise (a) clear and adequate explanations, or justifications, for an allocation decision, and (b) treatment of recipients with dignity and respect during the implementation of decision procedures (e.g., Moorman, 1991).

It is noteworthy that there is not yet complete certainty regarding the aspects of interpersonal treatment about which people are concerned. Greenberg (1993a) elaborated on the construct of interactional justice, arguing that people have concerns about interpersonal treatment not only during the enactment of decision procedures, but also during the enactment of the outcome, or distribution, phase of an allocation sequence. In other words, Greenberg (1993a; also see Greenberg, 1993b, 1994) argued that we can conceptualize social and structural elements pertaining to both procedures and distributions (he labeled the social considerations pertaining to procedures "informational justice" and the social considerations pertaining to outcomes "interpersonal justice"). In a related vein, several studies in the broader psychological literature (e.g., Mikula, Petrik, & Tanzer, 1990) suggest that people's concerns about the fairness of interpersonal treatment generalize beyond decision-making contexts to routine social interaction (also see Lind & Tyler, 1988, for a similar point). Although they have not yet completely done so, justice researchers will need to reconcile these various conceptualizations. In particular, there would be value in conceptual and empirical work following the lines of Greenberg (1993a, 1993b, 1994) and Mikula et al. (1990) to better understand the aspects of interpersonal treatment which affect people's fairness judgments. At least for the most part, researchers now seem to agree that the initial definition of the content domain of interactional justice was too narrow.

It is noteworthy that, whereas Bies and Moag argued that the enactment of decision procedures can be distinguished from their formal structure, Lind and Tyler (1988) presented an alternative model—the group value model—of procedural justice. (This model has been subsequently relabeled the relational model, Tyler & Lind, 1992.) Like Bies and Moag, Lind and Tyler (1988) argued that the Thibaut and Walker and the Leventhal models of procedural justice were insufficient in that they did not consider the importance of interpersonal elements of process. However, Lind and Tyler made no explicit distinction between the structural and interpersonal components, but rather viewed both as integral elements of process considerations. For example, in their book reviewing the prior two decades of research, Lind and Tyler (1988) stated that "procedural justice involves more than questions of how decisions are made. It also involves questions of how people are treated by authorities and other parties" (p. 214).

In their initial chapter, Bies and Moag (1986) acknowledged (also see Tyler & Bies, 1990) that it might be best to consider interactional justice as part of a broader conceptualization of procedural justice because people may only come to know procedures through their enactment, and thus the two elements will be highly interrelated perceptually. Nevertheless, they maintained that "interactional fairness will generalize to the procedure itself only when a person attributes responsibility for the action to the organization, a systemic attribution, rather than the decision maker. On the other hand, if a person attributes the deception and rudeness solely to the decision maker and not the organization, then there should be less implications for the procedure itself" (p. 52).

Summary

It is possible to distinguish between the definitions of the concepts of interactional justice and procedural justice, but this appears to depend on the definition of procedural justice that one adopts. If one follows a conceptualization based on the procedural justice models advanced by Thibaut and Walker (1975) and by Leventhal (1980), which emphasized the formal structure of decision procedures, then it is possible to distinguish the concept of interactional justice in terms of its theoretical definition. If, however, one follows the conceptualization of procedural justice offered by Lind and Tyler (1988; Tyler & Lind, 1992), which encompasses both structural and social or interpersonal considerations, then the distinction between procedural justice and interactional justice becomes less clear. Whether researchers should reserve the definition of procedural justice for referring to people's concerns about formal decision structure, and thus invoke a separate construct (interactional justice) to represent people's concerns about interpersonal treatment, will of course depend on the answers to the remaining three questions posed in this article.

Underlying Theoretical Mechanism

Bies and Moag's (1986) initial analysis did not clearly delineate the psychological mechanisms that could distinguish people's concerns about the structural and interpersonal components of decision procedures. Moreover, there has been relatively little subsequent theorizing and research to directly address this issue. Nevertheless, speculations in line with both sides of the issue—that people care about structural and interpersonal elements for the same versus for different underlying reasons—can be identified.

One argument for the notion that different psychological mechanisms may underlie people's concerns about the structure of procedures and their concerns about interpersonal treatment derives from the observation that these aspects differ in terms of their causal link to outcomes (e.g., see Bies & Moag, 1986; Brockner & Wiesenfeld, 1996; Folger & Cropanzano, 1998; Lind & Tyler, 1988). Specifically, given that decision procedures are the means by which allocation decisions are made, the formal structure of procedures can influence the outcomes. In contrast, interpersonal treatment does not necessarily have a direct causal influence on outcomes (although it may be perceived to have such an influence).

In view of the distinction in terms of causal influence on outcomes, it is possible that people value the fair structure of decision procedures and fair interpersonal treatment for different reasons. In line with the earlier "control" models of procedural justice (Leventhal, 1980; Thibaut & Walker, 1975), people may value a fair structure primarily for instrumental reasons (see the self-interest model of procedural justice, Lind & Tyler, 1988). For example, people may value a decision procedure that is structured fairly because they expect that it will yield favorable outcomes in the long run (see Cropanzano & Greenberg, 1997; Folger & Cropanzano, 1998; Lind & Tyler, 1988; Tyler & Lind, 1992). In contrast, in line with Lind and Tyler's relational model of procedural justice, people may value fair interpersonal treatment primarily for symbolic reasons: In particular, it may signal to recipients that they are valued members of a social group, and consequently enhance their sense of belonging and self worth. Given that, within Lind and Tyler's (1988) initial group-value model of procedural justice, the structural and interpersonal treatment components of procedures were not explicitly distinguished, it is possible that the criteria within their model that most heavily tap interpersonal concerns (e.g., "standing") have contributed most strongly to the empirical support for their model.

On the other side of the coin, Folger and Cropanzano (1998) have recently expanded Folger's (1986, 1993) referent cognitions theory (RCT), theorizing that the structure of decision procedures and interpersonal treatment are more similar than dissimilar. According to their new fairness theory, procedures and interactions serve similar functions in that they inform recipients about the intentions of decision-making agents. More specifically, in line with Folger's earlier theorizing on RCT, when there is a discrepancy between what recipients expect and what they receive (for example, when outcomes are less than expected), this may give rise to counterfactual thinking about what they "would" have received if alternative decision procedures had been used. If recipients believe that different procedures both "should" and "could" have been used, then they are more likely to blame the agent for the negative outcomes. Consequently, according to fairness theory, either fair decision procedures or fair conduct may mitigate the negative impact of receiving less than is expected, because both minimize the agent's accountability. Indeed, Folger and Cropanzano suggest that conduct may tell people even more about the agent's intentionality than do procedures per se, given that conduct is more discretionary (than either procedures or outcomes). According to fairness theory, then, because process and conduct both inform recipients about an agent's accountability, these elements may be more similar than dissimilar.

Fairness theory not only expands on the earlier RCT, it also includes an important revision: According to fairness theory, there is not necessarily a one-to-one correspondence between the event—that is, outcomes, procedures, and interactions—and the counterfactuals about what would, should, and could have happened. For example, within the initial RCT framework, evaluation of one's outcomes was typically assumed to induce counterfactual thinking about what would have happened had alternative procedures been used. According to Folger and Cropanzano (1998), considerations about procedures or interpersonal interactions can also generate such counterfactual thinking. In other words, outcomes, procedures, and interactions can each serve as the negative impact variable within fairness theory. Accordingly, Folger and Cropanzano have reconceptualized the statistical interaction effect between outcomes and procedures (e.g., Brockner & Weisenfeld, 1996) originally predicted by RCT in more fundamental terms. In other words, the original interaction, which stated that procedural justice mitigates the negative effect of unfavorable outcomes—a procedure x outcome interaction—is recast as a negative impact x accountability interaction.

In contrast to fairness theory, Bies and Moag (1986) argued that decision-maker conduct will only be similar to the formal structure of procedures when people attribute responsibility for the conduct to the organization and not to individual leaders. One implication from Bies and Moag's initial writing, then, is that differential source attributions are key in the conceptual distinction between the concepts. Put more simply, perhaps the only time interactional justice is distinguishable from procedural justice is when people attribute enactment to individual leaders (an agent of the system) and procedures to the organization (the system). As will be described in the next sections, this theme has been picked up in the measurement of the concepts (e.g., Moorman, 1991) and serves as a basis for much of the research aiming to show differential consequences. For the present, an important direction for future theorizing and research on whether interactional justice and procedural justice are distinct concepts is to determine if the distinction is more one of *source* (agent versus system) than of *content*. If the distinction between these concepts depends solely on a distinction between the sources of justice, then the fundamental distinction between the concepts becomes questionable. As we will discuss later, some researchers (e.g., Blader & Tyler, 2000; Byrne & Cropanzano, 2000) have begun to examine this question empirically.

Summary

At this point in the development of the justice literature, it is not yet clear whether people care about the structure of decision procedures and the interpersonal treatment they receive from authorities for the same or for different underlying psychological reasons. This observation goes against the argument for viewing these considerations as representing separate constructs—namely, procedural justice and interactional justice respectively.

QUESTION 2: CAN RESEARCHERS OPERATIONALIZE AND MEASURE THE FOCAL CONSTRUCTS INDEPENDENTLY?

Assuming that a new concept can be convincingly distinguished at the conceptual level, researchers should be able to operationalize it to determine the degree to which it is distinct from related concepts at the empirical level. To accomplish this, researchers typically examine a variety of data, such as the interrelation between theoretically related concepts and the internal consistency and factor structure of the new measure. In their initial chapter, Bies and Moag (1986) themselves called for research to uncover the empirical overlap between procedural justice and interactional justice measures because they acknowledged the possibility that the conceptual distinction might not hold up at the empirical level. Such a failure could arise either because people do not naturally make the conceptual distinction in the course of their everyday lives, because the distinction does not exist in reality, or both.

Unfortunately, despite previous calls for greater constancy in measurement of justice concepts (Greenberg, 1990; Lind & Tyler, 1988), there are as yet no standard measures of procedural justice and interactional justice on which researchers have conducted systematic validation efforts. Instead, there is substantial variability across studies in the measures used to tap these constructs, with most studies reporting measures developed specifically for that particular study. Of course, given the diversity of contexts in which fairness concerns are apparently applicable, Greenberg (1993c) questioned whether the development of standard measures of interactional justice and procedural justice is even appropriate. Nevertheless, the variation across studies limits the ability of researchers to engage in systematic construct validation research. It is noteworthy that, during the time this chapter was in press, a new justice measure has appeared in the literature (Colquitt, in press). This new measure holds the promise of helping to address many of the issues identified in this section.

The bulk of the published data, albeit based on a variety of measures, is consistent with the idea that people can and do distinguish between the structural aspects of procedures and the quality of interpersonal treatment that they receive from authorities. Still, the degree of overlap between these perceptions is often quite high. For example, several studies report uncorrected intercorrelations between measures of procedural justice (defined as the formal structure of decision procedures) and interactional justice (defined as the quality of interpersonal treatment received from authorities) that exceed .60 (e.g., Bobocel & Holmvall, 1999; Moorman, 1991; Skarlicki & Folger, 1997). In other studies, the scale intercorrelations are well below that level (e.g., Cropanzano & Prehar, 1999; Malatesta & Byrne, 1997; Masterson, Lewis-McClear, Goldman, Taylor, 1997). Internal consistency estimates for the multi-item measures used in past research are typically above the conventional .70 level. The factor structure of measures is not always presented in the published studies, but, in those studies that do present factor analytic data (e.g., Moorman, 1991), the factor structure of measures tapping the structural and social components is consistent with a two-dimensional versus a one-dimension model.

This pattern of data is supportive of the argument for independent constructs. Yet, given the variation in justice measures, it is ultimately difficult to draw firm conclusions at this time about the degree to which people's concerns about the formal structure of decision procedures and interpersonal treatment are interrelated. More importantly, the variation in measures makes it difficult to be certain about the purported relation between each of these components and the important dependent variables of interest (e.g., organization commitment, supervisor trust). The latter issue will be described more fully in the next major section. In the interest of guiding future research on improved measurement, in the remainder of this section we identify four ways in which existing justice measures vary.

First, it is not clear whether all measures reported in the literature adequately tap the content domain that they purport to tap. Following the conceptual definitions offered by Bies and Moag (1986), Moorman (1991) developed two multiple-item scales to index the procedural justice and interactional justice concepts (comprising seven items and six items, respectively). These measures, which have been used in several subsequent studies, do appear to tap the content domains as defined by Bies and Moag. Several alternative scales are, however, not so clear. That is, measures that claim to assess interactional justice often include items that are conceptualized by other researchers as a criterion of procedural justice and vice versa. For example, consistency in treatment, one of Leventhal's criteria of fair decision structure, is included as an index of procedural justice in some studies and as an index of interactional justice in others; in addition, voice, or input, another criterion of fair structure within the Leventhal (1980) and Thibaut and Walker (1975) models, is often used to represent procedural justice, although sometimes it is used as an index of interactional justice.

Second, measures across studies differ in whether they require people to report their general judgments of fairness across a number of decision-making contexts or their perceptions of the fairness of a specific event. For example, Moorman's (1991) scales require respondents to make general judgments by asking them to self-report their perceptions of justice across a variety of resource allocation procedures. Alternatively, other researchers (e.g., Cropanzano & Prehar, 1999; Masterson et al., 1997, 2000) have measured perceptions of interactional and procedural justice referring to a specific allocation context, such as performance evaluation. Likewise, in experimental studies in which the constructs are manipulated, researchers measure participants' reactions to a specific decision episode (e.g., Barling & Phillips, 1993; Moye, Masterson, & Bartol, 1997). Presumably, researchers are interested in understanding the psychology of fairness perceptions (i.e., causes, effects, mediation) regardless of whether participants are providing general judgments—which require a summary or integration of some kind on the part of respondents—or reacting to a specific event. However, one can readily speculate on how the results could differ depending on which form of judgment is required. As one example, researchers may observe higher interrelations between measures of the two justice concepts when general judgments are required because respondents could have more difficulty distinguishing them when they are summarizing over several allocation contexts. Instead, when rating the fairness of a specific event (e.g., one's recent performance evaluation), people could be better able to distinguish between the formal structure of the procedure and interpersonal treatment. The contrast between "general judgments of fairness" and judgments of fairness of "specific events" is an important one for researchers to consider in designing their research and in interpreting their findings. It is possible that the specific event approach could be the one most suitable for addressing the question of distinct concepts.

Third, there is a variation in whether the measures assess fairness perceptions "directly" or "indirectly" (using Lind & Tyler's, 1988, terms). For indirect (or composite) measures, fairness perceptions are calculated by averaging respondents' ratings of the criteria assumed to cause such perceptions (e.g., "how consistent are organizational procedures?", "how biased are procedures?", and so on). For direct measures, respondents are asked to provide a general evaluative response toward the structure of decision procedures (e.g., "how fair are organizational procedures?") or toward the treatment they receive from authorities (e.g., "how fairly does your supervisor treat you?"). What can be more problematic, however, is that sometimes both methods are used in the same study, with one concept being measured directly and the other indirectly. Psychologists have discussed the possible problems that can arise when making comparisons between measures of concepts that are operationalized at such different levels of specificity (see Cooper & Richardson, 1986; Fishbein & Ajzen, 1975). For example, spurious conclusions can be drawn about the extent of interrelation between the two justice constructs, as well as about the relation between each justice construct and criterion variables of interest. Indeed, direct and indirect measures might even "dissociate," leading to opposite conclusions.

Finally, measures of the two justice concepts typically differ systematically along two dimensions: the content of justice and the source of justice. In other words, measures of procedural justice assess perceptions of the formal structure of procedures, using the organization or system as the referent (e.g., "to what degree are the procedures used in your *organization* free of bias?"). In contrast, measures of interactional justice assess perceptions of interpersonal treatment, using the behavior of their particular supervisor as the referent (e.g., "to what degree does your *supervisor* provide you with timely explanations of decisions?"). As noted earlier, researchers have begun to stress this point, suggesting the possibility that the more fundamental distinction between measures of interactional justice and those of procedural justice may relate to the difference in source of justice rather than the content of justice. Indeed, in the next section, we describe how some researchers have begun to test this possibility empirically.

Summary

Taken together, the evidence on whether researchers can independently operationalize the structural and the interpersonal aspects of procedures is promising. For the most part, the data suggest that, in at least some conditions, people can and do distinguish these two attributes of procedures, although at times the perceptions are highly related. Nevertheless, measures of these constructs have been developed largely on an ad hoc basis, and there has been little systematic research on construct validation. We identified four ways in which existing measures of the concepts vary across studies, all of which impede drawing firm conclusions about the extent to which it is meaningful to conceptualize the structural and interpersonal aspects as separate constructs.

QUESTION 3:
DO MEASURES OF INTERACTIONAL JUSTICE AND PROCEDURAL JUSTICE HAVE DIFFERENT EFFECTS?

As noted at the outset of this article, a third way to demonstrate the distinction between two concepts is to examine whether they have different patterns of relations with theoretically relevant dependent, or criterion, variables of interest. Thus, if measures or manipulations of interactional justice (defined as the quality of interpersonal treatment) explain additional variance in criterion variables once the contributions of procedural justice (defined as the structure of procedures) and presumably distributive justice are accounted for, or if measures of the two concepts relate to different variables, then the distinction between these concepts will necessarily become clearer. In this section, we review three relevant lines of inquiry.[1]

Tests of Main Effects

Support for the notion that it is meaningful to distinguish the concepts of interactional and procedural justice appeared to gain particular momentum in the research literature in the early 1990s. In one study, Moorman (1991) used causal modeling techniques to assess the links between employees' perceptions of fairness and their tendency to engage in organizational citizenship behaviors. In brief, Moorman found that employees' perceptions of interactional, but not of procedural or distributive justice, were linked to supervisor-rated citizenship behaviors. Although not predicted a priori, Moorman's findings were consistent with the argument that the role of interpersonal aspects of decision-maker conduct may have been neglected in prior theorizing and research on procedural justice. Indeed, other researchers subsequently suggested that effects previously attributed to structural aspects of procedures might instead be due to the interpersonal component (e.g., Barling & Phillips, 1993).

A number of researchers have drawn on Moorman's findings and have argued that both the structure of decision-making procedures and the social enactment of those procedures are important independent, or predictor, variables that can be differentiated by their effects on different organizational variables (e.g., Cropanzano & Prehar, 1999; Malatesta & Byrne, 1997; Masterson et al., 1997, 2000; Moye et al., 1997). In particular, consistent with Bies and Moag's (1986) original reasoning, this more recent work has made the argument that people's perceptions of the structure of decisions may contribute most strongly to reactions directed at the system (e.g., affective commitment to one's work organization). In contrast, perceptions of interpersonal treatment may contribute most strongly to reactions directed at specific agents of the system (e.g., satisfaction with, or commitment to, one's work supervisor).

The basis for this reasoning has been set within the theoretical framework of social exchange (Blau, 1964), and the essence of the logic is as follows: To the extent that employees view the organization as responsible for creating fair procedures, a positive social exchange relationship should develop between the employee and the organization; in turn, this should cause employees to develop positive attitudes and behaviors directed toward the organization. Similarly, to the extent that employees perceive interpersonal treatment to be under the control of individual supervisors, a positive social exchange relationship between employee and supervisor should develop; in turn, positive attitudes and behaviors directed toward the supervisor should ensue.

Malatesta and Byrne (1997) used structural equation modeling to test this idea in a survey of employee-supervisor dyads. They found that employees' perceptions of procedural justice (defined as the formal structure of procedures) related to their level of affective organizational commitment. In contrast, employees' perceptions of interactional justice (defined as interpersonal treatment displayed by one's supervisor) influenced their self-reported supervisory commitment and supervisor-reported organizational citizenship behavior.

A similar pattern of data has been reported by two additional groups of researchers. In a field survey on performance appraisal, Masterson et al. (1997; Study 1) found that employees' perceptions of interactional justice but not of procedural justice predicted their ratings of supervisor-focused outcomes, namely, supervisor legitimacy. In contrast, procedural justice perceptions but not interactional justice perceptions predicted organization-focused outcomes, namely affective organizational commitment.

Masterson et al. (2000) replicated and extended their earlier findings by examining the mediating mechanism through which the justice concepts could relate to different organizational variables. Consistent with the notion that a social exchange process develops between employees and the source to whom they attribute justice (i.e., the organization or the supervisor), the researchers found that the relations between procedural justice and organization-directed outcomes were mediated by perceived organizational support. In contrast, the relations between interactional justice perceptions and supervisor-directed outcomes were mediated by the quality of leader-member exchange. If in fact people's concerns about the structure of procedures and about interpersonal treatment do represent separate constructs, then one would expect this disjunctive pattern of results. In contrast, job satisfaction was predicted similarly by the two justice perceptions, presumably because it is influenced by justice perceptions derived from both sources (i.e., the organization and the supervisor).

Cropanzano and Prehar (1999) tested similar hypotheses in a different sample of employees. As expected, and consistent with the Masterson et al. (1997, 2000) findings, employees who perceived the structure of their performance appraisal procedures to be fair reported higher levels of trust in management and satisfaction with the system. In contrast, employees' ratings of interactional justice were more strongly related to self-reported satisfaction with their supervisor and with supervisor-reported job performance. Moreover, as expected, the relation between interactional justice and supervisor-directed variables was fully mediated by leader-member exchange, whereas the relation between procedural justice and organization-directed variables was not. Unlike some of the preceding studies, Cropanzano and Prehar took the additional step of ruling out any potentially confounding role of distributive justice perceptions in these results by statistically controlling them prior to testing the primary predictions. Again, this pattern of data supports the argument for distinct concepts.

Although to date most of the research examining differential relations of the structural and interpersonal components with organizational variables has employed cross-sectional correlational designs, some experimental work also exists. For example, Moye et al. (1997) conducted a laboratory experiment in which they manipulated the two components of justice within the context of an organizational decision-making simulation. Participants engaged in a 15-minute brainstorming session to generate slogans for a new product, and their performance was ostensibly rated by a supervisor of the company interested in marketing the product. Procedural justice was manipulated by varying the procedural rules used by the supervisor to evaluate participants' performance; in particular, the procedures either did or did not violate three of Leventhal's (1980) procedural justice criteria: consistency, accuracy, and opportunity for appeal. Crosscutting this manipulation was the manipulation of interactional justice. In communicating participants' evaluations, the supervisor in the high interactional justice condition was respectful, offered a justification for the decision, and framed the feedback positively, whereas in the low interactional justice condition, these elements were lacking. (In their study, Moye et al. held the level of outcome constant, by informing all participants that they had performed at the 70th percentile).

As in studies reviewed earlier, Moye et al. (1997) predicted that the manipulation of structural characteristics would influence organization-directed outcomes (satisfaction with and attraction to the organization) whereas the manipulation of interpersonal components would influence leader-directed outcomes (trust in and satisfaction with the supervisor). Contrary to their predictions, however, there were no significant main effects of the procedural justice manipulation on either the organization-directed or supervisor-directed outcomes. In contrast to the manipulation of procedural justice, the manipulation of interactional justice had positive main effects on all four dependent variables—those directed at the organization as well as those directed at the supervisor. It is noteworthy that Barling and Phillips (1993) found the same pattern of results in an earlier vignette study that similarly manipulated interactional, procedural, and distributive justice. The manipulation of interactional justice but not of procedural justice had a positive effect on all dependent variables although, in their study, the dependent variables were not categorized a priori as organization-focused versus supervisor-focused.

Taken together, the results of the few experimental studies that have examined the differential effects hypothesis are not consistent with the results of the correlational field studies reviewed earlier. The correlational studies consistently show the dissociation in line with differentiable constructs whereas the experimental studies fail to do so. Clearly, more research is required to fully understand the reasons for the inconsistency in findings, but, for the present, this correlational/experimental discrepancy reduces one's ability to draw firm conclusions regarding differential consequences.

Disentangling Source of Justice and Type of Justice Effects

As noted in the preceding sections, some researchers have begun to test whether the more fundamental distinction between measures of interactional justice and procedural justice involves one of source (organization, supervisor) rather than of content. For example, Byrne and Cropanzano (2000) have recently argued that both sources of justice can provide both types of justice. To explore this idea, they examined perceptions of procedural and interactional justice emanating from both the organization and the supervisor. Consistent across two studies, the researchers found evidence for both source of justice and type of justice effects. In brief, justice emanating from the organization (i.e., procedural justice) predicted organizational-level criterion variables (e.g., organizational commitment) and justice emanating from the supervisor (i.e., interactional justice) predicted supervisory-level criterion variables (e.g., supervisory commitment). In addition, Byrne and Cropanzano (2000) found that when both sources of justice were taken into account, procedural justice was the better predictor of organizational level variables whereas interactional justice was the better predictor of supervisory level variables. In a recent study, Blader and Tyler (2000) found a converging pattern of results in line with the idea that source of justice and type of justice are independent dimensions. Contrary to the idea that it is appropriate to equate procedural justice with the organization and interactional justice with the supervisor, then, these initial findings suggest that both sources of justice can provide both types of justice. If this pattern continues to be observed, it will add to the complexity of discriminating the two justice constructs.

Statistical Interaction Effects

Whereas recent studies for the most part have examined the main effects of perceptions of procedural and interactional justice on different organizational variables, some researchers have begun to investigate the joint effect of these variables. For example, Skarlicki and Folger (1997) conducted a field study to examine the links between employees' interactional, procedural, and distributive justice perceptions on the one hand and their organizational retaliatory behaviors on the other. Interestingly, retaliatory behavior (as rated by participants' coworkers) was highest when employees perceived all three types of justice to be low, but this effect was lessened when either the procedures or the interactions were perceived as fair. More specifically, Skarlicki and Folger found a 3-way interaction among the justice measures, such that procedural and interactional justice had "substitutable" effects, with either being sufficient to mitigate the negative effect of low distributive justice perceptions. In other words, as predicted by referent cognitions theory, the researchers found a process x outcome interaction such that the perception of either fair procedures or fair interactions mitigated the enhanced retaliatory behavior that was observed when perceived distributive justice was low. Although their research did not test process directly, the pattern of Skarlicki and Folger's results is consistent with the notion that perceptions of interactional and procedural justice have a similar underlying function. In line with fairness theory, both procedures and interactions may convey information about intentionality; as such, they may mitigate the otherwise negative effect of unfair outcomes on retaliatory behavior. In summary, Skarlicki and Folger's data do not support conceptualizing procedures and interactions as independent justice concepts.

Summary

On the basis of our review, the bulk of the research stimulated by Bies and Moag's (1986) initial article on interactional justice pertains to the study of its consequences. However, whether people's concerns about the structural and interpersonal aspects of procedures translate into different experiences and consequences is not clear. The recent field research examining the differential effects hypothesis is intriguing in this regard, although the results of this line of research remain inconclusive. This is in part due to the construct validity problems and methodological inconsistencies outlined in the earlier section. Moreover, most of the research is based on a cross-sectional correlational methodology, which does not allow conclusions regarding causality. Finally, like the experimental work described in this section, the pattern of results reported by Skarlicki and Folger (1997) does not support the idea of separate justice concepts.

QUESTION 4: DO INTERACTIONAL JUSTICE AND PROCEDURAL JUSTICE HAVE DIFFERENT DETERMINANTS?

The final question that one may ask to determine whether two constructs are distinct has to do with determinants: Is it possible to demonstrate unique determinants of each of the constructs in question?

Unfortunately, there is a paucity of research on this question. Although there is a large literature demonstrating the link between various structural criteria argued to influence the perception of procedural justice (e.g., consistency, accuracy, voice; for comprehensive reviews, see Cropanzano & Greenberg, 1997; Folger & Cropanzano, 1998; Lind & Tyler, 1988), there is considerably less systematic research examining the question of unique causes of procedural and interactional justice perceptions. Moreover, several studies have found that the criteria (e.g., explanations) purported to influence people's perceptions of interactional justice can have the same effect on people's overall evaluations of procedural justice (e.g., Bies & Shapiro, 1987, Study 3; Bies & Shapiro, 1988; Bobocel, Agar, Meyer, & Irving, 1998). This pattern suggests a high degree of overlap between the two constructs, which argues against making the distinction.

The question of different antecedents has been tested most directly in the few studies that have experimentally manipulated both the structural and interpersonal criteria, measuring participants' overall evaluations of the fairness of the procedures and the quality of interpersonal treatment. For example, in the 2 x 2 experiment described earlier by Moye et al. (1997), the manipulation of consistency, accuracy, and appeals had the predicted significant effect on participants' perceptions of procedural justice, whereas the manipulation of respect, justification, and positive decision frame significantly influenced ratings of interactional justice.

Moreover, no interactions were found between these manipulations, all of which points to distinct concepts.

Given the possibility that in many situations the interpersonal criteria may also influence people's construal of the decision structure, it could in fact be quite difficult to demonstrate unique causes associated with each construct. This may be particularly true in field research in which respondents are reporting summary judgments of fairness. Many theorists have, in fact, acknowledged that the purported determinants of interactional justice may indirectly influence the perception of procedural justice (Bies & Moag, 1986; Cropanzano & Greenberg, 1997; Folger & Cropanzano, 1998; Tyler & Bies, 1990). This could explain why researchers have not systematically examined the question of antecedents. Nevertheless, to argue that it is meaningful to distinguish the concepts of interactional justice and procedural justice, researchers must be able to identify, at the empirical level, some determinants that are directly associated with one construct but not the other (Schwab, 1980). Ideally, this would be observed in both directions, with variable A affecting construct X but not construct Y, and variable B affecting construct Y but not construct X.

Summary

There is some empirical evidence to support the idea that people evaluate the fairness of the structure of a decision procedure using different criteria than those used to evaluate the quality of interpersonal treatment. Overall, however, few studies have addressed this issue.

CONCLUSIONS AND DIRECTIONS FOR FUTURE RESEARCH

We return now to the central question inspiring this article: Are the concepts of interactional justice and procedural justice fundamentally different? As we have shown, some studies seem to support the argument for making a distinction between these two concepts whereas others seem to oppose it. But, when taken together, the picture they paint is not completely clear.

On the basis of our analysis, it appears that the concept of interactional justice can be distinguished from procedural justice at a conceptual level, if we confine the definition of procedural justice to represent people's concerns about the structure of decision procedures and reserve the term interactional justice to represent people's concerns about the social or interpersonal aspects of decision making. However, if one adopts the definition of procedural justice initially advanced by Lind and Tyler (1988), which incorporates both aspects of procedures, then the distinction between the concepts becomes more blurred and the possibility of concept redundancy seems likely. How, then, do researchers come to consensus on whether to include the two attributes of procedures under the rubric of a single concept (procedural justice) or to conceptualize each as representing a different justice concept (procedural justice and interactional justice)? As we have argued, there are several considerations to be made jointly.

On the one hand, we see that, at this point in the development of the literature, there is virtually complete agreement among justice researchers that people are concerned not only about the structural aspects of procedures but also the interpersonal treatment they receive from authorities. In addition, researchers agree that the conceptual distinction between the structural and social attributes of procedures holds up empirically. In other words, under certain conditions, people are able to distinguish the structure of procedures from their enactment. In these ways, it is our view that research on the concept of interactional justice has had a particularly important influence in the justice literature. Indeed, we see the research stimulated by Bies and Moag's (1986) initial analysis as having helped to make explicit the central—perhaps preeminent—role of people's concerns about interpersonal treatment.

On the other hand, whereas researchers may agree that it is meaningful to think of procedures and their social enactment as separable components of the decision-making process, and even that it is possible to adequately measure people's perceptions of these attributes, this alone does not warrant utilizing two separate justice concepts. It is in this regard that the research examining differential consequences of these attributes holds substantial promise. Nevertheless, it is not yet clear that the two components can be distinguished in terms of their psychological function. Ultimately, the lack of theory and research on mechanism is perhaps the most problematic issue for the argument in favor of viewing procedural and interactional justice as two separate justice concepts.

On the basis of our review, there are several directions for future research that would be especially fruitful for resolving the debate about the differentiability of the concepts of interactional justice and procedural justice. We close this chapter with a consideration of these directions.

To the extent that people are concerned about the structural and interpersonal attributes of decision-making procedures for different underlying reasons, then support for the argument for two justice concepts becomes clearer. To date, there has been little systematic theoretical work regarding differential psychological mechanisms that may underlie the observed effects of measures of the two attributes. Indeed, as noted in an earlier section, Folger and Cropanzano's (1998) recent revision of RCT provides some theoretical reason to consider the attributes as more similar than dissimilar. On the basis of our review, it seems clear that to resolve the present debate, there is a need for more theoretical development regarding the psychological functions that the attributes of procedures and interpersonal interactions serve. Furthermore, we encourage research that is designed to test the proposed underlying mechanisms. If the two attributes serve the same underlying psychological function, then there is no need for researchers to use separate concepts to represent them.

Whereas the research examining the differential effects hypothesis is promising, there certainly would be added value in more research in this vein. As noted by Schwab (1980, p. 33), the accuracy of substantive validity conclusions—that is, conclusions about the relations between a new construct and criterion variables of interest—depends on construct validity—that is, research focusing on determining the relations between the results obtained from measures and the concepts or constructs that the measures are purported to assess. To date, the literature on the justice concepts has emphasized substantive validity (by examining links between measures of the concepts and organizational variables), with less attention paid to issues of construct validity of the measures. To fully understand the similarities and differences between people's concerns about the structural and social aspects of procedures, more emphasis on construct validation of the measures designed to index these aspects is needed. For example, we have highlighted several inconsistencies in the measures used across studies. One direction for research is to further examine the extent to which such differences in operations (e.g., general judgments of fairness versus reactions to specific events) may account for the empirical findings. Of particular interest, it will be important to continue to rule out empirically the possibility that the distinction between measures of the structural and social attributes of procedures hinges on different source attributions (i.e., to the organization and supervisor, respectively). If the distinction were purely one of different source attributions, then this could argue against distinct justice concepts.

In addition to attention to measurement of the focal attributes, there would also be value in research that draws on a wider variety of research methodologies. We believe in the value of convergence. For example, most of the research examining the differential effects hypothesis is based on a cross-sectional survey methodology. Research using experimental or longitudinal methods would complement this line of inquiry by reducing third variable threats to internal validity such as monomethod bias or survey wording artifacts (Cook & Campbell, 1979). Importantly, it would also test presumptions about causality that underlie this line of research.

In conclusion, our analysis suggests that whereas people are concerned with both the structure of decision procedures and the social enactment of those procedures, the research is not yet clear on whether these are two fundamentally different concerns and consequently whether researchers should use separate concepts to represent them. Having taken stock of the key issues here, our hope is that the present analysis will move the literature productively toward a resolution of this important question.

ACKNOWLEDGMENT

This project was supported by a research grant from the Social Sciences and Humanities Research Council of Canada. The authors are grateful to all of the participants of the 1999 Roundtable on Organizational Justice held in Nice, France, for the lively discussion of an earlier version of this article. We are also grateful to Colin MacLeod and the editors of this series for their helpful comments. This version of the article was prepared while RB was on research leave at the Free University of Amsterdam.

NOTE

1. Note that in all of the studies reviewed in this section, researchers conceptualized procedural and interactional justice as Bies and Moag (1986) suggested; that is, as reflecting people's concerns about the structural and social aspects of process, respectively.

REFERENCES

Adams, J.S. (1965). Inequity in social exchange. In L. Berkowitz (Ed.), *Advances in experimental social psychology* (Vol. 2, pp. 267-299). New York: Academic Press.

Barling, J., & Phillips, M. (1993). Interactional, formal and distributive justice in the workplace: An exploratory study. *Journal of Psychology, 126,* 649-656.

Bies, R.J. (1987). The predicament of injustice: The management of moral outrage. In L.L. Cummings & B.M. Staw (Eds.), *Research in organizational behavior* (Vol. 9, pp. 289-319). Greenwich, CT: JAI Press.

Bies, R.J., & Moag, J.S. (1986). Interactional justice: Communication criteria of fairness. In R.J. Lewicki, B.H. Sheppard, & M.H. Bazerman (Eds.), *Research on negotiation in organizations* (Vol. 1, pp. 43-55). Greenwich, CT: JAI Press.

Bies, R.J., & Shapiro, D.L. (1987). Interactional fairness judgements: The influence of causal accounts. *Social Justice Research, 1,* 199-218.

Bies, R.J., & Shapiro, D.L. (1988). Voice and justification: Their influence on procedural fairness judgements. *Academy of Management Journal, 31,* 676-685.

Blader, S.L., & Tyler, T.R. (2000, August). *A four-component model of procedural justice: What makes a process fair in work settings?* Paper presented at the annual meeting of the Academy of Management, Toronto, Ontario.

Blau, P. (1964). *Exchange and power in social life.* New York: Wiley.

Bobocel, D.R., Agar, S.E., Meyer, J.P., & Irving, P.G. (1998). Managerial accounts and fairness perceptions in conflict resolution: Differentiating the effects of minimizing responsibility and providing justification. *Basic and Applied Social Psychology, 20,* 133-143.

Bobocel, D.R., & Holmvall, C.M. (1999, April). *Distributive, procedural, and interactional justice: Exploring the nomological network of organizational justice constructs.* Paper presented at the 14th annual conference of the Society for Industrial and Organizational Psychology, Atlanta, GA.

Brockner, J., & Wiesenfeld, B.M. (1996). An integrative framework for explaining reactions to decisions: The interactive effects of outcomes and procedures. *Psychological Bulletin, 120,* 189-208.

Bryne, Z.S., & Cropanzano, R. (2000, April). *The relationship of organization justice to commitment, organizational politics, and citizenship behaviors: A test of three models.*

Paper presented at the 15th annual meeting of the Society for Industrial and Organizational Psychology. New Orleans, LA.

Colquitt, J.A. (in press). On the dimensionality of organizational justice: A construct validation of a measure. *Journal of Applied Psychology.*

Cook, T.D., & Campbell, D.T. (1979). *Quasiexperimentation: Design and analysis for field studies.* Rand-McNally.

Cooper, W.H., & Richardson, A.J. (1986). Unfair comparisons. *Journal of Applied Psychology, 71,* 179-184.

Cronbach, L.J., & Meehl, P.E. (1955). Construct validity in psychological tests. *Psychological Bulletin, 52,* 281-302.

Cropanzano, R., & Ambrose, M.L. (in press). Procedural and distributive justice are more similar than you think: A monistic perspective and a research agenda.. In J. Greenberg & R. Cropanzano (Eds.), *Advances in organizational justice.* Lexington, MA: The New Lexington Press.

Cropanzano, R., & Greenberg, J. (1997). Progress in organizational justice: Tunneling through the maze. In I.T. Robertson & C.L. Cooper (Eds.), *International review of industrial and organizational psychology.* New York: John Wiley & Sons.

Cropanzano, R., & Prehar, C.A. (1999, April-May). *Using social exchange theory to distinguish procedural and interactional justice.* Paper presented at the 14th annual meeting of the Society for Industrial and Organizational Psychology, Atlanta, GA.

Deutsch, M. (1985). *Distributive justice: A social psychological perspective.* New Haven, CT: Yale University Press.

Fishbein, M., & Ajzen, I. (1975). *Beliefs, attitude, intention and behavior.* Reading, MA: Addison-Wesley.

Folger, R. (1986). A referent cognitions theory of relative deprivation. In J.M. Olson, C.P. Herman, & M.P. Zanna (Eds.), *Relative deprivation and social comparison: The Ontario symposium* (Vol. 4, pp. 33-55). Hillsdale, NJ: Erlbaum.

Folger, R. (1993). Reactions to mistreatment at work. In J.K. Murnighan (Ed.), *Social psychology in organizations: Advances in theory and research* (pp. 161-183). Englewood Cliffs, NJ: Prentice-Hall.

Folger, R., & Cropanzano, R. (1998). *Organizational justice and human resource management.* Thousand Oaks, CA: Sage.

Folger, R., & Greenberg, J. (1985). Procedural justice: An interpretive analysis of personnel systems. In K.M. Rowland & G.M. Ferris (Eds.), *Research in personnel and human resources management* (Vol. 3, pp. 141-183). Greenwich, CT: JAI Press.

Greenberg, J. (1982). Approaching equity and avoiding inequity in groups and organizations. In J. Greenberg & R.L. Cohen (Eds.), *Equity and justice in social behavior* (pp. 389-435). New York: Academic Press.

Greenberg, J. (1990). Organizational justice: Yesterday, today, and tomorrow. *Journal of Management, 16,* 399-432.

Greenberg, J. (1993a). The social side of fairness: Interpersonal and informational classes of organizational justice. In R. Cropanzano (Ed.), *Justice in the workplace: Approaching fairness in human resource management* (pp. 79-103). Hillsdale, NJ: Erlbaum.

Greenberg, J. (1993b). Stealing in the name of justice: Informational and interpersonal moderators of theft reactions to underpayment inequity. *Organizational Behavior and Human Decision Processes, 54,* 81-103.

Greenberg, J. (1993c). The intellectual adolescence of organizational justice: You've come a long way, maybe. *Social Justice Research, 6,* 135-148.

Greenberg, J. (1994). Using socially fair treatment to promote acceptance of a work site smoking ban. *Journal of Applied Psychology, 79,* 288-297.

Homans, G.C. (1961). *Social behavior: Its elementary forms.* New York: Harcourt, Brace & World.

Konovsky, M.A., & Folger, R. (1989). Effects of procedural and distributive justice on reactions to pay raise decisions. *Academy of Management Journal, 32,* 115-130.

Leventhal, G.S. (1980). What should be done with equity theory? In K.J. Gergen, M.S. Greenberg, & R.H. Willis (Eds.), *Social exchange: Advances in theory and research* (pp. 27-55). New York: Plenum.

Lind, E.A., & Tyler, T.R. (1988). *The social psychology of procedural justice.* New York: Plenum.

Malatesta, R.M., & Byrne, Z.S. (1997, April). *The impact of formal and interactional justice on organizational outcomes.* Paper presented at the twelfth annual conference of the Society for Industrial and Organizational Psychology, St. Louis, MO.

Masterson, S.S., Lewis-McClear, K., Goldman, B.M., & Taylor, M.S. (1997, August). *Organizational justice and social exchange: An empirical study of the distinction between interactional and formal procedural justice.* Paper presented at the National Academy of Management Meeting, Boston, MA.

Masterson, S.S., Lewis, K., Goldman, B.M., & Taylor, M.S. (2000). Integrating justice and social exchange: The differing effects of fair procedures and treatment on work relationships. *Academy of Management Journal, 43,* 738-748.

Mikula, G., Petrik, B., & Tanzer, N. (1990). What people regard as unjust: Types and structures of everyday experiences of injustice. *European Journal of Social Psychology, 20,* 133-149.

Moorman, R.H. (1991). Relationship between organizational justice and organizational citizenship behaviors: Do fairness perceptions influence employee citizenship? *Journal of Applied Psychology, 78,* 845-855.

Moye, N.A., Masterson, S.S., & Bartol, K.M. (1997, August). *Differentiating antecedents and consequences of procedural and interactional justice: Empirical evidence in support of separate constructs.* Paper presented at the National Academy of Management Meetings, Boston, MA.

Schwab, D.P. (1980). Construct validity in organizational behavior. In B. Staw & L.L. Cummings (Eds.), *Research in organizational behavior* (Vol. 2, pp. 3-43). Greenwich, CT: JAI Press.

Skarlicki, D.P., & Folger, R. (1997). Retaliation in the workplace: The roles of distributive, procedural, and interactional justice. *Journal of Applied Psychology, 82,* 434-443.

Thibaut, J., & Walker, L. (1975). *Procedural justice: A psychological analysis.* Hillsdale, NJ: Erlbaum.

Tyler, T.R., & Bies, R.J. (1990). Beyond formal procedures: The interpersonal context of procedural justice. In J.S. Carroll (Ed.), *Applied social psychology and organizational settings* (pp. 77-98). Hillsdale, NJ: Lawrence Erlbaum Associates.

Tyler, T.R., Boeckmann, R.J., Smith, H.J., & Huo, Y.J. (1997). *Social justice in a diverse society.* Boulder, CO: Westview.

Tyler, T.R., & Lind, E.A. (1992). A relational model of authority in groups. In M.P. Zanna (Ed.), *Advances in experimental social psychology* (Vol. 25, pp. 115-191). San Diego, CA: Academic Press.

PART II

UNDERSTANDING DIVERSITY THROUGH ORGANIZATIONAL JUSTICE

CHAPTER 5

CULTURAL INFLUENCES ON PERCEPTIONS OF DISTRIBUTIVE AND PROCEDURAL JUSTICE

Dirk D. Steiner

ABSTRACT

This chapter presents a framework for studying culture's influence on organizational justice. I explore how culture influences perceptions that one's outcomes are fair or unfair (distributive justice) and that the procedures used to determine these outcomes are fair or unfair (procedural justice). First, I review definitions of culture and identify 13 dimensions of culture that seem relevant for organizational justice research. Special attention is focused on expanding dimensions of culture beyond those typically studied by organizational researchers. Perceptions of justice are then depicted as resulting from a comparison of expectations about treatment compared to perceptions of actual treatment. The role of expectations in various conceptualizations of distributive and procedural justice is examined. Culture is proposed to influence expectations about appropriate justice rules to be used in particular contexts. Researchable hypotheses that link the 13 cultural dimensions and specific justice rules are presented and summarized. In addition, suggestions are provided for researchers that focus on examining the influence of culture on expectations for various kinds of treatment in organizational contexts.

INTRODUCTION

- *Help wanted ads seeking candidates between 20 and 25 years old and requesting an application with a handwritten letter and a photo.*
- *News reports of companies that hire regularly based on graphology, astrology, morphology or any a plethora of other 'ologies' that represent the latest fads.*
- *Grades posted by the names of students in the halls of the universities.*

Such are examples of some of the common practices among French institutions that surprised me from my American perspective when I began encountering organizational realities in France. They surprised me of course because they go against my conception and experience of what constitutes fair and appropriate organizational practices. In fact, I viewed these French practices as inherently unfair. Were they also viewed as unfair by the French people who encountered them on a daily basis? Some of my initial inquiries suggested that the French did not react as strongly to the (un)fairness of these practices as I did. In fact the realization that organizational policies did not incite the same reactions in France as they would back in the United States is what initiated my interest in organizational justice research. These differences in reactions also suggested the importance of cultural factors in determining perceptions of justice.

My purpose in this chapter is to present a framework for studying culture's influence on organizational justice. Essentially, I will explore how culture influences perceptions that one's outcomes are fair or unfair (distributive justice) and that the procedures used to determine these outcomes are fair or unfair (procedural justice). As such, organizational justice is examined from the reactive point of view (cf. Greenberg, 1987) wherein one is interested in how people react when they receive outcomes or observe outcome allocations. (The proactive perspective considers allocators and the decisions they make, Greenberg, 1987.) The perspectives developed here are influenced by theory and research on organizational justice and on cross-cultural organizational studies. However, I do not intend to present an exhaustive review of various cross-cultural studies in the field of organizational justice as a number of excellent reviews have already been written (see for example James, 1993; Kabanoff, 1997; Leung, 1997; McFarlin & Sweeney, in press; Morris & Leung, 2000). Rather, my goal is to propose theoretical perspectives that are useful for thinking about how and why culture will impact perceptions of what is fair in organizations. Such a general framework may be useful for understanding the various empirical results that have been published and did not have a common framework to guide them. But such a framework seems especially necessary to help provide innovation in the way we think about organizational justice and to provide a basis from which to formulate hypotheses relative to cultural influences on justice.

A cross-cultural perspective on organizational justice is valuable for several reasons. At a basic level, cross-cultural research can contribute to an understanding of justice principles and to defining the extent of generalizability of research findings (Bond & Smith, 1996). Further, because culture influences how we interpret events and define appropriate behaviors (Lytle, Brett, Barsness, Tinsley, & Janssens, 1995), it is likely that it has important effects on perceptions of fairness. On a practical level, cross-cultural research on organizational justice can help multinationals to understand how the policies they institute are perceived by their employees world wide and the consequences of these perceptions (Ryan, McFarland, Baron, & Page, 1999). Similarly, cross-cultural research in organizational justice can contribute to knowing how to develop policies that will be well received in different countries.

The framework presented here shares perspectives of previous research, but attempts to go beyond them in several ways. Relative to previous treatments of culture in justice, I have attempted to present a more comprehensive framework in terms of the aspects or dimensions of culture studied. In addition, until recently, researchers have focused more on distributive than on procedural justice. This chapter addresses both aspects of justice. Finally, my presentation adopts a rather cognitive, information-processing perspective of justice. The chapters in this volume by Ambrose and Kulik and by Van den Bos provide more complete treatments on the cognitive question of how one determines whether one has been fairly treated. My chapter suggests that culture plays an important role in this determination.

WHAT IS CULTURE?

Because this chapter aspires to consider cultural influences on perceptions of justice, a definition of culture is a relevant starting point. First, it is important to recognize that culture is a rather vast concept. In reviewing various definitions of culture, Triandis (1980) focused on one provided by Herskovits: "Culture is the man-made part of the human environment" (cited in Triandis, 1980, p. 1-2). Triandis further indicated that such a definition allows one to recognize that physical objects and subjective responses are both the products of culture. Clearly, it is not possible to consider all the cultural influences implied by this definition, nor are they all relevant for our purposes here.

As an initial means of constraining the consideration of culture, the focus here is on national culture. It is necessary to recognize of course that there is no such thing as a pure culture, that people within a country do not all share the same background or cultural identity. For example, a number of researchers have been interested in how individual differences on cultural variables influence justice perceptions (cf. Morris, Leung, Ames, & Lickel, 1999; Ramamoorthy & Carroll, 1998). It is also necessary to recognize that national boundaries change and so what we mean by culture is in no way static. My approach to culture is similar to that of Doney, Cannon, and Mullen (1998) who stated that it refers to "a large number of people conditioned by similar background, education, and life experiences" (p. 607). Further, in an attempt to understand what differentiates cultures, authors suggest that they appear to be distinguished by explicit and implicit rules that are learned and that govern how one should behave (Lonner & Malpass, 1994) or by "ideals, values, and assumptions about life that guide specific behaviors" (Brislin, 1993, p. 23). A comprehensive taxonomy of the features of such rules or of the ideals, values and assumptions would be useful, but does not apparently exist. Various authors provide some guidance (e.g., Hofstede, 1980), but the extant conceptualizations of the dimensions of culture appear incomplete, and innovation is clearly needed. I therefore propose an approach to examining culture's influence that attempts to be more comprehensive than current efforts in this domain.

Dimensions of Culture

As noted above, culture is a vast concept and includes physical objects as well as subjective responses (Triandis, 1980). Triandis (1980) further identified at least five systems of variables that define various dimensions along which cultures differ. These include the ecology, the subsistence system, the sociocultural system, the individual system, and the interindividual system. The sociocultural system, defined as encompassing "institutions, norms, roles and values" (p. 9), appears to be the most relevant category for the study of organizational justice. Indeed, most cross-cultural researchers in this field have limited their study to the consideration of the values component of this system, and have relied almost exclusively on the system of cultural values developed by Hofstede (1980).

Hofstede's (1980) dimensions of cultural values comprise one of the most widely used perspectives for studying organizations cross-culturally. Indeed, this perspective is cited regularly in cross-cultural studies of distributive justice. Based on a large, multination survey, Hofstede identified four dimensions along which cultures differ according to their values. *Individualism-collectivism* refers to identity shaped by personal choices/achievements or by identifying with groups to which one belongs. *Uncertainty avoidance* concerns the degree of tolerance for ambiguity. It characterizes cultures where there is a preference for predictability, clear instructions, and expectations in the behavior of others. *Power distance* refers to inequalities in societies and is represented by the perceived amount of power or influence a hierarchical superior has over a subordinate in an organization. *Masculinity-femininity* indicates an emphasis on competition and success rather than on social relationships and quality of life. Despite criticisms of the definitions and operationalizations of the Hofstede dimensions (e.g., d'Iribarne, 1997; McFarlin & Sweeney, in press; Smith & François, 1998), they are so widely used and other researchers have identified such similar dimensions (see Smith, Dugan, & Trompenaars, 1996) that their continued consideration appears justified.

Whereas Hofstede's approach is certainly valuable, and its applicability to organizational justice will be developed below, it is also important for the advancement of research on cultural influences in organizational justice (as well as in organizational psychology) to consider other values and other aspects of the sociocultural system. In fact, too many cross-cultural researchers have limited their consideration of cultural influences to Hofstede's conceptualizations, and within this system have typically only considered two of the dimensions, individualism-collectivism and power distance (Triandis & Bhawuk, 1997). Leung (1997) has also commented on aspects of culture beyond values that should be considered in cross-cultural research, and Morris and Leung (2000) point out that more specific treatments of dimensions such as individualism-collectivism allow for more precision in cross-cultural predictions. Further, Ronen (1997) asserted that the consideration of so few cultural variables has contributed to the inability of organizational psychology to develop a strong cross-cultural paradigm. To enrich our thinking, I first consider broader value perspectives. Then, I explore additional cultural dimensions that may contribute to thinking about cultural differences in organizational justice.

Other efforts at defining cultural values allow for expanding beyond the four Hofstede dimensions. For example, in the Chinese Culture Connection studies (cited in Smith et al., 1996), which had a greater representation of Asian cultures, Bond and his associates also identified four factors. These factors indicated a great deal of overlap with the dimensions identified by Hofstede; however, they also identified *Confucian dynamism*, which was not represented in Hofstede's dimensions. High scores represent an emphasis on thrift, persistence, and a future-orientation, whereas low scores indicate a more static, tradition-oriented mentality. Another effort was conducted by Trompenaars (summarized in Smith et al., 1996) who also used a large data base, including former Soviet bloc nations not studied by Hofstede, to test for seven hypothesized dimensions of cultural valuing. Again, overlap is indicated with the various dimensions of Hofstede, but it would seem useful to retain three more dimensions after consideration of various studies using the Trompenaars approach relative to the Hofstede results (cf. Smith, 1997; Smith et al., 1996). These additional dimensions are: (1) *achievement-ascription* (merit as a basis for advancement vs. being born with or without privileges); (2) *internal-external locus of control* (Rotter, 1966; the degree to which individuals are viewed as responsible for their own fates); and (3) *time perspective* (are important life events in the past, present, or future?; Cottle, 1968).

For additional cultural dimensions beyond values, it is useful to consider the work by Lytle et al. (1995), which may be the most comprehensive attempt to date to catalogue the cultural dimensions that are potentially relevant to organizational researchers. These researchers identified 77 dimensions (although they are not all unrelated and could potentially be reduced to a smaller set) used by various researchers which were grouped into the six categories of: (1) Definitions of self and others; (2) motivational orientation; (3) relations between societal members; (4) patterns of communication; (5) orientation toward time, change, and uncertainty or risk; and (6) patterns of institutions and social systems. It is certainly beyond the scope of this paper to consider all 77 dimensions, although many of them may be relevant to organizational justice. To restrict consideration to a more manageable number of dimensions, I have chosen to study the value dimensions by Hofstede and others presented in the preceding paragraphs. These dimensions also figure in the catalogue of Lytle and her colleagues. Additional dimensions selected bring the total to 13 examined here to illustrate possible cultural influences on organizational justice. My choices are influenced in part by past research, but are also motivated by a desire to broaden the cultural dimensions typically considered in organizational psychology. The dimensions to be examined here are presented in Table 1 and are discussed in the following sections (more in depth definitions are provided by Lytle et al., 1995).

Definitions of Self and Others

This category generally has to do with self-concepts and how a culture conceptualizes human nature. I have included four cultural dimensions from this category. Ascription versus achievement and locus of control were presented above. *Human nature as good or bad* is a potentially interesting cultural dimension in the realm of organizational justice because it characterizes the degree of trust or distrust people tend to have in others. The *pragmatic versus idealistic* dimension represents the degree to which the society focuses on the end results rather than on an idealistic orientation (Lytle et al., 1995).

Motivational Orientation

Lytle et al. (1995) group motivational needs and ways of relating to achievement and failure in this category. I examine only the masculinity-femininity dimension of Hofstede from this category.

Relations Between Societal Members

Hofstede's dimensions of individualism-collectivism and power distance represent this category which addresses how individuals typically relate to others in a society.

Table 1
Dimensions of Culture Relevant to Organizational Justice

A. Definitions of self and others
    1. Ascription vs. Achievement (Parsons & Shills; Triandis)
    2. Locus of Control (Rotter)
    3. Human Nature Good or Bad (Kluckholhn & Strodtbeck; Triandis)
    4. Pragmatic vs. Idealistic (England; England & Koike)
B. Motivational orientation
    1. Masculinity vs. Femininity (Hofstede)
C. Relations between societal members
    1. Individualism-Collectivism (Hofstede; Triandis)
    2. Power Distance (Hofstede)
D. Patterns of communication
    1. High vs. Low Context (Hall)
E. Orientation toward time, change, and uncertainty or risk
    1. Confucian Dynamism (Hofstede & Bond)
    2. Past/present/future orientation (Kluckhohn & Strodtbeck)
    3. Uncertainty Avoidance (Hofstede)
F. Patterns of institutions and social systems
    1. Traditional/charismatic/legal-bureaucratic (Weber)
    2. Authoritarian vs. Democratic

Source: Adapted from Lytle et al. (1995); all references cited in Lytle et al. (1995).

Patterns of Communication

In this category, the cultural dimensions deal with the importance of different elements in communication. The degree of *context (high versus low)* is the dimension of communication patterns retained for consideration here. It is a dimension that refers to the degree to which the context carries a great deal of information, and therefore all need not be stated explicitly in communications. In low context cultures, communications carry little hidden meaning.

Orientation Toward Time, Change, and Uncertainty or Risk

Lytle et al. group into this category general orientations regarding the past, present, and future as well as dimensions concerned with the role and importance of change and uncertainty in determining one's actions. Here, I treat the already discussed Confucian dynamism, time orientation, and uncertainty avoidance dimensions of culture.

Patterns of Institutions and Social Systems

This category tends to refer to types of governments and larger societal systems. Weber's *traditional/charismatic/legal-bureaucratic* distinction is one of the two cultural dimensions retained for this category. Traditional societies are characterized by defining who is the legitimate authority by tradition and authority handed down from the past. In charismatic societies, the authority is the person who gains such status because of exemplary character. This authority defines rules and situations of intervention. Legal-bureaucratic societies have impersonal rules established through procedures that apply to members of the society. The second dimension retained in this category is *authoritarian versus democratic* which contrasts societies where power is concentrated in one or several elite individuals versus those where the people either directly or indirectly have power.

These different cultural dimensions are not necessarily independent. Even several of Hofstede's dimensions are intercorrelated. Further, values and social systems and other cultural dimensions are subject to mutual influence. It is useful to consider the various dimensions, even though they may be correlated, because the influence of one or the other of the dimensions is likely to be more direct for certain aspects of justice perceptions. Following a presentation of a general framework for considering organizational justice, we will examine how the cultural dimensions can influence organizational justice perceptions.

A FRAMEWORK OF CULTURE'S INFLUENCE ON ORGANIZATIONAL JUSTICE

The following propositions summarize the perspective presented in this chapter:

Proposition 1. Perceptions of injustice are produced by violations of expectations.

Proposition 2. Culture determines expectations regarding fair treatment and influences the importance of various types of violations of the expectations.

Each of these propositions will be developed in detail following this general overview. The first proposition suggests a rather universal, culture-free cause for perceptions of injustice: the violation of expectations. We have expectations about what our or others' rewards should be as a function of which distributive rule (see next section) we believe should be applied in a given situation. We also have expectations regarding the procedures (developed in the next section) that should be applied in determining the allocations. When these expectations are met or exceeded in our perception of the reality of the situation, the situation will be perceived as fair; when they are not met, unfairness will be perceived. Culture intervenes in the second proposition by influencing which of the various distributive and procedural rules will be activated to determine the expectations and their importance when evaluating the actual situation for violations.

It is useful to note that Morris and Leung (2000) have recently presented a review showing how culture has been studied in organizational justice research. Similar to the framework I present here, their model indicates that cultural factors influence which justice rule should be applied. However, they did not explicitly examine how one processes justice information, and so the role of expectations was not developed.

Let us now examine each of the propositions in detail.

Proposition 1. Perceptions of Injustice Are Produced by Violations of Expectations

The opening comments to this paper, indicating my surprise at French practices, illustrate this basic tenet. My American cultural background led me to expect that hiring practices should emphasize candidates' capabilities to perform the job rather than their handwriting or things that facilitate unfair discrimination (age, photograph) by American definitions. The use of such practices violated my expectations of what constitutes fair practices in these situations.

This basic statement of the role of expectations in perceptions of unfairness is supported by numerous authors in the field of organizational justice. Indeed, Furby (1986) maintained that meeting expectations is a key part of justice and other authors in this volume also discuss the important role expectations play in justice (cf. Ambrose & Kulik; Van den Bos). The examples from my French experiences illustrate expectations regarding procedures. Initially, researchers dealt with expectations regarding outcomes one should receive. It is probably worthwhile at this point to clarify the nature of these different expectations in organizational justice.

Considering the *distributive* justice perspective, the early work on relative deprivation identified the importance of comparing what one receives to some reference point (what others receive; see Cropanzano & Randall, 1993), and of course Adams' (1965) equity theory did much to define how one makes the comparison between one's own situation and that of a comparison other. From the perspective of relative deprivation, the reference point defines expectations about what one should receive. Further, the words "expect" and "expectation" occur frequently in Adams' (1965) presentation of distributive justice. According to equity theory, individuals expect to be compensated for their contributions, and they expect that the rules of exchange will be equivalent for similar others. In other words, what we *expect* to receive in a given situation is defined by such things as our inputs into the situation and our perceptions of what we perceive to be appropriate returns for these inputs. Using comparable others refines these perceptions.

Of course, other research has indicated that an equity perspective is not sufficient for understanding distributive justice. Equality, whereby everyone receives the same compensation, and consideration of special needs are two other distributive perspectives that individuals may find appropriate according to the circumstances (e.g., Deutsch, 1985; Lerner, 1977). These other distributive rules are not at all problematic for the current perspective. When the circumstances appropriate for the equality or special needs rules arise, our expectations are modified accordingly. Rather than expecting that our inputs will determine our compensation, we now expect to receive the same thing as everyone else, or we expect to have our special needs considered.

Perceptions of *procedural* injustice also arise from violations of expectations. First, several perspectives suggest that individuals expect fair treatment (Shapiro, 1998). According to Leventhal (1980), a procedural rule defines what *should* be done for a procedure to be considered fair. Voice, or process control (Thibaut & Walker, 1975), is a well-known procedural rule, as are the six procedural rules defined by Leventhal (1980), which are consistency, bias-suppression, accuracy, correctability, representativeness, and ethicality. But just as we have seen with distributive justice where the appropriate rule to apply is determined by the situation, Leventhal proposed that the context would define which procedural rule should be applied. And when the expected rule is not applied, procedural justice is violated (perceptions of unfairness result). Although Folger's Referent Cognitions Theory (see Bobocel & Holmvall in this volume) suggests that concerns about procedures arise when outcomes are lower than expected, the idea that one then considers procedures that "should" and "could" have been used to evaluate the agent also suggests that we have expectations about procedures.

Interactional justice (Bies & Moag, 1986) is now frequently considered to be a subcomponent of procedural justice (see Cropanzano & Greenberg, 1997; for a specific treatment in this volume, see the chapter by Bobocel & Holmvall). The dimensions of social sensitivity and justification by information are therefore considered here as two additional procedural justice rules. Once again, individuals *expect* fair treatment in their interactions with others (Bies & Moag, 1986).

The different procedural rules are presented in Table 2. They are illustrated with questions that indicate the nature of expectations one might develop about each of them. Figure 1 summarizes the general framework developed in these pages. The first proposition addresses the role of the distributive and procedural rules in determining expectations of treatment. These expectations are then compared to a perceived reality to determine the nature of reactions in terms of perceived justice or injustice. Meeting or exceeding expectations produces positive perceptions of fair-

Table 2
Expectations Regarding Procedural Rules with Questions Illustrating the Role of Expectations

1. **Voice**—will I participate in the decision?
2. **Consistency**—will all persons receive the same treatment at all times?
3. **Bias-suppression**—will a bias result against my group?
4. **Accuracy**—will accurate information be used; will a competent individual decide?
5. **Correctability**—will I have a second chance?
6. **Representativeness**—will my interests be considered?
7. **Ethicality**—are our moral and ethical values respected?
8. **Social Sensitivity**—will I be treated with dignity and respect?
9. **Informational Justification**—will I receive information regarding the basis for the decision?

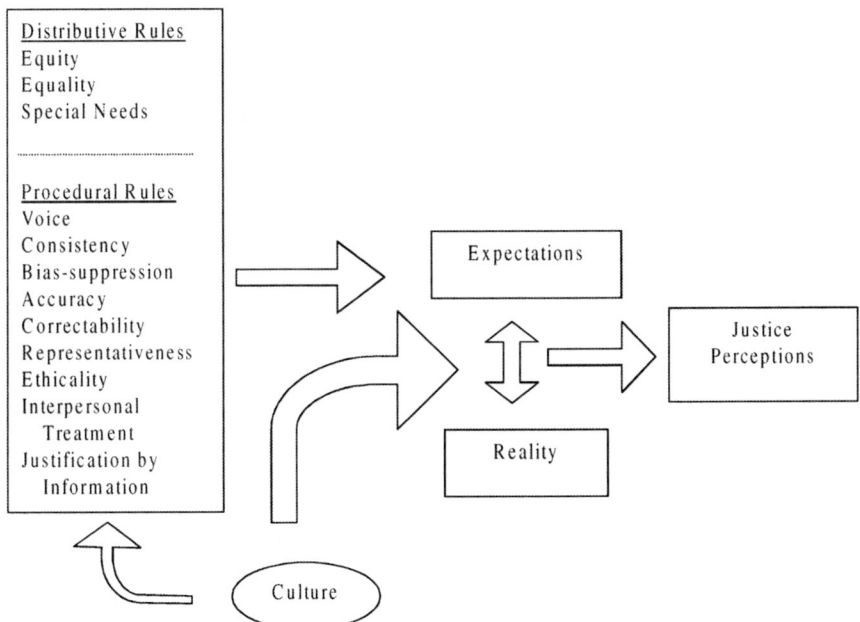

Figure 1. Schematic model of the influence of culture on organizational justice rules which determine justice expectations.

ness. Unfairness is experienced in greater degrees as a function of how far reality is believed to deviate from expectations.[1]

The Influence of Culture

We have seen that for both distributive and procedural justice, the context plays a role in determining the appropriate rule to be applied. A number of factors contribute to defining the context; culture is just one of these factors (see also Morris et al., 1999; Morris & Leung, 2000) and the only one to be treated here. As Cropanzano (1998) pointed out, culture can be viewed as a lens through which one interprets events, such as organizational policies and procedures that are relevant for perceptions of justice. Similarly, other authors have proposed that culture has a role in guiding the interpretation of events and in establishing appropriate behaviors (Lytle et al., 1995). Indeed, in cross-cultural research on distributive justice, researchers have been especially interested in the influence of culture on the preference for the equity or equality rule (special needs have only rarely been examined, Schwinger, 1986), and a rather large number of cross-cultural comparisons show that such cultural effects exist. On the other hand, relatively little cross-cultural research has examined cultural effects on the various procedural rules, despite the importance of doing so, either to assess the generalizability of American findings or to develop theory relating to differences (Lind, Tyler, & Huo, 1997).

The second proposition addresses explicitly the role of culture in perceptions of justice.

Proposition 2: Culture Determines Expectations Regarding Fair Treatment and Influences the Importance of Various Types of Violations of the Expectations

In this proposition, and as shown in Figure 1, culture influences expectations by determining which distributive rule should be applied in a given context and according to which procedural rules. For example, my (American) culture may lead me both to believe that the equity rule should be applied to determine my pay raise and to believe that consistency should be applied—the same rule for everyone. Culture is further depicted as influencing how these expectations are confronted to a perception of reality, that is, a construal of what one believes happened in a given situation. Morris et al. (1999; Morris & Leung, 2000) do a thorough job of developing culture's role in the construal of behavior, so it will not be addressed completely here. Suffice it to say, for example, that culture affects how one interprets one's inputs and outcomes in an equity theory perspective.

The various cultural dimensions will be examined first for distributive and then for procedural justice. Table 3 summarizes the cultural dimensions that are hypothesized to influence the various distributive and procedural rules. A "P" appears in the cells where a cultural dimension is hypothesized to be particularly influential on a justice dimension based on prior research or commentary; an "N" indicates a new relationship between culture and justice proposed here. A cursory glance of the table shows that there are many more N's than P's, indicating again that few cultural dimensions have been considered previously in cross-cultural research on organizational justice.

Distributive Justice

In the area of distributive justice, interest has focused on the conditions that are likely to produce preferences for (i.e., greater application and weighting of) the distributive rules of equity, equality, or special needs. Typically, applying one of these rules precludes the application of another one, although rewards based in part on two or all of the rules are possible. For example, researchers generally agree that conditions that emphasize productivity tend to result in preferences for equity, whereas conditions that emphasize group relations tend to produce preferences for equality in reward distributions (Kabanoff, 1991; Stake, 1983). The consideration of needs has not received as much attention by researchers, but one can note special situations such as reduction of pay, or contexts such as social programs where needs are acceptable as a basis for reward distribution (Elliott & Meeker, 1986; Schwinger, 1986; Steiner, Haptonstahl, Trahan, & Fointiat, 1996).

Cultural norms appear to influence the prevalence of the equity norm or other distributive norms. People from different cultures are likely to have different expectations about how rewards should be distributed (Leung, Su, & Morris, in this volume). Cropanzano and Greenberg (1997) reviewed a number of studies and found that researchers typically argue that equity is likely to predominate in North American organizations in order to spur productivity. In the context of compensation, Miles and Greenberg (1993) discussed the general preference for the equity rule in some countries (United States and Great Britain), equality in others (Scandinavian countries), and still other types of rules elsewhere (age, education, gender and so on in Japan). Several studies indicate that special needs are more likely to be considered in India than in the United States, but that the degree of this consideration may also be influenced by one's caste (Berman, Murphy-Berman, & Singh, 1985; Murphy-Berman, Berman, Singh, Pachauri, & Kumar, 1984; Pandey & Singh, 1997; but see Leung, 1997). In the current framework, these preferences are conceived as producing expectations for how rewards will be distributed.

In terms of the dimensions of culture presented in Table 1, preferences for the different distributive rules have most frequently been examined

TABLE 3
Cultural Dimensions and Their Hypothesized Influences on Distributive and Procedural Justice

Justice Rule	Achievement-Ascription	Locus of Control	Human Nature: Good vs. Bad	Pragmatic vs. Idealistic	Masculinity-Femininity	Individualism-Collectivism	Power Distance	High vs. Low Context	Confucian Dynamism	Time Perspective	Uncertainty Avoidance	Traditional/Charismatic/Legal-bureaucratic	Authoritarian vs. Democratic
A. Distributive Rules													
1. Equity vs. Equality vs. Needs	N	N	N		P	P	P				P	N	
B. Procedural Rules													
1. Voice	N	N	N		N	P	P	N			N	N	N
2. Consistency	N		N		P		N				N	N	N
3. Bias-Suppression			N			N						N	N
4. Accuracy	N		N		P		N				N	N	N
5. Correctability	N	N	N				N		N			N	N
6. Representativeness						N							N
7. Ethicality			N	N			N						N
8. Social Sensitivity			N		N		N						N
9. Informational Justification			N				N	N			N	N	N

P = Relationship postulated or examined in previous research.
N = New relationship proposed in this chapter

from the perspective of Hofstede's values (e.g., James, 1993; Miles & Greenberg, 1993). The most reliable finding appears to be with regard to the cultural dimension of individualism-collectivism, with individualistic countries using equity and collectivistic countries preferring group harmony and therefore equality or needs (James, 1993; Miles & Greenberg, 1993). However, Leung (1997) also reports on research he conducted with Bond, which found that one's level of contribution, and the in-group out-group status of the target member, are important contextual factors that moderate this general finding. Chen (1995) has also found that the preferred distribution rule for Chinese and American respondents depended on whether the rewards allocated were material or socioemotional in nature. Such findings point out that culture is not the only contextual factor that influences expectations regarding justice rules.

Miles and Greenberg (1993) examined hypotheses relating Hofstede's cultural dimensions to preferences for the equity over the equality rule in reward distribution by identifying previously conducted studies on these rules within European Community countries. They proposed that cultures characterized by individualism, low power distance, low uncertainty avoidance, and masculinity would be most likely to operate according to equity—rather than equality-based distributions. There was not much supportive evidence for the predictions, but they concluded that this review of previous studies was an unsatisfactory test of the hypotheses. Indeed, the studies they identified did not allow for controlling for contextual factors that influence preferences and did not always pit equity against equality as a choice for research participants. Experimental conditions and contextual factors influence the preference for the various distributive rules even *within* a culture (see also Leung & Bond, 1984; Leung, 1997; McFarlin & Sweeney, in press; Steiner et al., 1996).

Besides the Hofstede dimensions examined in the above-cited studies, it is difficult to find guidance from previous research for hypotheses concerning other cultural dimensions' effects on distributive justice. Other dimensions have on the whole simply not been studied in organizational justice contexts. I propose that countries with an emphasis on achievement are likely to prefer equity in order to reward merit, whereas cultures emphasizing ascription will focus more on the rules of needs or equality that permit recognizing privileges from birth rather than individual accomplishments.[2] Similarly, cultures where the people tend to have a more internal locus of control may prefer the use of equity because of the necessity to feel that what one does (contributes) is related to consequences (outcomes). On the other hand, if fate and external sources are expected to determine what happens, perhaps any of the three distributive rules are acceptable—others decide anyway. If human nature is viewed as generally bad, one may believe that rewards should be based on particular needs and therefore prefer granting outcomes to close in-group or family members whom one trusts. Finally, in traditional or charismatic societies, rather than in legal-bureaucratic ones, some version of special needs may prevail over equity concerns, as it is the authorities themselves in these countries who determine rules of functioning. Again, these new relationships are indicated by an "N" in Table 3.

Procedural Justice

As noted previously, Leventhal (1980) indicated that the weighting of the procedural rules varies based on a number of factors characterizing the situation. Of particular relevance for a consideration of the influence of culture are Leventhal's suggestions regarding the roles of legitimate authorities, perceived probabilities that a rule will be violated, and the regularity of governmental scandals, all of which may sensitize people to possible violations of the procedural rules. Leventhal also discussed the possible influence of monolithic versus pluralistic social systems. A system which imposes clear rules for many things will not arouse concerns of fairness as much as pluralistic systems which allow for a variety of approaches. These various ideas sound very much like notions of power distance (legitimate authorities), uncertainty avoidance (clarity of rules), and patterns of institutions that were developed as relevant cultural dimensions here.

Similarly as for the distributive rules, culture is depicted as influencing which procedural rules one expects to be applied in a given situation (see Figure 1). It has frequently been suggested that voice is important across all cultures (see Shapiro & Tinsley in this volume; Thibaut & Walker, 1975), although as we will see, certain cultural dimensions have also been proposed as influencing its importance. In contrast to the distributive rules where the use of one tends to preclude the use of the others, the procedural rules can all be applied more or less independently of one another. It is even possible that one expect all of them to be applied. A reexamination of Table 2 will allow the reader to see that the independence of these rules is possible. It will also facilitate an understanding of how culture may impact expectations regarding these rules. Finally, the grid in Table 3 presents the hypothesized influences of the cultural dimensions on the procedural justice dimensions, with P's again representing hypotheses based on previous work and N's for new relations proposed here.

Little theoretical or empirical work exists to guide the hypotheses for procedural justice proposed in Table 3. Lind et al. (1997) made this remark concerning relational issues in procedural justice, and we have already noted that cross-cultural researchers have paid more attention to distributive rather than to procedural justice. Some of the hypotheses in Table 3 are inspired by speculations made by McFarlin and Sweeney (in press), but their speculations revolved exclusively around Hofstede's four values. Thus, McFarlin and Sweeney suggest that selling oneself or having one's say (having voice) will be more important in individualistic than collectivistic cultures and in countries with low power distance (in this volume, Shapiro & Tinsley make the same argument concerning power distance). McFarlin and Sweeney further suggest that masculine, achievement-oriented countries (such as the United States) in contrast with feminine countries (e.g., Arabic countries) may be more preoccupied with the clear definition of performance standards and appropriate criteria, suggesting the importance of the procedural dimensions of consistency of application and accuracy. The greater the importance of these different justice rules in different cultures, the stronger should be the expectations that they will be respected.

There are a number of other possible cultural influences indicated in Table 3. Given the lack of research to guide hypotheses for the other dimensions, I speculate about the influences that seem most likely; others are certainly possible. First, because *achievement versus ascription* has to do with one achieving advantages rather than being born with them, it is hypothesized that in achievement-oriented societies people will expect and prefer procedures that allow their achievements to be recognized and accurately evaluated. Thus, people from achievement-oriented cultures are hypothesized to expect: (1) the possibility of participating in decisions (voice), (2) having all individuals evaluated according to the same criteria (consistency), (3) having all aspects of their contributions evaluated (accuracy), and (4) the possibility of a second evaluation (correctability). When people are born with advantages, input into decisions and the criteria for evaluation are less relevant. *Locus of control* is also hypothesized to influence preferences of and expectations for voice and correctability. In places where it is believed that one controls one's fate, voice and a second chance are consistent with having such control. Similarly, in this volume, Shapiro and Tinsley make the argument that determinism, which corresponds to an external locus of control, will produce a lower value for voice. They cite the Philippines, China, and Asia in general as areas characterized by high determinism.

Human nature as good versus bad is hypothesized to influence all nine procedural rules. Indeed, this conception of human nature is closely associated with trust or mistrust, and a large body of research in organizational justice focuses on the importance of trust in authority figures as the central reason for valuing procedural justice (e.g., Lind, 1992; Van den Bos, Vermunt, & Wilke, 1997). Thus, it is proposed that people will be particularly sensitive to violations of the nine procedural rules in areas where human nature is considered to be good and therefore there is a culture of trust. Where there is a general mistrust, on the other hand, people would not have great expectations regarding the respect of the procedural rules.

The *pragmatic versus idealistic* dimension emphasizes results and outcomes versus ideals or morality. As such, it is proposed as relevant to the ethicality rule. Societies that place greater emphasis on morality may be more sensitive to potential violations of their ethical values.

Some hypotheses regarding Hofstede's dimensions of *masculinity-femininity, individualism-collectivism,* and *power distance* were presented previously. In addition, masculinity, with its emphasis on achievement and success, may produce a greater importance of voice because people from these countries will want to make their achievements clearly known. On the other hand, femininity may result in a greater emphasis on social sensitivity because of the importance of social relationships and quality of life. Collectivism may cause individuals to be more concerned about protecting members of their group thus creating a sensitivity to bias-suppression, whereas individualism may result in a greater preoccupation for having one's own interests represented (representativeness). Power distance, similar to human nature as good or bad with its concern for relations to authority, is depicted as influencing a number of the procedural justice rules. So, in countries where a great power distance is perceived between the self and an authority, there may be low expectations regarding fair treatment for all (consistency), the use of accurate information by competent authorities (accuracy), the possibility for reconsideration (correctability), the use of ethical standards, social sensitivity in one's relations with the authority, and the providing of information regarding the bases for decisions.

High versus low context is potentially influential in the areas of voice and informational justification. In low context cultures, these two procedural rules are likely to be more important as individuals will expect and value more explicit, concrete communication. In high context cultures, individuals may make inferences from the nature of the situation and not need a well-defined opportunity to express a point of view or receive information. In this volume, Shapiro and Tinsley make a similar proposition concerning context and voice.

Confucian dynamism and *time perspective* are both depicted as influencing expectations regarding the correctability rule. The opportunity to try again may be associated with the perseverance value of Confucian dynamism and a longer time perspective. Time perspective may affect expectations regarding when it is acceptable for fair treatment to occur (short term vs. long term, Shapiro, 1998; Stone, 1998), and may emphasize preservation of the existing (past orientation), spontaneity (present), or planning (future; see Lytle et al., 1995). A future-oriented time perspective may place greater emphasis on correctability—allowing for the situation to become fair at a future time. *Uncertainty avoidance*, which characterizes cultures that prefer clear, well-defined rules rather than tolerating ambiguity, is likely to impact the preferences for the application of a number of the procedural rules. I hypothesize that it will be associated with the importance of the procedural rules that emphasize a clear definition of procedures, such as consistency of application, the use of accurate information, and providing information on the procedures. High uncertainty avoidance may also incite organizations to create greater voice opportunities for their employees. Getting as much information as possible may allow for reducing uncertainty. Along these lines, in the selection context, Ryan et al.

(1999) found that a greater variety of tests were used more extensively in countries high on uncertainty avoidance.

The final two cultural dimensions in the grid refer to forms of government. Once again, these dimensions have much to do with relations to authority, already noted as central to procedural justice concerns, and are therefore expected to influence expectations regarding many of the procedural rules. The *traditional/charismatic/legal-bureaucratic* dimension is hypothesized to influence preferences and expectations for seven of the procedural justice rules. This dimension essentially refers to the person who has power—someone who gains it by tradition, by personal characteristics, or by impersonal rules. It is therefore the legal-bureaucratic cultures, with their emphasis on impersonal rules for everyone, that are likely to put in place procedural rules. These forms of institutions influence whether one expects to have voice, whether the same procedures apply to everyone, whether biases are likely against particular groups, whether the authority is viewed as competent to evaluate, whether an error can be corrected, whether one's interests will be considered, and whether information is likely to be provided regarding procedures. Consistent with these hypotheses, Pearce, Bigley, and Branyiczki (1998) found that more modern cultures (e.g., the United States) compared to traditionalist ones (e.g., China or Russia) used more meritocratic principles and procedural justice. The *authoritarian versus democratic* dimension considers whether power is concentrated in one or a few elite individuals or whether the people have power. This dimension therefore likely influences voice, representativeness, the respect for ethical values, and the presence of justifying information. It is also likely that people in more democratic societies expect a minimum of social sensitivity in their interactions with authority.

Distributive vs. Procedural Justice

Culture may also influence the relative importance of distributive or procedural issues in determining one's overall perceptions of justice. The various theories that are used to explain why one is interested in procedures at all and not just distributions may be more or less valid in different cultures. For example, the resource model emphasizes maximizing positive outcomes and proposes that we believe that fair procedures ensure the greatest returns in the long term (Tyler, 1994). A rather future-oriented time perspective may be necessary for this model to hold. A Confucian dynamism with emphasis on perseverance may also improve the chances that the resource model is applicable. On the other hand, the relational model emphasizes our desire for high status in the group and suggests that fair procedures indicate that we are valued by the group (Tyler, 1994). Being valued by the group may be more relevant in collectivistic societies.

On a more general level, cultures that have a general mistrust of human nature may place greater emphasis on outcomes than procedures, relying on concrete results as indicative of fair treatment more than on rather abstract rules.

General Expectations of Unfair Treatment

The framework I have developed proposes that culture influences expectations about which rules of organizational justice one expects to be applied. It is also possible that cultures differ on the general expectation that people will be treated fairly. It seems likely that in the United States people generally believe that they will be treated fairly in their relationships with employers and that they can do something about it when they encounter unfair treatment. We can imagine that in some countries, people believe that they have little power and that they are likely to be exploited in all relations with authority. The dimensions of culture hypothesized here to influence expectations regarding many of the procedural justice rules may well be dimensions that influence an overriding expectation about whether fair treatment will occur. Thus, if human nature is viewed as generally bad, power distance is high, and the government is traditional or authoritarian, examining a particular situation to understand concerns of organizational justice may not be particularly relevant: People may have adapted to being exploited and putting up with unfair treatment across many situations.

DIRECTIONS FOR RESEARCH

Because of the complexity of culture, it is difficult for cross-cultural research in any field to determine clearly which aspect of culture is responsible for a particular finding. Nations vary on a large number of cultural dimensions, any of which may take precedence in a given situation to produce a particular result. Also complicating this matter is the strong possibility that several dimensions act together or even interact to influence the salience of a justice dimension. And yet another complication in the particular area of organizational justice is that other contextual factors may be more influential than culture (Lytle et al., 1995; Triandis & Bhawuk, 1997) or interact with cultural dimensions to determine the salience of the various dimensions of justice. Therefore, a particular context may suggest the importance of voice, for example, across all cultures. Given the complexity of the situation, how should we proceed to testing the framework presented in these pages?

I suggest that the model and the grid of hypotheses presented here may be used to identify some productive research projects. First, research could focus on examining explicitly the role culture has in determining justice expectations. Thus, for different organizational contexts, we should determine which justice rules are expected in cultures differing on key dimensions. In contexts such as performance appraisal, internal promotions, or personnel selection, we could assess expectations regarding the application of various justice rules. As a specific example, one might study whether people from feminine countries, such as Sweden and Norway (Hofstede, 1980), have greater expectations concerning the social sensitivity that should take place in a selection interview compared to people from more masculine countries such as Japan. Then, after gaining knowledge of the expectations about justice rules in different countries, it would be possible to study justice perceptions when these expectations are violated. For example, do Norwegians perceive greater injustice when they observe a simulated interview that violates social sensitivity than do Japanese respondents? This latter approach allows for manipulating the various justice rules experimentally to study the consequences of them in different cultures. Experimental tests are needed in the cross-cultural literature on justice for a better understanding of causality in justice judgements (see also Van den Bos in this volume).

The approach based on categorization theory presented by Ambrose and Kulik in this volume is also likely to be a fruitful approach for studying the role of culture in determining expectations for justice rules. Ambrose and Kulik propose that we have cognitive categories for procedural situations. It is likely that these categories differ culturally, and studying the differences in categories may in fact highlight the differences in expectations. Using the selection interview example again, when determining the category concerning a selection interview for Norwegians compared to Japanese, we may find that there are elements of social sensitivity present for the former but not for the latter.

Elsewhere, we have applied a number of the ideas presented in this chapter to the specific context of perceived justice in personnel selection (Steiner & Gilliland, in press). In a few cases, we proposed somewhat different effects of culture on justice expectations than those presented here because of the selection context and the application of justice to that context.

CONSEQUENCES OF JUSTICE PERCEPTIONS

A model of the influence of culture on perceptions of justice should not end with justice perceptions as the final dependent variable. Researchers in organizational justice have also been concerned with what happens as a consequence of feeling that one has been fairly or unfairly treated (a number of these are presented in Greenberg & Lind, 2000). It is beyond the scope of this chapter to develop fully the influence of culture on the link between the perception of injustice and a response to it. Instead, I will outline here some general notions of how culture may intervene. These notions merit a more thorough treatment in the future.

One example of a cross-cultural perspective on the consequences of justice is research indicating that procedural justice may be more predictive of organizational citizenship behaviors for Americans whereas distributive justice may be more predictive of these behaviors among Mexicans (Konovsky, Elliott, & Pugh, cited in McFarlin & Sweeney, in press; Konovsky & Pugh, 1994). Similarly, Leung, Smith, Wang, and Sun (1996) found that distributive and procedural justice, but not interactive justice, were predictive of job satisfaction among Chinese employees of a joint venture hotel.

On a more general level, responses to injustice may be culturally determined. Whether one uses legal challenges, for example, is likely to be influenced by the nature of the government and the extent to which the legal system clearly defines such options for individuals who perceive an injustice. Further, reactions to injustices are determined by perceptions that one *can* respond and that one *desires* to respond (Shapiro, 1998). Culture may influence both of these perceptions. For example, James (1993) reviewed results of several studies that found that reactions of anger to experienced injustice vary culturally. Further, this tendency to experience anger was greater in low power distance countries where individuals also reacted more negatively to unfair treatment by others (Gundykunst & Ting-Toomey, cited in James, 1993). Power distance seems to be related here to the desire to respond.

The cultural dimensions of Table 1 that seem most relevant to the perception that one can respond to an injustice are achievement-ascription (if ascription, one may feel there is nothing one can do to change the situation), locus of control (internals believe they can act on the situation), pragmatic versus idealistic (idealistic principles may dictate that one has an obligation to act), a more legal-bureaucratic system, and a more democratic government. The desire to respond may be reinforced in achievement-oriented cultures where individuals may react in order to further their chances of achieving.

CONCLUSION

Beyond the complexities of cross-cultural research that stem from the multitude of dimensions on which cultures differ, another concern in any type of cross-cultural research is that societies change, particularly their governments and their laws, and the emphasis placed on various justice rules are likely to change as well (see also Cropanzano & Greenberg, 1997). Nonetheless, conducting cross-cultural research at the present time is of value, as we noted in the opening pages of this chapter. Lytle et al. (1995) do a good job of describing how one chooses the countries to study in order to rule out alternative explanations. Unfortunately, given the number of cultural factors that may operate at any given time, it is likely that studying a large number of countries is necessary to clearly understand culture's impact on justice. It may be more feasible to study smaller sets of countries at a time with the necessity of integrating various results when enough similar efforts have been completed.

I recognize that there are a number of potentially important cultural factors that have not been considered here. The nature of social identifications is one such factor. In particular, the degree of identification with various minority, religious, or gender groups varies culturally due to the group's (or nation's) particular history. For example, James' (1993) review pointed out the salience of racial and gender distinctions in the United States, the salience of religious distinctions in Arabic countries, and the lack of salience of gender in Sweden and Iceland. These identifications may influence concerns of consistency of application, bias suppression, accuracy, representativeness, ethicality or even the importance of distributions relative to procedures.

In addition to government structures, the legal environment may vary by culture, but also by time. Concerning the legal environment, employment law is likely to be highly relevant to questions of organizational justice as laws may dictate appropriate practices in areas of compensation, personnel selection, and other organizational policies. Laws may influence not only how one perceives what is fair and unfair, but also how one responds when confronted with unfair treatment. National employment laws are particularly likely to vary regarding the treatment of women and minorities and are also likely to vary regarding the degree to which they provide guidance regarding what is considered to be a discriminatory practice and how to respond to it. For example, French law protects similar minority groups as defined by American EEOC laws, but the French system does less to define operationally how one knows whether discrimination has occurred and what one does if one is a victim. In France in 1998 there were only four formal complaints of racial discrimination in hiring practices although individuals openly discuss many more cases in the media. It may be that the feeling of empowerment to bring suit against a discriminatory company is relatively absent in France relative to the United States.

In conclusion, the role of culture in both distributive and procedural justice appears to be important. This chapter has attempted to provide a framework for examining broader aspects of culture than have been previously considered in the organizational justice literature. Further, relatively little research has been conducted to date considering the influences of culture on procedural justice. It is hoped that the current conceptualization is useful to researchers as they think about and study culture's role in creating expectations and preferences for the various rules of justice.

NOTES

1. Several points made in the research summarized by Van den Bos in this volume suggest the possibility that expectations will be more important for determin-

ing justice perceptions in certain situations. First, expectations may be more important for procedural than for distributive fairness because procedural justice is evaluated in more absolute terms and not in reference to a comparison other as is the case for distributive justice. Second, expectations might be more important for distributive justice in the absence of comparative information than when such information is present. And third, still in the context of distributive justice, expectations might be more important in situations where comparative information is not relevant, such as when comparison others do not exist or are unknown to the individual. This latter situation might arise for example when one is the only job candidate or when one does not have the opportunity to know the outcome of the selection process for other candidates.

2. It is also possible that the impact of this dimension is more important on the construal of reality, with individuals in ascription-oriented societies believing that one's privileges are an input to be considered in the equity ratio (cf. Morris et al., 1999; Morris & Leung, 2000).

REFERENCES

Adams, J.S. (1965). Inequity in Social Exchange. In L. Berkowitz (Ed.), *Advances in experimental social psychology* (Vol. 2). New York: Academic Press.

Berman, J.J., Murphy-Berman, V., & Singh, P. (1985). Cross-cultural similarities and differences in perceptions of fairness. *Journal of Cross-Cultural Psychology, 16,* 55-67.

Bies, R.J., & Moag, J.S. (1986). Interactional justice: Communication criteria of fairness. In R.J. Lewicki, B.H. Sheppard, & M. Bazerman (Eds.), *Research on negotiation in organizations* (Vol. 1, pp. 43-55). Greenwich, CT: JAI Press.

Bond, M.H., & Smith, P.B. (1996). Cross-cultural social and organizational psychology. *Annual Review of Psychology, 47,* 205-235.

Brislin, R. (1993). *Understanding culture's influence on behavior.* Fort Worth, TX: Harcourt Brace.

Chen, C.C. (1995). New trends in rewards allocation preferences: A sino-U.S. comparison. *Academy of Management Journal, 38,* 408-428.

Cottle, T.J. (1968). The location of experience: A manifest time orientation. *Acta Psychologica, 28,* 129-149.

Cropanzano, R. (1998, April). *Organizational justice and culture.* Paper presented at the 13th Annual Conference of the Society for Industrial and Organizational Psychology, Dallas.

Cropanzano, R., & Greenberg, J. (1997). Progress in organizational justice: Tunneling through the maze. In C.L. Cooper & I.T. Robertson (Eds.), *International review of industrial and organizational psychology: 1997.* New York: John Wiley & Sons.

Cropanzano, R., & Randall, M.L. (1993). Injustice and work behavior: A historical review. In R. Cropanzano (Ed.), *Justice in the workplace: Approaching fairness in human resource management* (pp. 3-20). Hillsdale, NJ: Erlbaum.

Deutsch, M. (1985). *Distributive justice: A social-psychological perspective.* New Haven, CT: Yale University Press.

D'Iribarne, P. (1997). The usefulness of an ethnographic approach to the international comparison of organizations. *International Studies of Management and Organization, 26,* 30-47.

Doney, P.M., Cannon, J.P., & Mullen, M.R. (1998). Understanding the influence of national culture on the development of trust. *Academy of Management Review, 23,* 601-620.

Elliott, G.C., & Meeker, B.F. (1986). Achieving fairness in the face of competing concerns: The different effects of individual and group characteristics. *Journal of Personality and Social Psychology, 50,* 754-760.

Furby, L. (1986). Psychology and justice. In R.L. Cohen (Ed.), *Justice: Views from the Social Sciences* (pp. 153-203). New York: Plenum.

Greenberg, J. (1987). A taxonomy of organizational justice theories. *Academy of Management Review, 12,* 9-22.

Greenberg, J., & Lind, E.A. (2000). The pursuit of organizational justice: From conceptualization to implication to application. In C.L. Cooper and E.A. Locke (Eds.), *Industrial and organizational psychology* (pp. 72-108). Oxford: Blackwell.

Hofstede, G. (1980). *Culture's consequences: International differences in work-related values.* Beverly Hills, CA: Sage.

James, K. (1993). The social context of organizational justice: Cultural, intergroup, and structural effects on justice behaviors and perceptions. In R. Cropanzano (Ed.), *Justice in the workplace: Approaching fairness in human resource management* (pp. 21-50). Hillsdale, NJ: Lawrence Erlbaum Associates.

Kabanoff, B. (1991). Equity, equality, power, and conflict. *Academy of Management Review, 16,* 416-441.

Kabanoff, B. (1997). Organizational justice across cultures: Integrating organization-level and culture-level perspectives. In P.C. Earley & M. Erez (Eds.), *New perspectives on international industrial/organizational psychology.* San Francisco: New Lexington Press.

Konovsky, M.A., & Pugh, S.D. (1994). Citizenship behavior and social exchange. *Academy of Management Journal, 37,* 656-699.

Lerner, M.J. (1977). The justice motive: Some hypotheses as to its origins and forms. *Journal of Personality, 45,* 1-52.

Leung, K. (1997). Negotiation and reward allocations across cultures. In P.C. Earley & M. Erez (Eds.), *New perspectives on international industrial/organizational psychology.* San Francisco: New Lexington Press.

Leung, K., & Bond, M.H. (1984). The impact of cultural collectivism on reward allocation. *Journal of Personality and Social Psychology, 47,* 793-804.

Leung, K., Smith, P.B., Wang, Z., & Sun, H. (1996). Job satisfaction in joint venture hotels in China: An organizational justice analysis. *Journal of International Business Studies, 27,* 947-962.

Leventhal, G.S. (1980). What should be done with equity theory? In K.J. Gergen, M.S. Greenberg, & R.H. Willis (Eds.), *Social exchanges: Advances in theory and research* (pp. 27-55). New York: Plenum.

Lind, E.A. (1992, March). *The fairness heuristic: Rationality and "relationality" in procedural evaluations.* Paper presented at the Fourth International Conference of the Society for the Advancement of Socio-economics, Irvine, CA.

Lind, E.A., Tyler, T.R., & Huo, Y.J. (1997). Procedural context and culture: Variation in the antecedents of procedural justice judgments. *Journal of Personality and Social Psychology, 47,* 793-804.

Lonner, W.J., & Malpass, R.S. (1994). *Psychology and culture.* Needham Heights, MA: Allyn and Bacon.

Lytle, A.L., Brett, J.M., Barsness, Z.I., Tinsley, C.H., & Janssens, M. (1995). A paradigm for confirmatory cross-cultural research in organizational behavior. In B.M. Staw & L.L. Cummings (Eds.), *Research in organizational behavior* (Vol. 17, pp. 167-214). Greenwich, CT: JAI Press.

McFarlin, D.B., & Sweeney, P.D. (in press). Cross-cultural applications of organizational justice. In R. Cropanzano (Ed.), *Justice in the workplace, Vol. II: From theory to practice*. Hillsdale, NJ: Lawrence Erlbaum Associates.

Miles, J.A., & Greenberg, J. (1993). Cross-national differences in preferences for distributive justice norms: The challenge of establishing fair resource allocations in the European community. In K.M. Rowland et al. (Eds.), R*esearch in personnel and human resources management* (Suppl. 3, pp. 133-156). Greenwich, CT: JAI Press.

Morris, M.W., & Leung, K. (2000). Justice for all? Progress in research on cultural variation in the psychology of distributive and procedural justice. *Applied Psychology: An International Review, 49*, 100-132.

Morris, M.W., Leung, K., Ames, D., & Lickel, B. (1999). Views from inside and outside: Integrating emic and etic insights about culture and justice judgment. *Academy of Management Review, 24*, 781-796.

Murphy-Berman, V., Berman, J.J., Singh, P., Pachauri, A., & Kumar, P. (1984). Factors affecting allocation to needy and meritorious recipients: A cross-cultural comparison. *Journal of Personality and Social Psychology, 46*, 1267-1972.

Pandey, J., & Singh, P. (1997). Allocation criterion as a function of situational factors and caste. *Basic and Applied Social Psychology, 19*, 121-132.

Pearce, J.L., Bigley, G.A., & Branyiczki, I. (1998). Procedural justice as modernism: Placing industrial/organizational psychology in context. *Applied Psychology: An International Review, 47*, 371-396.

Ramamoorthy, N., & Carroll, S.J. (1998). Individualism/collectivism orientations and reactions toward alternative human resource management practices. *Human Relations, 51*, 571-588.

Ronen, S. (1997). Personal reflections and projections: International Industrial/Organizational Psychology at a crossroads. In P.C. Earley & M. Erez (Eds.), *New perspectives on international industrial/organizational psychology*. San Francisco: New Lexington Press.

Rotter, J.B. (1966). Generalized expectancies for external versus internal control of reinforcement. *Psychological Monographs, 80*, (Whole No. 609).

Ryan, A.M., McFarland, L., Baron, H., & Page, R. (1999). An international look at selection practices: Nation and culture as explanations for variability in practice. *Personnel Psychology, 52*, 359-391.

Schwinger, T. (1986). The need principle of distributive justice. In H.W. Bierhoff, R.L. Cohen, & J. Greenberg (Eds.), *Justice in social relations* (pp. 211-225). New York: Plenum Press.

Shapiro, D. (1998, April). *Discussant comments on round table: Innovating organizational justice: Cultural, value and stakeholder perspectives*. Presented at the 13th Annual Conference of the Society for Industrial and Organizational Psychology, Dallas.

Smith, P.B. (1997). Leadership in Europe: Euro-management or the footprint of history? *European Journal of Work and Organizational Psychology, 6*, 375-386.

Smith, P.B., Dugan, S., & Trompenaars, F. (1996). National culture and the values of organizational employees: A dimensional analysis across 43 nations. *Journal of Cross-cultural Psychology, 27,* 231-264.

Smith, P.B., & François, P-H. (1998, August). *Une exploration du rôle des encadrants en France [An exploration of the role of managers in France].* Paper presented at the Conference of the Association Internationale de Psychologie du Travail de Langue Française, Bordeaux, France.

Stake, J.E. (1983). Factors in reward distribution: Allocator motive, gender, and Protestant Ethic endorsement. *Journal of Personality and Social Psychology, 44,* 410-418.

Steiner, D.D., & Gilliland, S.W. (in press). Procedural justice in personnel selection: International and cross-cultural perspectives. *International Journal of Selection and Assessment.*

Steiner, D.D., Haptonstahl, D.E., Trahan, W.A., & Fointiat, V. (1996, April). *Allocations and fairness in reward distributions: Culture and gender effects.* Paper presented at the 11th Annual Conference of the Society for Industrial and Organizational Psychology, San Diego.

Stone, D.L. (1998, April). *Values and current conceptions of social justice.* Presented at the 13th Annual Conference of the Society for Industrial and Organizational Psychology, Dallas.

Thibaut, J., & Walker, L. (1975). *Procedural justice: A psychological analysis.* Hillsdale, NJ: Lawrence Erlbaum Associates.

Triandis, H.C. (1980). Introduction to *Handbook of Cross-cultural Psychology.* In H.C. Triandis & W.W. Lambert (Eds.), *Handbook of cross-cultural psychology: Perspectives* (Vol. 1). Boston: Allyn & Bacon.

Triandis, H.C., & Bhawuk, D.P.S. (1997). Culture theory and the meaning of relatedness. In P.C. Earley & M. Erez (Eds.), *New perspectives on international industrial/organizational psychology.* San Francisco: New Lexington Press.

Tyler, T.R. (1994). Psychological models of the justice motive: Antecedents of distributive and procedural justice. *Journal of Personality and Social Psychology, 67,* 850-863.

Van den Bos, K., Vermunt, R., & Wilke, H.A.M. (1997). Procedural and distributive justice: What is fair depends more on what comes first than on what comes next. *Journal of Personality and Social Psychology, 72,* 95-104.

CHAPTER 6

AN ORGANIZATIONAL JUSTICE ANALYSIS OF DIVERSITY TRAINING

Stephen W. Gilliland and Cindi Kaufman Gilliland

ABSTRACT

Diversity training in the United States has been seen as everything from a critical strategic business advantage to a source of discrimination lawsuits. In an attempt to understand such varied reactions to diversity training programs, we examine diversity training from an organizational justice perspective. Organizational justice principles of distributive, procedural, and interactional justice are extended to general training programs as a possible framework for understanding reactions to training. We then examine the administration and delivery of diversity training from the perspective of these justice principles. Research propositions and recommended training practices are provided. The final section of this chapter considers individual differences in reactions to diversity training based on beliefs in multiculturalism. We hypothesize how different multicultural beliefs (radical structuralists vs. functionalists) influence preferences for different justice principles and thereby shape reactions to diversity training. We also speculate on the value of studying multicultural beliefs in other areas of organizational justice beyond diversity training.

INTRODUCTION

Diversity management initiatives at 55 Orange County and California companies... resulted in increased understanding of diverse customers, increased creativity and commitment to the organization, and better retention and attendance.
—Ivancevich and Gilbert (2000, p. 82).

> Chicago-based printing giant R.R. Donnelley & Sons Co. is defending itself in a big racial discrimination suit . . . Donnelley's sin was that it instituted a company wide 'diversity training' program.
> —Lubove (1997, p. 122).

Diversity management has become a popular addition to current management practices. Estimates suggest that as many as half of the 136,605 U.S. companies with more than 100 employees are using some form of diversity program and the bill for this training may be as high as $10 billion a year (Lubove, 1997). Diversity management programs include a variety of systematic and planned efforts to recruit, promote, retain, and reward a heterogeneous mix of employees (Ivancevich & Gilbert, 2000). Perhaps the most commonly used approach to diversity management is diversity training (Cox, 1993). The goal of diversity training is to make employees more aware of similarities and differences among ethnic, racial, age, and gender groups and to sensitize employees to the impact of their actions on fellow employees. As suggested in the first quote, advantages of effective diversity management included better utilization of talents, increased creativity of problem solving, increased teamwork and cooperation, and ultimately, enhanced revenues (Gilbert & Ivancevich, 2000). Unfortunately, not all diversity management is successful. As indicated by the second introductory quote, diversity training can be more than ineffective; it can lead to negative reactions and lawsuits. Lubove (1997) observed, "So much diversity training has gone awry that there's now a cottage industry of trainers who go into companies to mop up the messes created by other diversity trainers" (p. 122).

Why is it that some diversity training initiatives can provide a competitive advantage, whereas others can result in lost morale and, in extreme cases, lawsuits? Additionally, why do some people leave diversity training with an increased awareness of individual differences and the value of diversity, whereas others leave feeling alienated, frustrated, or discriminated against? We believe that concepts from organizational justice literature may be particularly helpful in explaining varied reactions to different types of diversity training programs.

Organizational justice concepts have been extended to many areas of human resource management (Folger & Cropanzano, 1998), including training. Basic concepts in the organizational justice literature include the fairness of outcomes (distributive justice), the fairness of procedures (procedural justice), and fairness associated with explanations or interpersonal treatment (interactional justice). For example, Quinones (1995) examined perceptions of the fairness of training implementation processes (procedural justice). Organizational justice may be particularly applicable to diversity training, given the focus in this training on individual, group, and cultural differences in perceptions and behavior. Additionally, many diversity training initiatives have been implicitly or explicitly linked to affirmative action or prior evidence of discrimination, so fairness and justice are salient concerns prior to any experience with these programs. Finally, the negative effects of diversity training can be seen as resulting from experiences of injustice or being treated unfairly in the training process.

In this chapter, we examine issues of distributive, procedural, and interactional justice in the administration and delivery of diversity training. Specifically, we examine how different aspects of diversity training may violate or enhance perceptions of justice. We begin by providing a brief overview of diversity training within the broader context of diversity management. We then identify those aspects of organizational justice that we believe are particularly relevant to a training context. We outline research propositions that lay a foundation for future research to examine perceptions of justice in training initiatives. The main body of this chapter examines features of diversity training from the perspective of the different types of organizational justice. Specifically, we identify research issues and suggest practices to maximize justice in diversity training administration and delivery. Finally, in the discussion section we go beyond the systemic features of training and justice and consider individual differences in reactions to diversity training. We believe that by studying differences in reactions to diversity training we may gain greater insight into individual and cross-cultural differences in justice perceptions.

DIVERSITY TRAINING

Projections of increases in demographic diversity have provided considerable energy for the diversity management movement in the United States (D'Amico & Judy, 1998). Many organizations facing increasingly diverse workforces have adopted diversity management as a means of acknowledging and including different perspectives among employees. In addition to simply responding to demographic changes, diversity management has the potential for providing businesses with an important strategic advantage. In fact, a study of organizations in the S&P 500 found that businesses committed to promoting diversity demonstrated an average annualized return of 18.3% over a five-year period (Glass Ceiling Commission, 1995). On the other hand, those companies that did the least to promote women and minorities averaged only 7.9%. Other discussed advantages of diversity management include increased ability to attract women and minorities who are traditionally underrepresented in the workplace and increased ability to understand and market to the interest of a diverse customer base (Gilbert & Ivancevich, 2000). Finally, a number of widely publicized discrimination lawsuits against large U.S. corporations such as Texaco and

Denny's have demonstrated the negative effects of failing to manage diversity effectively. In addition to costly legal settlements, these lawsuits have resulted in tarnished images and product boycotts.

Diversity management is generally accomplished through a multitude of organizational changes and developmental efforts (Baytos, 1995). Organizations such as Avon and Xerox that are known for successful diversity management use many techniques for encouraging the recognition and celebration of individual differences. For example, many organizations establish diversity councils or task forces, develop formal cross-cultural mentoring programs, create family-friendly policies and benefits, and host events that celebrate specific cultures. In 1995 IBM launched eight executive-led task forces to address issues for women, men, blacks, Hispanics, Asians, Native Americans, gays and lesbians, and employees with disabilities (Grossman, 2000). One of the keys to success in these diversity management programs is top leadership support (Gilbert & Ivancevich, 2000).

Although diversity management has most typically been addressed as an American management practice, companies in other countries offer diversity training to promote multicultural understanding. In Sweden, diversity training is more likely to address cross-cultural variation in values, rather than within-culture, racial and gender differences in perspective. Steiner and Leung, Su, and Morris provide further discussions of managing cultural diversity and organizational justice in their chapters in this volume.

Most diversity management programs include some form of diversity awareness training (Cox, 1993). Diversity training is designed to sensitize participants to differences in values and communication patterns among people of different gender, racial, and cultural mixes. Effective training often involves developing communication and conflict management skills to resolve daily diversity issues faced by workers. Some diversity training has adopted a fairly narrow definition of diversity that emphasizes gender and race, whereas other programs more broadly consider diversity to also include age, physical challenges, and cultural background (Ivancevich & Gilbert, 2000). Additionally, some training emphasizes inclusivity and highlights the similarities as well as differences among people of different backgrounds.

Not all diversity training adopts such a positive, "bridge-building" approach. Some programs attempt to increase awareness by having participants experience discrimination and harassment during the training process. For example, in the early 1990s, the U.S. Department of Transportation inadvertently provided an example of how *not* to conduct diversity training. In an effort to expose racial and sexual prejudices, training included a gantlet in which men were "ogled and fondled" by women, sessions where blacks and whites were encouraged to exchange racial slurs, and trainers who verbally abused participants. Part of the problem is that diversity training has become a high-growth industry with "experts" arising from such varied backgrounds as management, education, social work, and acting. There are no formal credentials to become a diversity trainer and no recognized standards or practices for effective diversity training.

There are few solid efforts to systematically document the effects of diversity training. Although we cited some evidence earlier for positive effects of diversity management, there exists no systematic empirical assessment of the extent to which diversity training changes behavior or performance on the job (Grossman, 2000). On the other hand, there is some evidence that diversity management has not resulted in a positive change and in some cases diversity training has resulted in costly problems for organizations. The lawsuit against R.R. Donnelley & Sons that was cited in the introduction to this chapter provides evidence that diversity training can cause financial harm to an organization. Diversity training can also lead to decreased morale and increased resentment regarding diversity.

In spite of the lack of scientific evidence documenting the long-term effects of diversity training, it is clear that much variation exists in the types of activities that are included in diversity training. It is also clear that both positive and negative reactions can result from this training. We believe the organizational justice literature provides a rich foundation for understanding reactions to training programs in general, and to diversity training more specifically. We next discuss organizational justice principles and research as a means of understanding reactions to training.

ORGANIZATIONAL JUSTICE AND TRAINING

Organizational justice research addresses perceptions of fairness in organizational decisions and decision making procedures. Within the fields of organizational behavior and human resource management, organizational justice concepts have been studied within the contexts of performance appraisal, reward allocation, employee selection, and conflict management (e.g., Cropanzano, 1993; Folger & Cropanzano, 1998; Gilliland, 1993). However, organizational justice has only recently been examined in the context of training. Quinones (1995) examined the role of procedural justice perceptions associated with decisions to offer training opportunities and the relationship of these perceptions to training outcomes. He found that procedural justice perceptions were positively associated with motivation to learn and attitudinal and behavioral training outcomes. While this study demonstrates the applicability of the justice concept to training decisions, it does not address the full range of justice perceptions that may be associated with training administration and delivery.

Many researchers have distinguished three dimensions of organizational justice along the lines of distributive, procedural, and interactional justice (e.g., Bies & Moag, 1986). Additionally, researchers have attempted to identify the various rules or principles that underlie these justice dimensions (e.g., Gilliland, 1993; Greenberg, 1986). For example, equity, and to a lesser extent, equality principles tend to define distributive justice perceptions. Voice (input), consistency, and relevance are all principles commonly associated with procedural justice. Interactional justice tends to arise from explanations and interpersonally sensitive treatment. Although these general principles are common to organizational justice in many human resource decisions, we believe that a subset of these principles may be more relevant in the training context.

Distributive justice in training is probably more strongly determined by equality and needs than equity. We suggest this because the outcomes associated with training are generally not allocated on a meritorious basis, as are pay increases or job offers. That is, when evaluating the distributive justice of a job offer, a natural and salient comparison is whether the most qualified person was offered the job (Gilliland, 1993). Evaluation of outcomes (e.g., job offer) and inputs (e.g., qualifications) relative to comparison others is the foundation for equity assessments. On the other hand, training is often provided to everyone in a unit or to those with special needs, and less often to those most deserving based on inputs. This is probably particularly true of diversity training. Therefore, we believe that equality and needs will be the salient principles in evaluating the distributive justice of training decisions.

Proposition 1. Reactions to training assignments and training content will be guided more by the distributive justice principles of equality and needs than by equity.

Leventhal (1980) identified six rules that he believed established procedural justice in a reward allocation situation. Specifically, procedures should be consistent, correctable, representative of the concerns of recipients, based on ethical standards, based on accurate information, and free from biases. Other researchers have emphasized the importance of recipients having voice or input into the decision process (e.g., Thibaut & Walker, 1976) and the importance of the procedures being relevant or related to the job (Gilliland, 1994). In the training context, we believe that procedural justice will partly be determined by the consistency of the process. Whether training is seen as a perk or as a burden or imposition, individuals will want to see this training consistently administered. Similarly, they are likely to believe that both training administration and delivery should be free from prejudice and biases. Relevance is probably a salient concern with regard to training, as the training literature emphasizes the importance of making training relevant for participants (Goldstein, 1990). A final concern with regard to procedural justice and training is voice; that is, input into decisions and the opportunity to participate in the process. Involvement is one method of increasing training success and is also probably a salient justice concern.

Proposition 2. Perceptions of procedural justice of training administration and delivery will be most strongly influenced by principles of consistency, lack of bias, relevance, and opportunity for input.

With regard to interactional justice, the two primary dimensions that have been discussed in prior research are explanations or information and interpersonal sensitivity (e.g., Shapiro, Buttner, & Barry, 1994). These dimensions highlight the influence of social context on perceptions of fairness. Training is a highly interactive social context, such that interactional justice concerns are likely to be salient. In particular, explanations can increase the acceptance of training decisions and sensitivity of training delivery (or lack thereof) can influence perceptions of the training.

Proposition 3. Interactional justice in the form of explanations and interpersonal sensitivity will strongly influence reactions to training administration and delivery.

We have proposed a number of principles that will determine distributive, procedural, and interactional justice perceptions in the training context. Unfortunately, most of our proposals are intuitively rather than empirically derived. In an attempt to gain some empirical support for our proposed principles, we asked 16 employed MBA students to indicate whether they would describe training in their organizations as fair or unfair and why. Most (15) indicated that the training was fair. Content coding of students' "why" answers provided some support for our proposed justice principles (see Table 1). In terms of distributive justice, four individuals described equality issues and three described need-based decisions, whereas none indicated anything related to equity. The four proposed principles of procedural justice (consistency, lack of bias, relevance, and input) were all mentioned by at least one participant. Finally, although interactional justice was not evident in many of the statements, one individual mentioned providing ample information about training opportunities and another mentioned sensitivity of treatment. While we are not trying to make any claims about the scientific validity of these results, we do believe they provide some initial support for our proposed training justice principles. Clearly, more rigorous research is needed to further evaluate these principles.

It is possible that an application of organizational justice principles to training evaluation may help understand and predict participants' reactions to training programs. Traditionally, the training evaluation literature has addressed different types of training outcomes and evaluation designs for assessing training effectiveness (Noe, 1998). For example, Kraiger, Ford, and Salas (1993) distinguish cognitive, skill-based, and affective out-

TABLE 1
Training Justice Principles

Justice Principle	Number of Times Identified	Example Statement
Equality (distributive)	4	"Everyone receives the same 8 hour training"
Needs (distributive)	3	"They always try to train according to employees' and organization's needs"
Consistency (procedural)	2	"They were very committed to ensuring equal and fair treatment of employees was carried out"
Lack of bias (procedural)	1	"[Manager] does not discriminate in these matters as to employee rank or other factors"
Relevance (procedural)	2	"It's relevant to immediate job assignment"
Input (procedural)	3	"Employees get sent to training if they ask for it" and "Very open to questions"
Explanation (interactional)	1	"Everyone receives a lot of information about training opportunities"
Sensitivity (interactional)	1	"My manager takes an interest in individual employees' development plans"

comes and the different types of learning associated with these outcomes. However, far less attention has been given to developing models of the features of training programs and training administration that influence these outcomes. Organizational justice principles provide one possible framework for understanding attitudinal reactions to training. Our research propositions provide some guidance for research aimed at developing this framework.

Having discussed the dimensions of organizational justice that are likely to be salient in the training context, the next section of our paper focuses directly on justice and diversity training.

JUSTICE AND DIVERSITY TRAINING

The concepts of distributive, procedural, and interactional justice may lead to a greater understanding of the variation between individual reactions and organizational responses to diversity training. Specifically, we apply these justice dimensions to an examination of the content of diversity training programs as well as to how these programs are administered (see Table 2). We discuss the implications of program administration and con-

TABLE 2
Justice in Diversity Training Administration and Delivery

Justice Dimension	Key Issue	Justice Principle	Recommended Practice
Program Administration			
Distributive Justice	Deciding who goes	Equality	• Training for all as opposed to specific groups
Procedural Justice	Program development	Input	• Use of diversity council or task force
		Lack of Bias	• Decisions based on business relevance of diversity training
Interactional Justice	Communicating importance of diversity training	Information/ Explanation	• Upper management's words and actions must demonstrate commitment to diversity training • Communicate strategic importance of diversity training
Training Delivery			
Distributive Justice	Nature of program content	Equality	• Avoid material that is divisive • Develop a sense of inclusive community with respect for differences
Procedural Justice	Training techniques	Input	• Engage participants with hands-on techniques • Have participants contribute to content during training session
		Relevance	• Tie training to job specific tasks (e.g., servicing customers)
		Lack of Bias	• Avoid discriminatory role-plays or confrontations
Interactional Justice	Trainers' delivery	Sensitivity	• Committed to diversity without being overzealous • Balance individual respect with equal treatment
		Information	• Discuss importance of diversity given population demographics and value of diversity for organizational productivity

tent for justice perceptions, and in turn, the likely effect of these perceptions on the level of success of the diversity training itself.

Program Administration

Decisions made about the administration of diversity training are likely to impact issues of justice, which in turn will influence the success of the training outcomes. Specifically, decisions about who goes to training and why are likely to impact perceptions of distributive justice, and the procedures used to make these decisions and the ways the decisions are communicated are likely to affect procedural and interactional justice, respectively. Perceptions of justice, in turn, are likely to affect perceptions of the diversity training and ultimately the level of attitude and behavior change the training is able to evoke. We will discuss each of the three types of justice perceptions in turn.

Distributive Justice

Distributive justice issues are relevant when making administrative decisions such as who should attend diversity training sessions. For example, although some organizations have had success offering diversity training to specific employee subgroups such as women or people of color (Loden & Rosener, 1991), some research suggests that such targeted training may violate expectations of equality and may be perceived as unfair by those excluded from the training (Gentile, 1996). Diversity training targeted to specific groups has even been shown to create resentment among those receiving the special training (Thomas, 1991), probably because these individuals perceived the violations of expectations of equality as well. Generally, then, diversity training that does not exclude individuals based on demographic characteristics is likely to be perceived as more distributively just and should therefore create less resentment and "backlash."

Proposition 4. Diversity training that is provided to all employees as opposed to specific groups will be more likely to satisfy the equality distributive rule and will lead to greater acceptance.

Procedural Justice

Perceptions of procedural justice are also important to consider when making administrative decisions. We believe two dimensions of procedural justice are particularly salient. First, individuals in an organization who are given the opportunity to participate in decisions regarding diversity training are more likely to feel that the process has been fair. Many organizations have created diversity councils or task forces in which employees from all levels participate (Baytos, 1995). Decisions made by these groups to institute diversity training or to select who attends are likely to be perceived as more fair than similar decisions made unilaterally by upper management in the organization.

Second, it is important that individuals perceive a lack of bias in procedures used to make administrative decisions. If some individuals are selected to participate in diversity training while others are not, the procedures used to make these decisions must be perceived as consistent and relevant. For example, the sales force in an organization may be selected to participate first because they have the highest degree of contact with an increasingly diverse customer base. A decision made for this reason will probably be resented less than a decision made to select a certain department at random or for reasons that are not clearly explained.

Proposition 5. Procedural justice associated with diversity training will be enhanced to the extent to which employees are involved in administrative decisions and these decisions are consistent and free of bias.

Interactional Justice

Interactional justice in administrative decisions also impacts perceptions of diversity training. Specifically, the ways in which information about the training is communicated by management to others in an organization will impact their perceptions of it. First, it is important that upper management communicate their commitment to the diversity training (Baytos, 1995; Cox, 1994). If participants perceive that the program is unimportant to management, they are likely to feel that it is a waste of their time and are unlikely to be positively influenced by it. One excellent corporate example of senior management commitment to diversity is Levi Strauss, in which senior management not only attend a three-day workshop on diversity but then serve as faculty for the diversity classes all managers can take (Loden & Rosener, 1991).

Second, management must communicate the importance of the diversity training to its strategic goals. This can be accomplished by differentiating diversity from affirmative action (Thomas, 1991), and by identifying ways in which increased attention to diversity in an organization will serve strategic needs. For example, employees should be given information about how diversity training can enhance profitability by increasing work group creativity, decreasing absenteeism and turnover, and providing new marketing and customer service opportunities (Cox, 1994). In addition to increasing perceptions of interactional justice, this information should increase the perceived relevance and therefore the procedural justice of the diversity training.

Proposition 6. Upper management demonstrating their commitment to diversity and communicating the strategic importance of diversity will enhance interactional justice and acceptance of diversity training.

Training Delivery

The presentation of the actual diversity training session(s) is likely to strongly influence perceptions of distributive, procedural, and interactional justice among training participants, perhaps even more than decisions regarding program administration.

Distributive Justice

With regard to diversity training content, distributive justice suggests that reactions to training should be influenced by what issues it covers. Some diversity training is divisive in nature, focusing on issues of blaming others for their lack of cultural sensitivity or even on white male bashing (Baytos, 1995). This training violates perceptions of equality in much the same way as do discrimination and harassment in the workplace. Other examples of divisive training techniques include exercises in which participants are asked to name as many stereotypes about others as they can or are asked to discriminate against each other based on characteristics like eye color (Nemetz & Christensen, 1996). The ostensible purpose of such training is to sensitize individuals to the reality of prejudice and to the feelings created by discrimination, but a justice perspective suggests that these techniques are unlikely to be successful. Instead, individuals are likely to feel that they are being treated unfairly: unjustly blamed and penalized for society's woes in one case, subjected to unreasonable, hurtful prejudice and discrimination in the other.

Other diversity training programs contain content that does not single people out and violate perceptions of equality. By ensuring equal treatment for all, this training is more likely to be perceived as distributively just and is therefore more likely to meet organizational aims. These programs typically focus on intellectual as well as emotion-based learning (Cox, 1994), and provide practical information about building diversity awareness and behavior that reflects respect for diverse others (Thomas, 1991). Instead of emphasizing divisions among participants, this training content builds a sense of the workplace as an inclusive community in which all individuals are respected (Gentile, 1996). This creates the perception that there is something in diversity training for everyone, not just for women or for people of color, and thereby increases perceptions of equality and distributive justice. In this type of inclusive diversity training, stereotypes and discrimination are discussed, but their often unintentional nature is emphasized, and participants build consensus about how to avoid them (Nemetz & Christensen, 1996).

Proposition 7. Diversity training will be seen as more fair and will be associated with greater acceptance when the content of the training is inclusive and emphasizes a respect for differences rather than divisive and focuses on prejudices and biases.

Procedural Justice

Issues of procedural justice are also relevant for categorizing program content (see Table 2). There are many different techniques that trainers may use to present diversity training, and they have important implications for perceptions of procedural justice. Specifically, training that fully engages participants is more likely to be perceived positively and to impact attitudes (Baytos, 1995; Nemetz & Christensen, 1996). Trainers must balance the need to impart theoretical information about topics such as demographic shifts and results of "glass-ceiling" research with opportunities for participants to develop and practice practical, hands-on techniques for coping with diversity. Some examples of such techniques include "listening across differences" (i.e., a technique for developing cross-cultural listening skills), mentoring, conflict resolution, and cross-cultural interviewing (Gentile, 1996). Training that is too theoretical is likely to decrease perceptions of procedural justice because participants will feel they have not been given an opportunity to actively participate in the process and to gain specific, helpful skills. Additionally, it may be difficult to see the relevance of purely theoretical training.

Participants are also more likely to see diversity training as fair if it appears to be highly relevant to their jobs. For example, employees whose jobs involve low contact with others are unlikely to see cross-cultural communication skills they develop in diversity training as relevant to their job performance. By contrast, employees who frequently give customer service to members of other cultures could be expected to see the training as more relevant and therefore more procedurally just.

Participants should also perceive higher levels of procedural justice when they are allowed to participate in the design of diversity training. Trainers should be sure to seek input from diverse members of an organization when designing program content (Baytos, 1995). In addition, actual program participants can be given a greater voice in program content by simply asking them to name their personal and organizational goals for the training. An effective trainer will take careful note of participants' comments and will do his or her best to address them during the training session(s). This not only increases the perceived procedural justice of the training, but should also increase participants' interest and motivation while completing it.

Finally, to ensure procedural justice, it is important that trainers not appear biased for or against a particular group of individuals. Nemetz and Christensen (1996) describe some diversity trainers as radical structuralists. These trainers are typically social activists who focus on the domination and oppression of groups such as women and people of color by those in power, most typically white European males. Radical structuralists often employ techniques such as separating the genders and encouraging women to sexually harass men through role plays, or discussing the ways in which dominant social systems favor white men and oppress others. Such techniques have been demonstrated to lower the effectiveness of attitudinal change among many participants (Nemetz & Christensen, 1996), and this is most likely because these methods violate perceptions of procedural justice. Caucasian males undergoing this kind of training are likely to feel that they are being discriminated against by the trainer and by other participants and are therefore less likely to positively participate or to develop an appreciation for diversity.

Proposition 8. Diversity training will be seen as more fair and will be associated with greater acceptance when the training engages and involves participants, when the content is linked to specific job tasks, and when it does not involve confrontations and discriminatory role-playing.

Interactional Justice

Finally, issues of interactional justice in program content will affect how successful diversity training is likely to be. Justice research suggests that individuals are affected by how organizational agents behave toward them, so diversity trainers should give careful attention to how they treat session participants. Specifically, diversity trainers typically bring deep commitment to ideals of diversity and passion for their work into the training experience (Baytos, 1995). This brings energy and a sense of importance to diversity training, but trainers must be careful not to become overzealous and lose their neutrality.

In addition, trainers should ensure that they attend to all participants equally and respond to their comments constructively. Trainees should not be made to feel that some of them are "more diverse" than others or that their experiences are less valid than others' are. To increase perceptions of interactional justice, diversity trainers should consider all participants to be valued individuals deserving of respect and should treat them accordingly. For example, when a participant makes a comment demonstrating racial bias, the trainer should point out information discrepant with the bias without accusing the participant of racism or insensitivity or highlighting the participant's comment as a bold example for the group. Sensitive but direct communication by a diversity trainer should be much less likely to provoke reactions of "diversity backlash" among participants.

Another way to increase perceptions of interactional justice is to ensure that diversity training programs include information about the bottom-line importance of diversity. Justice research in other contexts, such as layoffs and pay cuts, demonstrates that information that sensitively and thoroughly explains the business necessity of the negative decision can increase perceptions of justice (e.g., Greenberg, 1990; Konovsky & Brockner, 1993). Many individuals do not believe that diversity is inherently a desirable goal or that business has any sort of moral obligation to foster it; these individuals are more likely to exhibit changes in attitudes and behavior when given information that explains the impact of diversity on profit and other organizationally important outcomes (Gentile, 1996). For example, many training programs emphasize shifts in population demographics and their implications for hiring and retaining workers, enhancing work group creativity, improving employee cooperation and work climate, and enhancing customer service and marketing capabilities. Inclusion of such information increases perceptions of distributive justice because it emphasizes the organizational relevance of diversity management and justifies the devotion of the individual's time and energy to the topic.

Proposition 9. Diversity training will be seen as more fair and will be associated with greater acceptance when trainers are committed but not overzealous and when information is included about the bottom-line importance of diversity for the organization.

Summary

The application of justice principles to diversity training provides a reasonable set of explanations for why some diversity training succeeds while other training fails. In Table 2, we have summarized the justice principles that apply to diversity training administration and delivery and have summarized some recommended practices. Although this application of organizational justice to diversity training is based on both justice research and research on diversity training, we know of no research that directly examines justice in diversity training. Given the wide variance in reactions to diversity training, it is important to understand what promotes positive reactions. The organizational justice framework we have suggested provides a theoretical foundation for this research, such that findings may generalize beyond narrow features of specific training programs. If our proposition regarding the role of equality in distributive justice perceptions is supported, diversity training may be one of the few areas of management in which equality is a more salient principle than equity. Consequently, justice researchers may learn something about the influence of context on the salience of distributive justice principles. With the potential contributions to both the diversity training and organizational justice literatures, we believe this is a fruitful direction for future research. Our research propositions and the issues and justice principles summarized in Table 2 can provide a template for such research.

INDIVIDUAL DIFFERENCES IN JUSTICE AND DIVERSITY TRAINING

Thus far, we have examined the influences of diversity training administration and training program content on justice reactions. It would be incomplete to suggest that perceptions of justice and injustice are determined

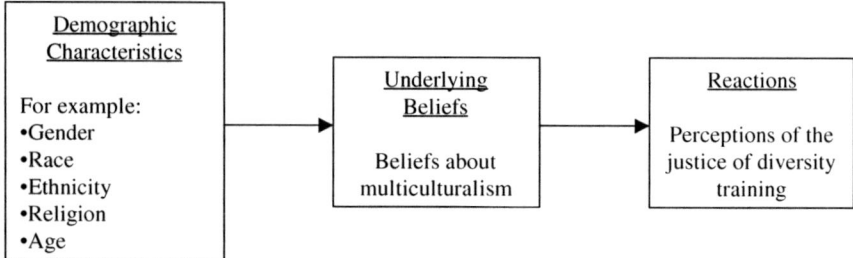

Figure 1. Proposed relationship between demographic characteristics, underlying beliefs, and justice reactions.

solely by these system characteristics. The fact that different people can walk out of the same diversity training session with very different reactions suggests that individual differences also influence justice perceptions in the diversity training context. In this section we explore some possible constructs that may explain these individual differences.

There are many possible sources of variation in reactions to diversity training. Gender, race, and ethnicity are some of the most obvious demographic characteristics that covary with training reactions. However, noting these demographic differences does little in terms of helping us understand the theoretical reasons for these differences. More important, simply studying demographic differences does not help illuminate the relationship between justice and diversity training. We believe that a more productive approach to studying individual differences is to focus on the beliefs or values that mediate the relationship between demographic differences and justice reactions to diversity training. Figure 1 captures our proposed relationship between demographic characteristics, underlying beliefs, and justice reactions.

We turned to the diversity literature to identify a framework for studying these underlying beliefs. Specifically, Nemetz and Christensen (1996) discussed variation in beliefs about multiculturalism and the effects of these beliefs on diversity training tactics. In the following sections we will highlight the variation that exists in beliefs about multiculturalism and then relate these beliefs to justice and reactions to diversity training. Therefore, our focus in this chapter is on the second arrow in Figure 1.

Beliefs about Multiculturalism

Nemetz and Christensen (1996) suggest that individuals interpret the world through paradigms or sets of frameworks that encompass beliefs and values. In particular, they contrast a radical structuralist view of society with a functionalist view. *Radical structuralists* see a plurality of interests and values in society and believe that any attempt at articulating common values will result in domination by those with greatest power. Therefore, separation is the only way to successfully deal with variation in the population, such as racial or ethnic differences. They tend to emphasize within-group similarity and between-group differences. From a moral perspective, radical structuralists tend to advocate moral relativism, such that each group must define its own moral truths.

On the other hand, *functionalists* prefer unity, social cohesion, and maintaining social order. From this perspective, integration is the logical means of dealing with variation in population characteristics. This homogenization of society attempts to minimize between-group differences. Similarly, functionalists identify universal moral codes and truths that can be applied to all humankind. These truths may change over time, but this change is evolutionary and incremental. Functionalist would see the greatest threat to society coming from conflict and the failure to adopt uniform cultural values.

In addition to these two extremes, *functional pluralists* represent something of a midpoint on the continuum. Common values are desired, but conflict and conflict resolution can be a useful means of deriving these common values. Diversity in values and opinions is acceptable, as long as this diversity is used to develop an ultimate consensus. Thus, like the functionalists, functional pluralists see integration as a goal, but are more willing to tolerate and debate cultural and moral variation as a means of ultimately attaining this goal.

After defining these beliefs about multiculturalism, Nemetz and Christensen (1996) illustrate how these different beliefs can result in dramatically different approach to diversity training. For example, radical structuralists often require participants to demonstrate and debate prejudices and biases based on common subgroups (e.g., gender or racial groups). Functionalist or functional pluralists are more likely to highlight the problems caused by discrimination and have participants discuss methods for avoiding stereotypes and prejudices. We believe it is also possible to use variation in beliefs about multiculturalism to understand perceptions of justice and reactions to diversity training.

Multiculturalism and Diversity Justice

Many of the recommendations we made with regard to promoting justice in diversity training are consistent with a functional pluralist and to a lesser extent functionalist perspective. In particular, we expect that people who tend toward functionalist beliefs would be concerned with equality, consistency, and lack of bias in diversity training. Thus, training that is inclusive and aims to build community and shared understanding should be positively received by those with functionalist beliefs. On the other hand, people who tend toward radical structuralist beliefs may find our recommended organizationally just training to be ineffective and unjust. Radical structuralists may see greater value in needs based training in which those with the greatest need for diversity awareness (e.g., white males) are forced to confront discrimination and prejudice. Distributive justice from a radical structuralist perspective may have more to do with needs-based distributions than equality-based distributions.

Proposition 10. In evaluating the distributive justice of diversity training, radical structralists will place greater emphasis on the needs principle, whereas functionalist will place greater emphasis on the equality principle.

Another difference between functionalists and radical structuralists may be in the need for input or participation in the training development and administration process. Given the radical structuralists' emphasis on plurality and group differences, individual input should be particularly salient for individuals with this belief structure. Input may be seen as a way of having unique views and beliefs expressed. Functionalists should be less concerned about voice in the decision and training delivery processes, since their emphasis is on consensus and unity. Interestingly, functional pluralists may react more like radical structuralists when it comes to the importance of input, given that diversity in opinion is seen as a means of attaining ultimate consensus.

Proposition 11. Radical structuralists and functional pluralists should place greater value on participation and input in diversity training than functionalists.

With regard to interactional justice and diversity training, sensitivity should be of greater concern for functionalists who attempt to avoid conflict and division than for radical structuralist who see confrontation (and even revolution) as necessary for change. It is unclear whether or not information and explanation will be valued differently by functionalist and radical structuralists. However, information from upper management such as we advocated in the program administration process, is more likely to be viewed with skepticism by radical structuralists than by functionalists. This may be more a function of the messenger than the message.

Proposition 12. Interpersonal sensitivity during diversity training will be a greater concern for functionalists than for radical structuralists.

Clearly we believe the study of multicultural beliefs and justice reactions to diversity training is a valuable direction for future research. Unfortunately, this research may be difficult to initiate given that the notion of beliefs in multiculturalism is relatively new in the management literature. Nemetz and Christensen (1996) suggest that considerable work needs to be done to develop psychometrically sound instruments that assess beliefs in multiculturalism. We suggest that there is also the need for greater construct definition and differentiation in this domain. We believe that Nemetz and Christensen have made an impressive first step in this regard, but considerable additional work needs to be done to develop a nomological network around multiculturalism beliefs. If this work is done, we may find that multiculturalism provides a useful framework for understanding individual differences in reactions to broader organizational justice issues.

Multiculturalism and Justice

In another chapter in this volume, Steiner discusses the influences of cultural values on justice perceptions. It might also be possible to extend the concept of beliefs in multiculturalism to perceptions of organization justice. Extending from our discussion of multiculturalism and diversity training justice, it is possible to speculate that functionalist view equality as a more salient determinant of distributive justice than radical structuralists. The functionalists' beliefs in unity and social cohesion should be most directly served by the equality principle. On the other hand, radical structuralist may be much more sensitive to needs-based distributions and may use needs as the primary determinant of distributive justice. It is unclear how the most common distributive justice rule, equity, is interpreted by functionalists and radical structuralists.

The salience of procedural justice principles may also vary as a function of beliefs about multiculturalism. Given the functionalists' emphasis on homogeneity and cohesion, consistency and lack of bias are probably salient procedural justice concerns. Alternatively, radical structuralists should be more interested in voice, input, and due process since these are the ways in which varying opinions can be heard and are ways in which those with low power can challenge those who hold more power.

Interactional justice may be more of a concern for functionalists than radical structuralists. Interpersonal sensitivity helps preserve cohesion and social structure and therefore should be valued by functionalists. Information and explanations, especially from management, will probably be more credible and promote greater acceptance from functionalists who believe in existing authority structures. Radical structuralists, who challenge authority and traditional power, will probably be more likely to challenge and discount explanations from authority figures (such as management).

This first, broad-brush attempt to consider variation in justice perceptions as a function of multiculturalism beliefs is obviously largely speculative. Our intention with this application is to generate ideas and suggest a venue for future theory development, not to develop a comprehensive theory. Considerable work needs to be done to develop the beliefs about multiculturalism construct and then to relate this construct to existing theories of organizational justice. Nonetheless, we are excited about this possible application of beliefs about multiculturalism to the study of individual differences in perceptions of organizational justice.

CONCLUSIONS

In this chapter we have sought to achieve two goals. First, we wanted to apply the concepts of organizational justice to the context of diversity training. Our hope is that justice theories and research will help us better understand reactions to diversity training. In the discussion of justice and diversity training we suggested that issues of distributive, procedural, and interactional justice are salient in both the administration and delivery of diversity training. Key justice concerns center on principles of equality, input, lack of bias, relevance, interpersonal sensitivity, and information. Along the dimensions of these principles, we argue that some diversity training programs and techniques fail because they violate justice perceptions and others succeed because they are consistent with justice principles. We encourage further research on diversity training that adopts a justice perspective and believe we have provided an initial framework for this research. In setting up this framework, we have also provided an initial template for researchers to examine organizational justice of training initiatives in general.

Our second goal was to demonstrate how an exploration of individual differences in reactions to diversity training could actually help us understand more general individual differences in justice perceptions. We suggested that beliefs regarding multiculturalism might provide an interesting framework for studying some individual differences. With the development of stronger construct definitions for the dimensions of beliefs about multiculturalism and with the development of psychometrically sound measures, we believe justice researchers may gain greater understanding of variation in perceptions of justice.

REFERENCES

Baytos, L.M. (1995). *Designing and implementing successful diversity programs.* Englewood Cliffs, NJ: Prentice-Hall.

Bies, R.J., & Moag, J.S. (1986). Interactional justice: Communication criteria of fairness. In R.J. Lewicki, B.H. Sheppard, & M. Bazerman (Eds.), *Research on negotiation in organizations* (Vol. 1, pp. 43-55). Greenwich, CT: JAI Press.

Cox, Jr., T. (1994). *Cultural diversity in organizations: Theory, research, and practice.* San Francisco: Berrett-Kohler.

Cropanzano, R. (1993). *Justice in the workplace: Approaching fairness in human resource management.* Hillsdale, NJ: Erlbaum.

D'Amico, C., &. Judy, R.W. (1998). *Workforce 2020: Work and workers in the 21st century.* Indianapolis, IN: Hudson Institute.

Folger, R., & Cropanzano, R. (1998). *Organizational justice and human resource management.* Thousand Oaks, CA: Sage.

Gentile, M.C. (1996). *Managerial excellence through diversity: Text and cases.* Chicago: Irwin.

Gilbert, J.A., & Ivancevich, J.M. (2000). Valuing diversity: A tale of two organizations. *Academy of Management Executive, 14*(1), 93-105.

Gilliland, S.W. (1993). The perceived fairness of selection systems: An organizational justice perspective. *Academy of Management Review, 18,* 694-734.

Gilliland, S.W. (1994). Effects of procedural and distributive justice on reactions to a selection system. *Journal of Applied Psychology, 79,* 691-701.

Glass Ceiling Commission. (1995). *A solid investment: Making full use of the nation's human capital.* Washington, DC: The Federal Glass Ceiling Commission.

Goldstein, I.L. (1990). *Training in organizations.* Monterey, CA: Brooks/Cole.

Greenberg, J. (1986). Determinants of perceived fairness of performance evaluations. *Journal of Applied Psychology, 71,* 340-342.

Greenberg, J. (1990). Employee theft as a reaction to underpayment inequity: The hidden cost of pay cuts. *Journal of Applied Psychology, 75,* 561-568.

Grossman, R.J. (2000). Is diversity working? *HR Magazine, 45*(3), 46-50.

Ivancevich, J.M., & Gilbert, J.A. (2000). Diversity management: Time for a new approach. *Public Personnel Management, 29(1),* 75-92.

Konovsky, M.A., & Brockner, J. (1993). Managing victim and survivor layoff reactions: A procedural justice perspective. In R. Cropanzano (Ed.), *Justice in the workplace: Approaching fairness in human resource management* (pp. 133-153). Hillsdale, NJ: Erlbaum.

Kraiger, K., Ford, J.K., & Salas, E. (1993). Application of cognitive, skill-based, and affective theories of learning outcomes to new methods of training evaluation. *Journal of Applied Psychology, 78,* 311-328.

Leventhal, G.S. (1980). What should be done with equity theory? New approaches to the study of fairness in social relationship. In K.J. Gergen, M.S. Greenberg, & R.H. Willis (Eds.) *Social exchange: Advances in theory and research* (pp. 27-55). New York: Plenum.

Loden, M., & Rosener, J. B. (1991). *Workforce America! Managing employee diversity as a vital resource.* Homewood, IL: McGraw-Hill.

Lubove, S. (1997). Damned if you do, damned if you don't. *Forbes, 160*(13), 122-134.

Nemetz, P.L., & Christensen, S.L. (1996). The challenge of cultural diversity: Harnessing a diversity of views to understand multiculturalism. *Academy of Management Review, 22,* 434-463.

Noe, R.A. (1998). *Employee training and development.* Boston: Irwin/McGraw-Hill.

Quinones, M.A. (1995). Pretraining context effects: Training assignment as feedback. *Journal of Applied Psychology, 80,* 226-238.

Shapiro, D.L., Buttner, E.H., & Barry, B. (1994). Explanations for rejection decisions: What factors enhance their perceived adequacy and moderate their enhancement of justice perceptions? *Organizational Behavior and Human Decision Processes, 58,* 346-368.

Thibaut, J., & Walker, L. (1975). *Procedural justice: A psychological analysis.* Hillsdale, NJ: Erlbaum.

Thomas, Jr., R.R. (1991). *Beyond race and gender: Unleashing the power of your total work force by managing diversity.* New York: AMACOM.

CHAPTER 7

JUSTICE IN THE CULTURALLY DIVERSE WORKPLACE:

The Problems of over and under Emphasis of Cultural Differences

Kwok Leung, Steven K. Su, and Michael W. Morris

ABSTRACT

We examine two broad, opposite approaches that often guide managers in managing diversity issues. One approach, the *universalist* approach, emphasizes similarity as the basis of justice, as embodied in the often-heard managerial motto that fairness is maintained by treating everyone exactly the same. In contrast to this is the *particularist* approach, which emphasizes accommodation to cultural differences: fairness is maintained by being aware of and taking into account cultural differences in managerial decisions. We analyze the problems of simplistic espousal of either of these extremes. First, we explore whether cultural differences should be emphasized as a way of understanding the causes of other people's behavior. Second, we explore whether the existence of different cultural groups should be emphasized when organizations allocate resources and rewards. And finally, we explore the extent to which cultural differences should be emphasized in managing the career development of subordinates.

INTRODUCTION

More and more often today, workplaces are environments in which people from diverse backgrounds interact with each other. Much research has examined diversity of ethnicity and gender in organizations (e.g., Cox, 1993; Pettigrew & Martin, 1987). However, diversity of national culture has also become important as organizations increasingly span national boundaries. In part this is due to the growing importance of global markets, in which customers for one company's products may reside in many different nations (e.g., American software, Japanese cars, and European fashion). Companies have also sought to capitalize on international labor markets and cheaper production costs by having operations in foreign countries.

Culturally diverse organizations are often difficult to manage. While members of different cultural groups need to work together to create a successful organization, they also compete for limited resources, such as salary and advancement opportunities. Moreover, cultural groups are typically not equally dispersed in the organizational hierarchy, and typically one cultural group dominates the apex of the organizational pyramid. Perceptions of inequality across groups may engender distrust, and exacerbate intergroup competition and hostility.

A number of theoretical models for understanding or managing workplace diversity have been proposed, but the more specific matter of how justice can be maintained in a culturally diverse workplace is only recently receiving significant attention (e.g., Tyler, Boeckmann, Smith, & Huo, 1997). Research has shown that minority members of organizations often view the organization as unfair and uninclusive (e.g., Barak, Cherin, & Berkman, 1998), whereas majority members often perceive affirmative action and diversity policies as unfair preferential treatment. Perceptions regarding fairness have important implications for people's willingness to maintain and cooperate in social relationships. For instance, judgments regarding the fairness of authority figures affect the degree to which their decisions are accepted (Lind, Kulik, Ambrose, & de Vera Park, 1993). In work contexts, perceptions of fairness in interpersonal treatment received from supervisors are positively related to job satisfaction and organizational citizenship behavior (Moorman, 1991). In short, if justice issues are not well managed in a diverse workplace, detrimental consequences ranging from poor morale and low job satisfaction to intergroup rivalry may result.

Emphasizing Cultural Similarities or Differences?

How can organizations maintain justice in culturally diverse workplaces? To provide a conceptual framework for addressing this very complex issue, we will examine two broad, opposite approaches that often guide managers in managing diversity issues. One approach, the *universalist* approach, emphasizes similarity as the basis of justice, as embodied in the often-heard managerial motto that fairness is maintained by treating everyone exactly the same. In contrast to this is the *particularist* approach, which emphasizes accommodation to cultural differences: fairness is maintained by being aware of and taking into account cultural differences in managerial decisions, such as those pertaining to employee evaluation and job assignments. This dilemma is similar to what Jones (1998) coined as the new American dilemma of race. One position advocates the formulation of democratic policies without regard to race, whereas another position calls for an explicit consideration of race in policy formulations.

Today, many global companies have had to decide whether to take a universalist approach that applies the same management practices globally, or a particularist approach that varies according to national context. For example, Japanese auto manufacturers have implemented many Japanese organizational policies in their North American factories, such as an extremely small number of job classifications and intensive functional cross-training (rather than individual specialization), continually increasing (rather than fixed by contract) performance standards, security of employment, and co-worker (rather than management) sanctioning of misbehavior (Florida & Kenney, 1991; Fucini & Fucini, 1990; Wilms, Hardcastle, & Zell, 1994; Young, 1992). Many Western firms operating in China have attempted to implement human resources management practices that are foreign to, if not resisted by, local employees (e.g., Leung & Kwong, in press). The imposition of management practices from parent firms on local subsidiaries is often defended in the name of standardization and control, but in a culturally diverse workplace, the imposition of the cultural values and practices of the dominant group risks generating resentment, the accusation of chauvinism, and charges of unfairness from less powerful groups.

To assess these issues, we will examine the interplay of organizational justice and cultural diversity in work settings. In our analysis, we draw upon several distinct bodies of academic literature. One important body of work is concerned with interactions between people of different social backgrounds or social classifications (e.g., Tajfel, 1982). Equally important is research that has demonstrated that, in interpreting the behavior of others, perceivers are deeply influenced by preexisting beliefs and schemas regarding race (e.g., Devine, 1989). In organizational settings, social classification and schematic confirmation processes have also been shown to have a profound influence on organizational outcomes such as success and advancement in organizations (for reviews, see Martin, 1993; Pettigrew & Martin, 1987). Finally, a separate and more recent body of research has examined the relationship between justice perceptions and national culture (For reviews, see James, 1993; Leung & Morris, in press; Steiner, this volume). Many studies have revealed notable cultural differences in the antecedents of justice judgments (e.g., Hamilton & Sanders, 1992; Hundley & Kim, 1997; Leung & Bond, 1984). Other work has broadened the justice concept by including interpersonal obligations or rules (Miller, 1994). In our analysis, these diverse streams of research will be integrated with the aim of developing a conceptual framework to guide future research.

Types of Justice Concerns that Arise in Organizations

Research on justice examines the manner in which people make judgments about the fairness of the actions of others. In recent decades, social psychologists and organizational researchers have examined the interpretive steps people take in making specific kinds of justice judgments (for a review, see Sheppard, Lewicki, & Minton, 1992). A tripartite notion of justice has been prominent in this literature. The perceived fairness of reward allocation has been addressed by models of *distributive* justice (Adams, 1965; Deutsch, 1985). The fairness of punishment and sanctions is addressed by models of *retributive* justice (e.g., Shaver, 1985; Vidmar & Miller, 1980). Also important are factors influencing perceptions of fair decision-making processes and the implementation of decisions, which are captured in models of *procedural* justice, which include both formal procedural elements as well as interpersonal treatment (Lind & Tyler, 1988; Thibaut & Walker, 1975; Tyler & Bies, 1990). In this line of research, researchers have analyzed the antecedents of fairness perceptions as well as their consequences, such as commitment, loyalty, and organizational citizenship (e.g., Kim & Mauborgne, 1997; Sheppard et al., 1992; Trevino, 1992).

The major purpose of this chapter is to discuss how concerns about the fairness of distribution, retribution, and procedure are manifested when the workplace is culturally diverse. Supervisors must decide whether to brush aside or to emphasize cultural differences in making managerial decisions and policies. While the conceptual simplicity of blanket espousal of either a universalist or particularist managerial philosophy is seductive, we will show that over emphasizing either extreme can lead to perceptions of injustice in three different domains. First, we discuss whether cultural differences should be emphasized as a way of understanding the causes of other people's behavior. Second, we consider whether the existence of different cultural groups should be accentuated when organizations allocate resources and rewards. And finally, we inquire into the extent to which cultural differences should be emphasized in managing the career development of subordinates.

UNDERSTANDING THE BEHAVIORS OF OTHERS

When one makes judgments about the fairness of an event, one also makes judgments about cause and effect. For any observed behavior, there may be many explanations for the cause of the behavior, some of which may trigger intense feelings of injustice. For example, when one observes a superior severely berating a subordinate, one must construct an explanation for the cause of the behavior. Does it occur because the superior is an unreasonable person? Does it occur because the situation causes the superior to do this? Does it occur because the superior's culture explicitly states that the subordinate should be berated, or that the act of berating means something different to the superior? Leung, Su, and Morris (2000) have shown that the extent to which a supervisor's critical behavior is attributed to external circumstances rather than to his stable negative dispositions increases the perception of justice.

This section focuses on the extent to which perceivers attribute the behaviors of others to their culture. Since cultural differences are usually salient in cross-cultural organizations, culture serves as an important potential explanation for behavior (Leung & Chan, 1999). How much of a person's workplace behavior can be attributed to his or her culture? Research showing that national culture is an important determinant of workplace behavior is both voluminous and prominent (see Hofstede, 1980 for an example). On the other hand, there is also the basis for a universalist argument that people of different cultures are essentially similar. Social psychologists have argued that behavior is often more strongly influenced by situational constraints than by individual characteristics (Ross & Nisbett, 1991). Similarly, organizational scholars (Weick, 1995) have suggested that organizations shape the mental schemas of their employees through extensive socialization. While different national cultures exist externally to the organization, the organization functions as a culture of its own, coordinating the behavior of its diverse membership.

Do ascriptions of cultural differences in workplace behavior reflect actual differences in behavior, or merely stereotypes held by perceivers? As behavior within organizations is complex and multifaceted, neither of these answers can adequately characterize all behaviors in culturally diverse organizations. As we will argue below, in certain domains differences in behavior will reflect cultural differences, while in other domains they reflect the perceiver's preconceived notions about how other cultural groups behave. While the causes of behavior are multifaceted, perceivers have a tendency to seek accounts that are simplified (Ross & Nisbett, 1991). It is the reduction of nuanced workplace behavior to simplified accounts that produces biases in attribution.

We present two types of biases in attribution, which correspond to whether cultural similarity or differences are emphasized. The first type occurs when the perceiver ignores or even dismisses cultural differences as a causal factor, although culture is the most probable explanation for the observed behavior. In other words, the perceiver gives insufficient weight to cultural differences, and misattributes the behavior of a person to other factors. We may term this bias the *universalistic attribution bias*, which has been the focus of much of the literature on cross cultural contact and training (e.g., Cushner & Brislin, 1996). For instance, people come to misperceive others from a different cultural group as rude because they apply their own cultural meaning systems to make sense of behaviors that are grounded in another cultural meaning system (e.g., Asante & Davis, 1985).

The second type of bias, which may be termed the *cultural attribution bias*, occurs when the perceiver's preconceptions about how people from other cultures behave leads him or her to make causal attributions that are consistent with these beliefs. The perceiver overemphasizes culture as a cause of behavior. Cultural attribution errors have been extensively documented in research on the role of stereotypes and preexisting mental categories in shaping cognitions and judgments. Research in this tradition suggests that people acquire cultural schemas, and that new information is interpreted in a way that is consistent with or confirms these schemas. To the extent that many of these schemas prescribe a causal relationship between culture and behavior, they cause people to overattribute the behavior of members from other cultural groups to their cultural backgrounds.

Universalistic Attribution Bias

In an intercultural situation, members of one cultural group typically engage in behaviors that are consistent with the justice norms of their culture. However, what is regarded as fair and appropriate in one culture may be regarded as an injustice in another. Perceivers, applying the behavioral norms of their own culture, are liable to misinterpret the social significance of the behaviors grounded in the meaning systems of other cultures. In the following, we describe a few examples of how such causal misattributions can occur between Asian and European/North American cultures.

Expression of Conflict

One of the most prominent themes in East Asian cultures shaped by Confucianist thought is the principle of *harmony* (Hsu, 1953). Whereas for Deutsch (1975) and other Western thinkers, harmony and productivity are distinct goals calling for different justice principles, in the Confucian tradition harmony is the key to productivity in a group. Harmony is a central construct in the values of ordinary members of Chinese societies. Cross-cultural surveys of value scales developed in the North American context (e.g., Huang, 1963) reveal that values related to social harmony are more strongly endorsed by Chinese students and workers than comparable groups in the West.

Because of the emphasis on ingroup harmony, conflict avoidance is common in Asian cultures (Leung & Tjosvold, 1998; Morris et al., 1999). In U.S. culture, differences of opinion are often voiced and argued, whereas in Asia, differences of opinions are more likely to be pursued indirectly. Asians and Westerners working together may give insufficient allowance to this cultural difference, resulting in misattribution and feelings of being unfairly treated. For instance, Asian norms require an especially high degree of deference to superiors. Bond (1991) noted that "The superior must always be accorded face, so one first agrees with whatever he or (occasionally) she said" (p. 83). In the face of such behavior, Westerners may be frustrated that their Asian colleagues appear to be passive, lacking initiative, and unwilling to challenge old ideas. Asians may see their Westerner co-workers as pushy, argumentative, and uncooperative. Consider the reaction of a Thai employee to his American Superior: "I've tried to explain all this to Max several times, but, like so many Americans I've known, he's not interested in listening when he thinks he's right. He wants this thing done yesterday. He practically screamed this at me at our last few meetings—once in front of a few of my employees" (Roongrerngsuke & Chansuthus, 1998, p. 198). In short, if differences in behavior are not placed in cultural context, managers may perceive their employees to be behaving inappropriately, making true collaboration and partnership difficult. Western managers are likely to regard their Asian subordinates as passive and evasive, whereas Asian managers may regard their western subordinates as confrontational and disrespectful.

Interpersonal Obligations and Rules

Cultures differ with respect to conceptions of morality. Some cultures give precedence to rule-like principles (e.g., do not steal) that apply to all situations regardless of the actors involved. Other cultures are very much concerned with the relational status of the actors involved, obliging the individual to act in the interests of close friends and family. Miller and Bersoff (1992) examined Indian and American reasoning in dilemmas between interpersonal obligations and moral rules. Most Indians gave priority to interpersonal expectations, whereas most Americans gave priority to rules. Indians possess a moral code in which interpersonal responsibilities are seen in as fully principled terms as justice obligations and may be accorded precedence over rules. These findings suggest that a personal morality of interpersonal responsiveness and caring can be meaningfully differentiated from rights-oriented cultural views (Miller, 1994).

If employees of different cultural backgrounds put different amounts of emphasis on moral rules and interpersonal obligations, the mutual perception of unethical behavior may easily occur. Imagine a situation in which one employee has to choose between following company policies and helping a close co-worker. Western employees will probably feel more obligation to observe rules and policies, whereas Asians might feel a greater obligation to "bend the rules" in order to help. Western managers may regard their Asian subordinates as cronyist, whereas Asian managers may regard their Western subordinates as bureaucratic and disloyal.

Allocation of Rewards

The *equity* principle, that rewards should be directly proportional to contributions, has long been given central attention in the justice literature (Adams, 1965). Cross-cultural research has now shown that there are substantial cultural differences regarding what constitutes a contribution, and that performance is just one of many criteria for allocating a reward (Leung & Morris, in press). For instance, relationships may also constitute a legitimate criterion for reward allocation. Although there can be no doubt that an employee's relationships enter into appraisals of employees in many Western settings, its role is generally left implicit and unarticulated. Not so in Chinese settings, where there are widely-used constructs to articulate how a person's value depends on relationships (Hsu, 1971). An employee who has *guanxi* with important others (this translates literally to "connections" but has more positive connotations) can expect a high level of obligation and commitment from them, which brings value to the organization (Farh, Tsui, Xin, & Cheng, 1998; King, 1991).

Seniority is another criterion that may be used in reward allocation. Ethnographers of the Chinese workplace have noted an almost filial respect for older, higher-tenure employees in an organization (Farh & Cheng, in press; Redding & Wong, 1986). Similarly, studies of Japanese organizations and trading partnerships have noted that higher-tenure employees play an almost paternal role and hence are perceived as valuable and deserving (e.g., Ouchi & Jaeger, 1978; Rohlen, 1974). Consistent with these reports, a recent comparative study by Hundley and Kim (1997) found that, when asked to consider the fairness of levels of pay for managers with different combinations of job performance, work effort, seniority, education, and family size, Koreans were comparatively more concerned with seniority, education, and family size, whereas Americans were comparatively more concerned with performance.

It is easy to envision how differences in expectations about how rewards should be allocated can lead to perceptions of injustice. Managers of one culture may reward employees according to a standard that is not recognized in the culture of some employees, causing them to attribute such allocations to biases and discriminatory tendencies.

Disciplinary Action

While all cultures have some forms of disciplinary actions, norms about punishment and disciplinary action may differ drastically across cultures. Whereas in the west it is accepted that punishment should be apportioned only to guilty individuals, and not to others who associate with them, there is a tradition in the East of recognizing punishment on a collective Level. Collective responsibility is a distinguishing feature of traditional Chinese law. Starting from 746 BC, the system of *yuan zuo* (holding offenders' superordinates, kinsmen, and neighbors responsible for a crime simply because they are related to the offenders) was widely practiced in China (see Zhang, 1984). The rationale underlying this practice was the belief that the would-be offender's in-group had the obligation to monitor his or her behavior, and therefore should have been able to prevent the crime.

Cultures also differ with respect to the preferred disciplinary methods. North American conceptions of retributive justice focus heavily on the idea of retribution directed at the transgressor. The culpable employee receives his/her just deserts (e.g., a fine), is incapacitated (e.g., fired), or receives a strong deterrent (e.g., demoted). East Asians, on the other hand, are more likely to regard retribution as having an educational and rehabilitative function. Hamilton and Sanders (1988) conducted a comparative survey of sanctioning choices among matched samples of American and Japanese respondents. Japanese respondents were more likely to justify punishment as a way of rehabilitating the criminal or of denouncing the act as wrong, Americans were more likely to justify punishment with the rationale of direct retribution or incapacitation. Furthermore, the classical work of Benedict (1946) and Doi (1973) emphasized that Japanese are embedded in social roles, relationships, and contexts and hence are highly vulnerable to shame. Informal disciplinary procedures, often involving social censure such as ostracism, are common and effective. For instance, in *naikan* therapy, a practice which began in correctional institutions and spread to other organizations, a wrongdoer is isolated for several days and asked to meditate on what has been received from others and on the troubles caused for others (Murase & Johnson, 1974). In Japanese corporations, there are milder forms such as assigning a wrongdoer to an isolated desk and not giving the person any work for a period of time.

In the work context, managers will inevitably have to decide whether and how to punish a transgression. In a culturally diverse workplace, the decision that is taken may be viewed as unjust by some portion of the employees. Westerners are more likely to perceive collective level punishment as unfair, and rehabilitation oriented punishments as too weak and ineffective. Asians are likely to perceive collective punishment as less unfair, and harsh punishments as inhumane.

Cultural Attribution Bias

People often form stereotypes about the types of behaviors or traits that are associated with people of other cultures. A second type of bias occurs when people overemphasize culture as a causal factor in behavior, and as a result, develop and utilize such stereotypes. Unfortunately, cultural stereotypes may be inaccurate descriptors of the cultural group as a whole, or inaccurate when applied to describe a specific individual. Such biases, if they affect the manner in which employees are appraised for ability or performance, may lead to objections regarding unfair evaluation.

Stereotypic Confirmation

Once established, stereotypic beliefs are extremely resistant to change. An impressive array of social psychological studies have documented the ways in which people maintain their beliefs in the face of contrary evidence. Once cued, schemas affect how quickly we perceive, what we notice, how we interpret what we notice, and what we perceive as similar and different. Race or ethnicity stereotypes function as schemas that guide how people evaluate others. Unfortunately, they are often biased against certain groups. For instance, white participants recognized positive stereotypic words (e.g., "smart," "ambitious") faster when they were preceded by "whites" rather than by "blacks" (Gaertner & McLaughlin, 1983). White participants were faster to respond that negative or stereotypic traits "could ever be true" of blacks and similarly that positive or stereotypic traits "could ever be true" of whites (Dovidio, Evans, & Tyler, 1986). In a study of the causal attributions made by white undergraduates about individuals with successful banking careers; both female and male participants attributed significantly less ability, more effort, and more luck to a white female, a black male, or a black female than to an identically successful white male (Yarkin, Town, & Wallston, 1982).

Ingroup Favoritism in Attribution

A separate stream of research argues that in the presence of salient group boundaries, people have a tendency to make more favorable attributions about others who belong to the same group. This ingroup bias in attribution, labeled as the *Ultimate Attribution Error* (Pettigrew, 1979) is well documented. When evaluating an outgroup member, people are more likely to attribute good outcomes to factors external to the person, such as good luck; and bad outcomes to internal causes, such as low skill (for a review see Brewer & Kramer, 1985). When participants are asked to explain the success or failure of blacks and whites in both academic and athletic pursuits, both black and white participants were more likely to attribute failure to a lack of ability if the activity was performed by someone not of their race (Whitehead, Smith, & Eichhorn, 1982) Similarly, Hindu Participants in India are more likely to make attributions to an actor's stable internal dispositions to explain positive acts of Hindus and negative acts of Muslims (Taylor & Jaggi, 1974).

In evaluating an employee's performance, appraisers from different cultural groups may make different attributions for the performance of the same individual. Appraisers from the cultural group as the employee may be more willing to make a more favorable evaluation. If performance evaluations lead managers to allocate less reward to outgroup members, the recipients may respond with accusations that the evaluation process is illegitimate. People are motivated to maintain positive self-image, and often do so by attributing negative feedback that they receive to racism (Crocker & Major, 1989).

Such biases may actually produce an appraisal process that is more difficult and stringent for members of certain cultures. Individuals disadvantaged by unfair organizational practices often recognize their disadvantage and react negatively (Martin, 1993). In a survey of managers from 12 large corporations (Fernandez, 1982), 83% of black managers, in contrast to only 10% of white managers, agreed with the proposition that minorities have to be better performers than whites.

Toward Remedies

Both the universal attribution error and the cultural attribution error occur because it is difficult to assess accurately and exactly the types of behavior which are culturally determined. Managers who attempt to "treat everyone the same" may fail to acknowledge cultural differences that truly exist. On the other hand, managers who are overly attentive to culture may create or act upon inaccurate stereotypes. The most straightforward remedy for cultural misunderstanding is for organizations to provide members with accurate information about cultural differences. Organizations often attempt to do this through formal or informal training in which members of one culture are taught how to deal with others of another culture, or by social activities in which employees of different cultures have more opportunity to become better acquainted with each other. Yet another approach is to train managers to engage in isomorphic attribution (Cushner & Brislin, 1996; Triandis, 1975): when evaluating someone of a different culture, perceivers attempt to make the same attributions that other members of that person's cultural group are likely to make.[1]

While these activities can be helpful, one inherent problem is that it is difficult to recognize and understand all relevant cross-cultural differences, let alone simulate them. Effective remediation is likely to require placing individuals who understand the other culture into key positions. This may involve placing bicultural individuals in boundary spanning positions, who then serve as cultural interpreters for others. Organizations may also require that employees are evaluated by superiors of their own culture, or alternatively that employees will be evaluated by two individuals, one of whom is of the same culture.

Finally, individuals in the organization can be counseled about the two themes that have appeared in this section. First, that cultural differences do exist, and can lead to misunderstandings and conflict between two well-intentioned persons. When one perceives conflict with a person of another culture, one should first explore whether it is due to a misunderstanding that can be explicated by a bicultural expert. Second, people take an active role in the perception process, as they impose their biased preconceptions in making sense of the world. In judging individuals of another culture, it may be advisable to solicit input from others who are unlikely to share the same prejudices.

SALIENCE OF CULTURAL IDENTITY IN INTERGROUP RELATIONS

Social psychological research has demonstrated that people have a natural tendency to mentally distinguish others according to salient social categories, such as race or national culture. In promoting a sense of fairness in a multicultural workplace, is it better to ignore differences in culture and assert that all groups are treated the same? Or, is it better to emphasize differences? In this section, we focus on two issues related to group identification. First, we discuss the tendency for people to view national culture as a dominant distinction, and its consequences for intergroup conflict. Later, we focus on the extent to which members of different cultures compare themselves to each other. Our discussion will suggest that perceptions of injustice may result both when organizations overemphasize cultural group distinctions and when they attempt to ignore them.

Making Cultural Distinctions Salient

Numerous studies have shown that the mere act of categorizing people can produce favoritism toward others in the same group and discrimination against those in other groups (Tajfel, 1982). People tend to protect the interests of the group to which they belong though behaviors such as allocating more resources to ingroup members and evaluating their own group more positively. More recent research has shown that group interest can cause perceivers to suspend or alter justice judgments. Platow, Hoar, Reid, Harley, and Morrision (1997) recently compared the endorsement of fair and unfair leaders in interpersonal and intergroup situations. As expected, fair leaders were endorsed more than unfair leaders in interpersonal situations. In intergroup situations, however, this pattern was attenuated or even reversed if the unfair leader allocated more to the ingroup. A similar bias exists for ethnic groups. Azzi (1993) reported that minority group members were more likely to regard a procedure granting them veto power as fair than were majority group members. Affirmative action procedures that favor minority applicants are regarded as more fair by people with a minority background (Arthur, Doverspike, & Fuentes, 1992). Tyler, Lind, Ohbuchi, Sugawara, and Huo (1998) examined how the evaluation of a third party in resolving a dispute was affected by whether the dispute occurred within the same cultural group or across cultural groups. The actual fairness of the treatment received from the third party affected their evaluation of the third-party decisions more when the dispute was within cultural groups than across cultural groups. In sum, intergroup research clearly shows that people tend to focus on the well-being of their own group, and often skew their standards of fairness to serve this goal. In the extreme case, outgroup members may be considered to be morally excluded, or undeserving of any justice at all (Deutsch, 1985; Opotow, 1990).

Organizations that make cultural boundaries salient risk engendering intergroup competition. Managers and employees may become more concerned with furthering the well being of their cultural group than with whether other groups perceive their behavior to be fair and develop a zero-sum mentality. Intercultural contact is fraught with opportunities for misunderstanding and unnecessary conflict (Leung & Chan, 1999), and a zero-sum approach is likely to exacerbate such tendencies (cf. Pruitt & Carnevale, 1993). Moreover, actions that have the appearance of helping the outgroup, such as affirmative action policies, are likely to be perceived as unfair.

Ignoring Cultural Distinctions

In cross-cultural organizations, it is often the case that employees of different nationalities are paid on widely different scales because labor market conditions in different countries are drastically different. This arrangement, however, poses a threat to the cohesiveness of multicultural teams because social comparisons may lead to perceptions of unfairness (Tyler et al., 1997, ch. 1). Whether a person regards his/her share of a reward as fair depends greatly on the size of the reward of others in a similar situation (Adams, 1965). In a diverse workplace, social comparisons across cultural groups are salient (Runciman, 1966). Berger, Zelditch, Anderson, and Cohen (1972) have proposed a status-value approach to distributive justice, which focuses on comparisons to generalized others and to nonsimilar referent groups. When two cultural groups are involved, with the dominant group occupying a higher socioeconomic status than the subordinate group, the status-value approach suggests that members of the subordinate group will compare themselves with the dominant group.

We argue that in this type of a situation, it may be advisable for organizations to emphasize cultural differences, especially if there is a basis for suggesting that members of the higher paid culture possess unique skills. If members of the lower paid culture will inevitably make cross-cultural comparisons of pay, cultural differences in ability to contribute to the success of the organization may provide the only justifiable explanation. An organization that espouses equal pay structures across cultural lines, but systematically pays one culture less, will only encourage dissatisfaction, a sense of injustice, and hostility (e.g., Gladwin & Walter, 1980; Walker & Mann, 1987).

International Joint Ventures

The predicament described above is best illustrated by international joint ventures between economically developed and developing countries.

Companies from affluent countries often set up joint ventures in developing countries to exploit their lower costs and emerging markets. These joint ventures are typically managed by expatriates, whereas middle managers and workers are local employees. Because of the economic disparity between developed and developing countries, expatriate managers are often paid many times more than local employees. The huge gap in compensation often result in feelings of injustice among the local staff and conflict between these two groups (Shenkar & Zeira, 1987).

Leung, Smith, Wang, and Sun (1996) surveyed Chinese employees in international joint venture hotels in the Hangzhou and Shanghai area. Chinese respondents regarded their salaries as reasonably fair in comparison to the salaries of expatriates, despite the much better compensation and benefits received by expatriate managers. One reason to explain this finding is that local employees did not use the expatriate managers as the referent group to determine the fairness of their pay. Consistent with this argument, results also showed that comparison with other local employees was related to job satisfaction, but comparison with the overseas employees was not. A follow-up study, which was conducted three years later, yielded different results (Leung, Wang, & Smith, in press). Unlike the first study, respondents regarded their salary as unfair when compared to the salaries of expatriate managers. Leung and colleagues argued that the increasing familiarity with joint ventures by Chinese employees may explain this change in fairness perception. When the first study was conducted, joint ventures were still a new phenomenon. Chinese employees may have regarded expatriate managers as possessing know-how that they did not have, and hence accepted their high salary. When the second study was conducted, joint ventures were widespread, and many Chinese employees had direct or indirect experiences with joint ventures. Many may have seen the gap between their knowledge and performance and those of expatriate mangers to be small or nonexistent.

These two studies suggest that social comparison processes underlying justice perception are not static, and that people in a disadvantaged position may gradually ignore cultural boundaries and take a universalist position in assessing the fairness of their compensation. Jost and Banaji (1994) review Marxist arguments about "false consciousness" that leads groups to accept unequal distributions of power and resources as fair. However, little research has examined the circumstances under which people move out of this mode of thinking and demand better treatment, and international joint ventures provide an ideal context for exploring these issues.

Toward Remedies

Cultural boundaries within organizations provide the potential for inter-cultural conflict, especially when economic realities require that individuals from one country be paid on a higher scale. Managers are placed in a delicate position whereby if they emphasize cultural distinctions, they risk exacerbating intergroup conflict. And if they avoid discussion of differences, employees may become resentful of their salary. We propose two potential remedies which recognize cultural boundaries, but also attempt to reduce perception of unfairness.

Identification with a Superordinate Group

Research suggests that one way to reduce intergroup conflict is to emphasize categorical identities that are common to the various cultures in an organization and to promote interdependence (Schneider & Northcraft, 1999). Smith and Tyler (1996) found that European and African Americans who identified more strongly with their ethnic groups were less supportive of policies that result in fewer resources for their own group. In contrast, for those who identified more strongly with the United States, the superordinate group, instrumental concerns became less important, and the interpersonal treatment they received became more important. Huo, Smith, Tyler, and Lind (1996) surveyed public-sector employees in the United States to compare the relative importance of the outcome received and the interpersonal treatment received. For respondents who identified more strongly with the organization they worked for, instrumental evaluations showed a smaller effect, and relational evaluation showed a larger effect on decision acceptance, and perception of procedural and distributive justice. In contrast, for respondents who identified strongly only with their ethnic groups, the pattern was reversed. Importantly, for respondents who identified with their own ethnic group as well as the superordinate group, instrumental evaluations decreased in importance, whereas relational evaluations became important.

These results suggest that identification with the superordinate group diminishes instrumental concerns and increases the motivation to cooperate. The cultivation of a strong common group identity may be crucial to the success of a diverse organization. A recent study by Chan and Goto (2000) echos the importance of the "we-ness" in a diverse workplace. A group of Hong Kong Chinese employees who had contact with expatriate co-workers were surveyed. They were asked to indicate what conflict resolution procedure they would use to resolve a conflict with a supervisor from Hong Kong, mainland China, and the United States. Results showed that respondents were more likely to use arbitration, a win-lose procedure, to pursue a conflict with an American or a mainland Chinese superior than with a local superior. Regression analysis showed that the more social distance was perceived between the respondent and the superior, the more likely that arbitration would be used. Because of this procedure's adversarial nature, if disputes in a diverse workplace are typically resolved by arbitration, relationships between different cultural groups are likely to be tense. Time and energy may be channeled to draining confrontations, leading to a decline in productivity and effectiveness.

Highlighting Cultural Boundaries

Perhaps one way to address the problem of social comparisons across different cultural groups in international joint ventures is to highlight national differences in labor market conditions. If members of different cultural groups understand that compensation is also based on macro economic factors and labor market conditions, the feelings of injustice experienced by the lower paid cultural group may be alleviated. This strategy may work especially well with people high in social dominance, who show a more positive attitude toward hierarchical relationships among social groups (Pratto, Sidanius, Stallworth, & Malle, 1994; Sidanius, 1993). Yet another way to reduce dissatisfaction is for the organization to examine why it is willing to pay the higher wages of the expatriate. Presumably, the expatriate has a certain skill set which is valuable, yet difficult to find among individuals from the host country. In such cases, the importance of this skill set should be clearly communicated to employees.

MANAGING THE CAREER DEVELOPMENT OF SUBORDINATES

One of the most critical functions of an organization is to select and help employees progress and develop. In an intercultural context, managers attempting to perform this function will once again have to determine whether to ignore or to vary their behavior according to differences in culture. One approach is to base selection and promotion upon performance, without regard to culture. An alternative approach is to focus specifically on culture. Both of these approaches pose potential dangers if implemented without careful consideration.

We argue that people with cultural backgrounds different from the dominant group may have more difficulty gaining access to resources, and may be confronted with more difficult situations in the organization. A policy that does not recognize these obstacles will make it more difficult for these employees to advance. Policies that make employees conscious of cultural differences may also have drawbacks. Managers may communicate lower expectations to certain cultural groups, producing self-fulfilling prophesies.

Ignoring Culture: Differential Access to Resources

It is well known that similarity breeds attraction (Rubin, 1973), and that people are drawn to others like themselves. The similarity-attraction hypothesis also applies to contact among different ethnic groups (Osbeck, Moghaddam, & Perreault, 1997). In a review of the literature, Crosby, Bromley, and Saxe (1980) conclude that people tend to provide more aid to recipients of the same race than to those of a different race. A study which examined the multivariate effects of demographic variables on variables related to success in the organization (Tsui & O'Reilly, 1989) suggests that this tendency generalizes to work settings as well. This field study of superior-subordinate dyads revealed that dissimilarity in superior-subordinate demographic characteristics (relational demography) is associated with lower effectiveness as perceived by superiors, less personal attraction toward the subordinates by superiors, and increased role ambiguity experienced by subordinates. Other studies show that people who are similar are more likely to associate with one another informally (Ibarra & Andrews, 1993), and such informal contacts provide access to critical resources in the organization (Burt, 1992).

Due to these similarity-attraction effects, subordinates from less powerful cultural groups often encounter more difficulties than their counterparts from the dominant group. Because such barriers are often unrecognized or underestimated, superiors who intend to be fair and who utilize reliable measures of performance may nonetheless systematically prevent employees of one culture from progressing. Over long periods of time, this may yield an organization in which members of one culture are persistently "underrepresented" at the higher levels, and make it more vulnerable to charges of discrimination.

Over-Consciousness of Cultural Differences

One of the most intriguing findings in social psychology concerns how expectations often become self-fulfilling prophesies (Snyder, 1984). Merely having the belief that certain characteristics are associated with performance may lead managers to be more encouraging toward employees with those characteristics. Moreover, those employees may internalize this expectation, and as a result, expend more effort to succeed. Such Pygmalion effects on work performance (Eden, 1990) are often beneficial. However, in a diverse workplace, the danger exists that supervisors may subscribe to the belief that one cultural group is unlikely to attain a high level of performance or have the attributes that are necessary for succeeding at a senior level. They may communicate implicitly their unfavorable expectations to members of this group, causing them to perform worse. At times, such cues may be extremely subtle. Word, Zanna, and Cooper (1974) showed that in a job interview, minority applicants received less eye contact, less forward body lean, and shorter interviews: behaviors that would lead applicants of any race to be judged as more nervous and less effective. Similarly, negative expectations on the part of supervisors have been demonstrated to suppress performance on the part of subordinates (Eden, 1990).

A related problem is overaccommodation, which refers to the adaptation of one cultural group to the behavioral and communicative style of another cultural group (e.g., Hashimoto & Rao, 1996). If cultural differences are overemphasized to the extent that judgments of efficiency are avoided, superiors may regard maladaptive behaviors of members of another cultural group, such as lateness and low quality of work, as part of their cultural background. Supervisors may be reluctant to provide constructive feedback and opportunities for learning and development to correct these problematic behaviors. At a result, these subordinates remain at a sub-optimal level of performance and fail to meet requirements for advancement in the organizations. In sum, self-fulfilling properties of negative stereotypes and overaccommodation to ineffective behavior may help to explain why some cultural groups are confined to rank-and-file jobs, leading to the perception of an unfair glass ceiling and the tension between the dominant and subordinate groups.

Toward Remedies

The problems addressed in this section share the common theme that managers impact the performance of subordinates in powerful, yet subtle ways that they may be unaware of. Managers may not recognize that employees' access to resources is affected by their cultural backgrounds. Also they may not realize that they send important cues that affect the behavior of their employees. One action that organizations can take is to make managers aware of their influence. Training may involve alerting managers to the self-fulfilling nature of negative expectations, and to encourage managers to develop positive expectations for other cultural groups.

Mentoring programs may also be effective in help members of disadvantaged groups to move up the organizational ladder (e.g., Murrel, Crosby, & Ely, 1999). The central idea is to provide personalized resources and opportunities to specific members of disadvantaged groups. Barriers, both explicit and implicit, that hinder them from advancing their careers are also removed. This strategy is often effective, but more so when the mentoring relationship is within cultural groups rather than across (Feldman, Folks, & Turnley, 1999). Unfortunately, some people may not be chosen for a mentoring program. Those not benefitting from any program intended to benefit one cultural group often perceive it as unfair preferential treatment. Not much is known about the factors that enhance the perceived fairness of these developmental programs in an intercultural context, and more work is needed to explore these issues in the future.

CONCLUSIONS

It is widely recognized that workplace diversity involves both benefits and costs. Schneider and Northcraft (1999) go one step further and argue that workplace diversity can be conceptualized as a social dilemma. For instance, a manager may reap the benefits of diversity management without paying the costs if other managers are actively practicing diversity management. However, if no one is willing to embrace diversity, many can suffer. This social dilemma analysis provides one important reason why some people may resist diversity programs. Our discussion has provided another important reason why people are intimidated by diversity management: it is difficult to strike a balance in managing a diverse workforce. Earlier analyses have centered on the universalist-particularist debate with regard to how much attention should be given to race (e.g., Jones, 1998). Our review suggests that this debate seems moot because both culture-blind and culture sensitive strategies can be counterproductive under specific circumstances. Specifically, over- and under-emphasizing cultural differences can have a negative effect on justice perception in the culturally diverse workplace. A contingency approach is needed to reap the benefits and minimize the costs of diversity, and this approach has been applied in three different domains. First we argue that to reduce cross-cultural miscommunication and misattribution, culture should be highlighted and organizations need to provide their members with accurate understanding of cross-cultural differences. A related suggestion is that misunderstandings may also be avoided if perceivers always start with the hypothesis that negative interactions with others of a different culture may be due to cross-cultural differences as their initial attempt to understand the problem. Second, to foster cross-cultural cooperation, managers should downplay culture and emphasize a superordinate identity to forge cooperation and mutual trust. In situations involving different nationals receiving differential salaries, such as in a joint venture set up by a firm form a developed nation in a developing nation, cultural differences in economic development should be emphasized from time to time to legitimize the lower salaries offered to those from developing nations. Finally, in the area of performance appraisal, managers should be sensitive to obstacles to members of certain cultural groups, and willing to adjust their performance evaluations to "level the playing field." Managers should also be aware that hypotheses about other cultural groups can be self-fulfilling. To this extent, managers should be encouraged to place more emphasis on hypotheses that encourage success and high performance on the part of members from a different cultural group.

We have reviewed a number of issues crucial to the maintenance of justice in a culturally diverse work place. However, it is not our intention to claim that the three domains we focus on—causes of behaviors, resource allocation, and career development—are exhaustive of the topics in this area. Many other topics are important and should also be subject to a similar conceptual analysis. For instance, occupational segregation by culture may exist in some organizations. That is, some jobs are reserved for people of one culture, and other jobs for those of another. Engineers of an Asian background often complain about a glass ceiling, which prevents them from moving into managerial positions (Leong, 1996). Obviously, this arrangement leads to strong feelings of injustice among those who are confined to low-status positions and should be addressed in more detail in future. In sum, we believe that the issues surrounding culture, justice, and the management of cultural diversity are multifaceted and complex, and we are just beginning to understand some of the dynamics involved. We hope that this review will stimulate more theorizing and empirical work in this important area of research.

NOTE

1. In the work setting, however, isomorphic attribution may not always be desirable. For instance, if punctuality is not emphasized in a given cultural group, one might isomorphically attribute the frequent lateness of an employee to this cultural norm rather than to irresponsibility and laziness. However, some jobs may require a high level of punctuality, and explicit discussion of the importance of punctuality rather than isomorphic attribution would be needed to solve this problem. Following this logic, there are two ways to deal with over- or under-emphasis on cultural differences in attribution in a diverse workplace, and to reduce the concomitant feelings of injustice and anger. For issues that have little to do with productivity and profitability, isomorphic attribution should be encouraged, which aims at better mutual understanding across different cultural groups. For issues that involve an optimal level for maximal benefit to the employees and the firm as a whole, explicit rules and standards for proper conduct should be articulated such that attributions of violations to irresponsibility will be expected.

REFERENCES

Adams, J. S. (1965). Inequity in social exchange. In L. Berkowitz (Ed.), *Advances in experimental social psychology* (pp. 267-299). New York: Academic Press.

Arthur, W., Jr., Doverspike, D., & Fuentes, R. (1992). Recipients' affective responses to affirmative action interventions: A cross-cultural perspective. *Behavioral Sciences and the Law, 10*, 229-243.

Asante, M., & Davis, A. (1985). Black and White communication: Analyzing work place encounters. *Journal of Black Studies, 16*, 77-93.

Azzi, A.E. (1993). Implicit and category-based allocations of decision-making power in majority-minority relations. *Journal of Experimental Social Psychology, 29*, 203-228.

Barak, M.E.M., Cherin, D.A., & Berkman, S. (1998). Organizational and personal dimensions in diversity climate: Ethnic and gender differences in employee perceptions. *Journal of Applied Behavioral Science, 34*, 82-104.

Benedict, R. (1946). *The chrysanthemum and the sword*. Boston: Houghton Mifflin.
Berger, J., Zelditch, M., Anderson, B., & Cohen, B.P. (1972). Structural aspects of distributive justice: A status-value formulation. In J. Berger, M. Zelditch, & B. Anderson (Eds.), *Sociological theories in progress* (Vol. 2, pp. 119-246). Boston: Houghton Mufflin.
Bond, M.H. (1991). *Beyond the Chinese face: Insights from psychology*. Hong Kong: University of Oxford press.
Brewer, M.B., & Kramer, R.M. (1985). The psychology of intergroup attitudes and behavior. *Annual Review of Psychology, 36*, 219-243.
Burt, R.S. (1992). *Structural holes*. Cambridge, MA: Harvard University Press.
Chan, D.K.S., & Goto, S.G. (2000). *Conflict resolution in the culturally diverse workplace: Some data from Hong Kong employees*. Manuscript submitted for publication.
Cox, T., Jr. (1993). *Cultural diversity in organizations*. San Francisco: Berrett Koehler.
Crocker, J., & Major, B. (1989). Social stigma and self-esteem: The self-protective properties of stigma. *Psychological Review, 96*, 608-630.
Crosby, F., Bromley, S., & Saxe, L. (1980). Recent unobtrusive studies of Black and White discrimination and prejudice: A literature review. *Psychological Bulletin, 87*, 546-563.
Cushner, K., & Brislin, R. W. (1996). *Intercultural interactions: A practical guide*. Thousand Oaks, CA: Sage.
Deutsch, M. (1975). Equity, equality, and need: What determines which value will be used as the basis of distributive justice? *Journal of Social Issues, 31*, 137-149.
Deutsch, M. (1985). *Distributive justice: A social-psychological perspective*. New Haven, CT: Yale University Press.
Devine, P.G. (1989). Stereotyping and prejudice: Their automatic and controlled components. *Journal of Personality and Social Psychology, 56*, 5-18.
Doi, T. (1973). *The anatomy of dependence*. Tokyo: Kodansha International.
Dovidio, J.F., Evans, N., & Tyler, R.B. (1986). Racial stereotypes: The contents of their cognitive representations. *Journal of Experimental Social Psychology, 22*, 22-37.
Eden, D. (1990). *Pygmalion in management: Productivity as a self-fulfilling prophecy*. Lexington, MA: Lexington Books/D. C. Heath and Company.
Ekman, P. (1992). An argument for basic emotions. *Cognition and Emotion, 6*, 169-200.
Farh, J.L., & Cheng, B.S. (in press). Paternalistic leadership in Chinese organizations: A historical analysis. *Indigenous Psychological Studies*. (In Chinese)
Farh, J.L., Tsui, A.S., Xin, K., & Cheng, B.S. (1998). The influence of relational demography and guanxi: The Chinese case. *Organization Science, 9*, 471-488.
Feldman, D.C., Folks, W.R., & Turnley, W.H. (1999). Mentor-protege diversity and its impact on international internship experiences. *Journal of Organizational Behavior, 20*, 597-611.
Fernandez, J.P. (1982). *Racism and sexism in corporate life: Changing values in American business*. Lexington, MA: Heath.
Florida, R., & Kenney, M. (1991). Transplanted organizations: The transfer of Japanese industrial organization into the U.S. *American Sociological Review, 56*, 381-398.
Fucini, J.J., & Fucini, S. (1990). *Working for the Japanese—Inside Mazda's American auto plant*. New York: Free Press.

Gaertner, S.L., & McLaughlin, J.P. (1983). Racial stereotypes: Associations and ascriptions of positive and negative characteristics. *Social Psychology Quarterly, 46*, 23-30.

Gilligan, C. (1982). *In a different voice: Psychological theory and women's development.* Cambridge, MA: Harvard University Press.

Gladwin, T.N., & Walter, I. (1980). *Multinationals under fire: Lessons in the management of conflict.* New York: John Wiley & Son.

Hamilton, V.L., & Sanders, J. (1988). Punishment and the individual in the United States and Japan. *Law and Society Review, 22*, 301328.

Hamilton, V.L., & Sanders, J. (1992). *Everyday justice: Responsibility and the individual in Japan and the United States.* New Haven, CT: Yale University Press.

Hashimoto, K., & Rao, A. (1996). Intercultural influence: a study of Japanese expatriate managers in Canada. *Journal of International Business Studies, 27*, 443-466.

Hofstede, G. (1980). *Culture's consequences: International differences in workrelated values.* Beverly Hills, CA: Sage.

Hsu, F.L.K. (1953). *Americans and Chinese: Two ways of life.* New York: Abelard-Schuman.

Hsu, F. (1971). Psychological homeostasis and jen: conceptual tools for advancing psychological anthropology. *American Anthropologist, 73*, 23-44.

Huang, S.C. (1963). *A comparison of selected values among Formosan and American adolescents.* Doctoral thesis, Ohio State University.

Hundley, G., & Kim, J. (1997) National culture and the factors affecting perceptions of pay fairness in Korea and the United States. *International Journal of Organizational Analysis, 5*, 325-341.

Huo, Y.J., Smith, H.J., Tyler, T.R., & Lind, E.A. (1996). Superordinate identification, subgroup identification, and justice concerns: Is separatism the problem, is assimilation the answer. *Psychological Science, 7*, 40-45.

Ibarra, H., & Andrews, S.B. (1993). Power, social influence, and sense making: Effects of network centrality and proximity on employee perceptions. *Administrative Science Quarterly, 38*, 277-303.

James, K. (1993). The social context of organizational justice: cultural, intergroup, and structural effects on justice behaviors and perceptions. In R. Cropanzano (Ed.), *Justice in the workplace* (pp. 21-50). Hillsdale, NJ: Erlbaum.

Jones, J.M. (1998). Psychological knowledge and the new American dilemma of race. *Journal of Social Issues, 54*, 641-662.

Jost, J.T., & Banaji, M.R. (1994). The role of stereotypes in system-justification and the production of false consciousness. *British Journal of Social Psychology, 33*, 1-27.

Kim, W.C., & Mauborgne, R. (1997, July-August). Fair process: Managing in the knowledge economy. *Harvard Business Review, 75*, 65-75.

King, A.Y.C. (1991). Kuan-hsi and network building: A sociological interpretation. *Daedalus, 120*, 63-84.

Leong, F.T.L. (1996). *Acculturation and Asian values in the United States.* Paper presented at the Conference on Global organizations. Hong Kong University of Science and Technology, Hong Kong.

Leung, K., & Bond, M.H. (1984). The impact of cultural collectivism on reward allocation. *Journal of Personality and Social Psychology, 47*, 793-804.

Leung, K., & Chan, D.K.S. (1999). Conflict Management Across Cultures. In J. Adamopoulos & Y. Kashima (Eds), *Social psychology and cultural context* (pp. 177-188). Thousand Oaks, CA: Sage.

Leung, K., & Kwong, J.Y.Y. (In press). Human resource management practices in international joint ventures in China: A justice analysis. *Human Resource Management Review.*

Leung, K., & Morris, M.W. (In press). Justice through the lens of culture and ethnicity. In L. Hamilton & J. Sanders (Eds), *Handbook of law and social science: Justice.* New York: Plenum.

Leung, K., Smith, P.B., Wang. Z.M., & Sun, H.F. (1996). Job satisfaction in joint venture hotels in China: An organizational justice analysis. *Journal of International Business Studies, 27,* 947-962.

Leung, K., & Stephan, W.G. (1998). Perceptions of injustice in intercultural relations. *Applied and Preventive Psychology, 7,* 195-205.

Leung, K., Su, S.K., & Morris, M.W. (2000). *When is criticism not constructive: The role of fairness perceptions and dispositional attributions in employee acceptance of critical supervisory feedback.* Manuscript submitted for publication.

Leung, K., & Tjosvold, D.W. (Eds.). (1998). *Conflict management in Asia Pacific Rim.* Wiley: Singapore.

Leung, K., Wang, Z.M., & Smith, P.B. (in press). Job attitudes and organizational justice in joint venture hotels in China: The role of expatriate managers. *International Journal of Human Resource Management.*

Lind, E.A., Kulik, C.T., Ambrose, M., & de Vera Park, M.V. (1993). Individual and corporate dispute resolution: Using procedural fairness as a decision heuristic. *Administrative Science Quarterly, 38,* 224-251.

Lind, E.A., & Tyler, T.R. (1988). *The social psychology of procedural justice.* New York: Plenum.

Martin, J. (1993). Inequity, distributive injustice, and organizational illegitimacy. In K. Murnighan (Ed.), *Social psychology in organizations: Advances in theory and research* (pp. 296-321). Englewood Cliffs, NJ: Prentice-Hall.

Miller, J.G., & Bersoff, D.M. (1992). Culture and moral judgment: How are conflicts between justice and friendship resolved? *Journal of Personality and Social Psychology, 62,* 541-554.

Miller J.G. (1994). Cultural diversity in the morality of caring: Individually-oriented versus duty-based interpersonal moral codes. *Cross-Cultural Research, 28,* 3-39.

Moorman, R.H. (1991). Relationship between organizational justice and organizational citizenship behaviors: Do fairness perceptions influence employee citizenship? *Journal of Applied Psychology, 76,* 845-855.

Morris, M.W., Williams, K.Y., Leung, K., Bhatnagar, D., Li, J.F., Kondo, M., Luo, J.L., Hu, J.C. (1999). Culture, conflict management style, and underlying values: Accounting for cross-national differences in styles of handling conflicts among US, Chinese, Indian and Filipino Managers. *Journal of International Business Studies, 29,* 729-748.

Murase, T., & Johnson, F. (1974). Naikan, Morita, and Western psychotherapy: A comparison. *Archives of General Psychiatry, 31,* 121-128.

Murrell, A.J., Crosby, F.J., & Ely, R.J. (1999). (Eds.) *Mentoring dilemmas: Developmental relationships within multicultural organizations.* Mahwah, NJ: Lawrence Erlbaum.

Opotow, S. (1990). Moral exclusion and injustice: An introduction. *Journal of Social Issues, 46,* 1-20.

Osbeck, L.M., Moghaddam, F.M., & Perreault, S. (1997). Similarity and attraction among majority and minority groups in a multicultural context. *International Journal of Intercultural Relations, 21,* 113-123.

Ouchi, W.G., & Jaeger, A.M. (1978). Type Z organization: Stability in the midst of mobility. *Academy of Management Review, 3,* 305-314.

Pettigrew, T.F. (1979). The ultimate attribution error: Extending Allport's cognitive analysis of prejudice. *Personality and Social Psychology Bulletin, 5,* 461-476.

Pettigrew, T.F., & Martin, J. (1987). Shaping the organizational context for black American inclusion. *Journal of Social Issues, 43,* 41-78.

Platow, M.J., Hoar, S., Reid, S., Harley, K., & Morrison, D. (1997). Endorsement of distributively fair and unfair leaders in interpersonal and intergroup situations. *European Journal of Social Psychology, 27,* 465-494.

Pratto, F, Sidanius, J., Stallworth, L.M., & Malle, B.F. (1994). Social dominance orientation: A personality variable predicting social and political attitudes. *Journal of Personality and Social Psychology, 67,* 741-763.

Pruitt, D.G., & Carnevale, P.J. (1993). *Negotiation in social conflict.* Buckingham: Open University Press.

Redding, G., & Wong, G.Y.Y. (1986). The psychology of Chinese organizational behaviour. In M.H. Bond (ed.). *The psychology of the Chinese people* (pp. 267-295). Hong Kong: Oxford University Press.

Rohlen, T. (1974). *For harmony and strength: Japanese white-collar organization in anthropological perspective.* Berkeley: University of California Press.

Roongrerngsuke, S., & Chansuthus, D. (1998). Conflict Management in Thailand. In K. Leung & D.W. Tjosvold (Eds.), *Conflict management in the Asia Pacific* (pp. 167-222). Singapore: Wiley.

Ross, L., & Nisbett, R. (1991). *The person and the situation: Perspectives of social psychology.* New York: McGraw-Hill.

Rubin, Z. (1973). *Liking and loving: An invitation to social psychology.* New York: Holt, Rinehart, & Winston.

Runciman, W.G. (1966) *Relative deprivation and social justice.* London: Routledge and Kegan Paul.

Schneider, S.K., & Northcraft, G.B. (1999). Three social dilemmas of workforce diversity in organizations: A social identity perspective. *Human Relations, 52,* 1445-1467.

Schwartz, S. (1992). Universals in the content and structure of values: Theoretical advances and empirical tests in 20 countries. In M.P. Zanna (Ed.), *Advances in experimental social psychology* (Vol. 25, pp. 1-65). San Diego, CA: Academic Press.

Shaver, K.G. (1985). *The attribution of blame.* New York: Springer-Verlag.

Shenkar, O., & Zeira, Y. (1987). International joint ventures: Implications for organization development. *Personnel Review, 16,* 30-37.

Sheppard, B.H., Lewicki, R.J., & Minton, J.W. (1992). *Organizational justice: The search for fairness in the workplace.* New York: Lexington Books/Macmillan.

Sidanius, J. (1993). The psychology of group conflict and the dynamics of oppression: A social dominance perspective. In S. Iyengar & W.J. McGuire (Eds.), *Explorations in political psychology.* Durham, NC: Duke University Press.

Smith, H.J., & Tyler, T.R. (1996). Justice and power: When will justice concerns encourage the advantaged to support policies which redistribute economic resources and the disadvantaged to willingly obey the law? *European Journal of Social Psychology, 26,* 171-200.

Snyder, M. (1984). When belief creates reality. In L. Berkowitz (Ed.), *Advances in experimental social psychology* (pp. 247-305). New York: Academic Press.

Tajfel, H. (1982). Social psychology of intergroup relations. *Annual Review of Psychology, 33*, 139.

Taylor, D.M., & Jaggi, V. (1974). Ethnocentrism and causal attribution in a south Indian context. *Journal of Cross Cultural Psychology, 5*, 162-171.

Thibaut, J., & Walker, L. (1975). *Procedural justice: A psychological analysis*. Hillside, NJ: Lawrence Erlbaum Associates.

Trevino, L.K. (1992). The social effects of punishments in organizations: A justice perspective. *Academy of Management Review, 17*, 647-676.

Triandis, H.C. (1975). Culture training, cognitive complexity, and interpersonal attitudes. In R.W. Brislin, S. Bochner, & W. Lonner (Eds.), *Cross-cultural perspectives on learning* (pp. 39-77). Beverly Hills, CA: Sage.

Tsui, A.S., & O'Reilly, C. A. (1989). Beyond simple demographic effects: The importance of relational demography in superior-subordinate dyads. *Academy of Management Journal, 32*, 402-423.

Tyler, T.R., & Bies, R.J. (1990). Beyond formal procedures: The interpersonal context of procedural justice. In J.S. Carroll (Ed.), *Applied social psychology and organizational settings* (pp. 7798). Hillsdale, NJ: Lawrence Erlbaum Associates.

Tyler, T.R., Boeckmann, R.J., Smith, H.J., & Huo, Y.J. (1997). *Social justice in a diverse society*. Boulder, CO: Westview.

Tyler, T., Lind, E. A., Ohbuchi, K., Sugawara, I., & Huo, Y.J. (1998). Conflict with outsiders: Disputing within and across cultural boundaries. *Personality and Social psychology Bulletin, 24*, 137-146.

Vidmar, N., & Miller, D.T. (1980). The social psychology of punishment. *Law and Society Review, 14*, 565-602.

Walker, I., & Mann, L. (1987). Unemployment, relative deprivation and social protest. *Personality and Social Psychology Bulletin, 13*, 275-283.

Whitehead, G.I., Smith, S.H., & Eichorn, J.A. (1982). The effect of subject's race and other's race on judgments of causality for success and failure. *Journal of Personality, 50*, 191-202.

Weick, K.E. (1995). *Sensemaking in organizations*. Thousand Oaks, CA: Sage.

Wilms, W.W., Hardcastle, A.J., & Zell, D.M., (1994, Fall). Cultural transformation at NUMMI. *Sloan Management Review*, 99-113.

Word, C.O., Zanna, M.P., & Cooper, J. (1974). The nonverbal mediation of self-fulfilling prophesies in interracial interaction. *Journal of Experimental Social Psychology, 10*, 109-120.

Yarkin, K.L., Town, J.P., & Wallston, B.S. (1982). Blacks and women must try harder: Stimulus persons' race and sex attributions of causality. *Personality and Social Psychology Bulletin, 8*, 21-24.

Young, S.M., (1992). A framework for successful adoption and performance of Japanese manufacturing practices in the United States. *Academy of Management Review, 17*, 677-700.

Zhang, J. (1984). Exploratory investigations on the characteristics of the judicial system in feudal China. *Theses of Law of China, 1*, 245-266.

CHAPTER 8

INTERVENING "FAIRLY" IN DISPUTES AMONG NATIONALLY-DIFFERENT EMPLOYEES:
Is this Possible?

Debra L. Shapiro and Catherine H. Tinsley

ABSTRACT

The international diversity of the "American" workforce is increasing exponentially, leading to more disputes between nationally-different employees; these disputes need to be managed. The rise of self-managing work teams means that third party-interventionists are increasingly peers, not only authorities. In this chapter we review literature that guides propositions regarding the extent to which procedural justice will be perceived as fair by non-U.S. as well as U.S. disputants. We examine cases where: (1) the dispute resolution procedure gives the disputants outcome control in addition to process control; (2) the third-party is a peer rather than an authority-figure; (3) the third-party shares nationality with only one of the disputants; and (4) all parties involved in the dispute resolution procedure—each disputant and the third party—are from different nations. After identifying the likelihood that national differences among disputants and third parties may impede a universal experience of procedural justice, we discuss possible remedies for intervening "fairly" for all disputants in such situations.

INTRODUCTION

We know that an abundance, perhaps the bulk, of managers' time is spent intervening in disputes among other organizational members (Mintzberg,

1975). In helping to resolve these disputes, the third party may intervene as a mediator, inquisitor, adjudicator, arbitrator (Sheppard, 1983), advisor, problem solver, investigator, or restructurer (Kolb, 1986; Kolb & Glidden, 1986). Although there is considerable overlap in these roles, they tend to vary in the amount of control that the third party retains or gives back to disputants. The choice as to how a third party will intervene is influenced by a variety of individual and situational characteristics (Kolb & Sheppard, 1985; Lewicki & Sheppard, 1985; Shapiro & Rosen, 1994; Sheppard, 1983; 1984; Sheppard, Saunders, & Minton, 1988).

We know that the dispute resolution procedure that disputants generally prefer, or see as most fair, is one that enables them to express their views (or "voice," cf. Folger, 1977; Houlden, LaTour, Walker, & Thibaut, 1978; Lind & Tyler, 1988; Tyler, 1987; Sander & Goldberg, 1993) and to participate in deciding the dispute's outcome (cf. Karambayya & Brett, 1989; Karambayya, Brett, & Lytle, 1992; Shapiro & Brett, 1993). Said differently, procedural justice is generally associated with high levels of process-control (voice)[1] and outcome (decision) control, respectively.

Yet, these conclusions have generally resulted from studies consisting of U.S. American participants, and of third-parties who were authority-figures (not peers). We know less about situations in which the disputants are not U.S. Americans, and the third-parties are not authorities. For two reasons, such situations are an increasing part of employees' disputing experiences. First, with regard to the nationality of disputing parties, the "American workforce" is no longer all-American (cf. Adler, 1997; Jackson, Alvarez, & Stone, 1992; Shapiro & Von Glinow, 1999). This is evidenced, for example, by the fact that the National Academy of Management's (NAOM's) membership in the last five years has grown more by non-U.S. citizens than by U.S. citizens. The internationalization of the workforce is due, in part, to such activities as multinational company growth and the popularity of international strategic alliances (Di Cieri & Dowling, 1995; Gregerson, 1992; Kanter & Corn, 1994). From 1990 to 1996, for example, the stock of foreign direct investment in the United States grew 132%, and the stock of U.S. foreign direct investment grew 109% (Economist Intelligence Unit, 1997).

Second, with regard to third-party authorities, the responsibility of resolving employee disputes is no longer (only) in the role of "manager"; rather, this responsibility increasingly belongs to employees who are part of self-managing work teams (SMWTs), or group assignments that give self-management responsibilities (e.g., the planning, organizing, and monitoring of work) to the group members (cf. Kirkman & Shapiro, in press; Manz & Sims, 1993; Wellins et al., 1990). The ease with which goods and services cross national borders has contributed to the exponential increase in SMWTs. Companies needing to be cost-conscious, because of global competitors from lesser developed, lower labor cost countries, have eliminated middle-to-higher (more costly) managers and pushed downward in organizations (to the team members) the decisions that had been traditionally made at higher levels. Cumulatively, these changes mean that employees' disputes at work are more likely today than even five years ago to consist of disputants from different countries and third-parties who are peers rather than authorities.

What are the implications of these changes for managing employee disputes—especially if the end-goal remains doing so in a way that provides *all* disputants procedural justice? Dispute resolution studies have found that disputants perceive the greatest procedural justice to occur when: (1) the procedure gives disputants, both, outcome control and voice (cf. Karambayya & Brett, 1989; Shapiro & Brett, 1993); or in contrast, (2) the procedure gives disputants only voice, leaving the ultimate settlement in the hands of the third party (cf. Houlden et al., 1978). The former and latter procedures are what U.S. Americans call "mediation" and "arbitration," respectively.[2] The reason why disputants do not always wish to have outcome control, Houlden et al. explain, is because the outcome-judgment of a neutral third-party is generally perceived as more fair than the judgments of disputants themselves. If disputants can agree on a third party who, being outside the conflict, is likely to have an unbiased perspective, then disputants may trust that this third party has the credibility to render a fair judgment. For reasons we will present in this chapter, the perception of the third party's neutrality and credibility, however, may be less likely to occur when the disputing parties are from different countries, or the third party is from a different country than one or more of the disputants.

It is important to note that when disputants are given either process-control or outcome-control, they are being given expression-opportunities.[3] Process- versus outcome control differ from each other only in terms of *what* disputants are substantively expressing. If disputants control the presentation of evidence—that is, if they express views on the facts or perceptions relating to the dispute—then they are exercising process control. If they control the final solution—that is, if they express views on how the dispute should be settled and consensually choose the dispute's settlement—then the disputants are exercising outcome control. For reasons we will present in this chapter, we believe that employees will prefer process-control and/or outcome control more so in some countries than in others; and as a result, employees from different countries will probably prefer different dispute intervention procedures.

Purpose of the Chapter

The purpose of this chapter is to review literature that will guide propositions regarding the extent to which both U.S. and non-U.S. disputants will perceive a third-party intervention to be procedurally fair. We consider cases when: (1) the dispute resolution procedure is akin to mediation; (2)

the third-party is a peer rather than an authority-figure; (3) the third-party shares nationality with only one of the disputants; and (4) all parties involved in the dispute resolution procedure—each disputant and the third party—are from different nations. After identifying the likelihood that national differences amongst disputants and third parties may impede a universal experience of procedural justice, we discuss possible remedies for intervening "fairly" for all disputants in such situations.

DISPUTANTS' NATIONAL DIFFERENCES: DO THESE INFLUENCE WHAT PROCEDURES ARE "FAIR"?

How can we begin to surmise whether disputants from different nations will differentially perceive a third-party intervention as fair? As a starting point, it is helpful to remember that voice is generally associated with greater levels of procedural fairness. Although the studies we cited before generally consisted of U.S. participants, this same finding has been observed in non-U.S. populations as well (cf. Thibaut & Walker, 1975). But *why* has the "voice-effect" (Folger, 1977) occurred? An understanding of this is necessary if we are to predict when disputants from different countries will value the chance to express their views.

The Voice Effect: Why?

Different (and competing) explanations have been offered for the voice-effect (see Shapiro, 1993, for a review and a reconciliation), but in general all agree that voice provides grievants two functions: (1) an instrumental function, since voicing one's views enhances the chance that listeners may accommodate these (cf. Shapiro & Brett, 1993; Brett, 1986); and (2) a relational function (also referred to as the "group-value perspective," cf. Lind, Kanfer, & Earley, 1990), since merely being given the chance to voice enhances grievants' feelings that their group or organization respects their standing. It is important to note that the first function described refers to a "chance" at influencing the listener's response to an expressed grievance, and thus voice gives rise to perceptions of *possible* instrumentality (see elaborations on this view by Barry & Shapiro, 2000; Shapiro, 1993). This is why voice has been said to lead to "indirect outcome control" (Brett, 1986; Shapiro & Brett, 1993), but perhaps should be called "potential outcome control." Importantly, this does *not* mean that voice leads to actual outcome control; rather, voice leads a party to believe she may possibly control the listener's (third-party's) decision, hence her outcome. Interestingly, disputants seem to overinflate their potential to influence a third party. Lind et al. (1990) found parties to believe they had potential outcome control, even after they were told the third-party's decision had already been made and would *not* take into consideration the opinions that the participants were invited to present.

The second function of voice that we noted above regards the tendency for those to feel more valued as members of their group or community when their opinions have, rather than have not, been solicited. And thus, the second function of voice could perhaps be more succinctly described as one that provides "voicers" an experience of positive affect (such as respect, cf. Tyler, 1987).

The belief that one's voice *may* be influential and is being respected is probably enhanced by listeners' interpersonally-sensitive behaviors (e.g., nodding one's head to show understanding, concern, or empathy). For this reason Shapiro and her colleagues (Barry & Shapiro, 2000; Shapiro, 1993) have theorized that voicers who perceive that their views are (rather than are not) being considered probably feel potentially instrumental *as well as* relationally valued. Either or both of the latter feelings may thus explain why the voice-effect has been found only when voicers perceived third-party consideration (cf. Barry & Shapiro, 2000).

Despite these two functions of voice, and the possibility that they influence each other, it is important to note that leaders who solicit subordinates' views do not always generate positive affect. A recent study by Peterson (1999) shows that *reduced* levels of satisfaction can be associated with employee voice if the leaders' request for employee input appears to be inappropriate. Similarly, Scandura, Von Glinow, and Lowe (1998) found that in Saudi Arabia (unlike the United States), employees were generally less satisfied with supervisors who used a participative, rather than authoritative, decision making style—apparently because they were culturally accustomed to seeing leaders behave more authoritatively. Conversely, Brockner et al. (in press) have found that the lack of voice in managers' decision making is generally associated with greater levels of perceived injustice (hence greater dissatisfaction) in some countries more than others—namely, in the countries where expressing views to authorities is the norm. These latter findings reinforce the likelihood that employees from different nations will probably react differently to third-party interventions that give or deny them opportunities for expression.

Summary of Reasons for the Voice-Effect

In summary, we have identified the two reasons most commonly offered for the voice-effect in the justice literature to date: (1) the function voice serves in giving people the *chance* to potentially influence their listener; and (2) the function voice serves in giving people feelings of positive affect (e.g., respect) associated with the group or community to whom they are expressing themselves. Additionally, we have identified the possibility that a listener's interpersonal sensitivity heightens voicers' sense that they are, both, potentially influential and relationally valued; and these feelings, in turn, enhance the perception of procedural justice. It follows, then, that procedural justice is less likely to be perceived when the opportunity for expression does *not* lead to positive cognitive- or affective-consequences. Indeed, we believe this is likely to be the case in some countries more than others. Next, we explain why.

WHY COGNITIONS AND FEELINGS ASSOCIATED WITH VOICE MAY DIFFER ACROSS COUNTRIES

As noted earlier, the relational model-based explanation for the voice-effect assumes that positive affect (e.g., feelings of being respected in one's group or community) results when one's opinion has, rather than has not, been solicited. Under the latter circumstances, the instrumental model-based explanation for the voice-effect assumes that positive affect (e.g., feelings of hope, or possible influence) will result too. Naturally, then, the voice-effect is less likely to occur if people believe, instead: (1) that expressing their views will result in *negative* consequences (e.g., the disruption of a working relationship or friendship, or of social harmony more generally); or (2) that expressing their views is a waste of time since they cannot possibly influence their environment, hence the dispute's outcome. Either or both of these beliefs will thus discourage disputing employees from seeking or accepting third-party interventions that give them control over the presentation of facts and/or the determination of a settlement. Because these beliefs are influenced by national culture (or more accurately, the *values* associated with a nation's culture), employees from some countries will be more or less likely to have them; and as a result, disputants of different nationalities will probably *not* equally value third-party interventions that give them the chance to express themselves. This thinking is consistent with those who have identified cultural values as one of the reasons people in different countries differ in the way they negotiate business transactions (Brett et al., 1998; Brett & Okumura, 1998; Tinsley & Pillutla, 1999).

Figure 1a visually summarizes the relationships associated with the voice-effect (described above), and reflects our belief that the positive consequences of voice will *depend on* (hence be moderated by) the national-based cultural values held by the disputant. Importantly, our figure refers to the exogenous variable as "the opportunity for expression." We have chosen this language to reflect the fact that, as we noted before, when disputants are given either process- or outcome-control, they are being given the opportunity to express their views. And process- versus outcome-control differ only in terms of *what* disputants are substantively expressing. Naturally, then, we would expect the cultural values that influence the desirability of process- or outcome-control to be similar; however, we will take care to note the few occasions when we expect differences. Next, we identify the cultural values that we believe are most likely to influ-

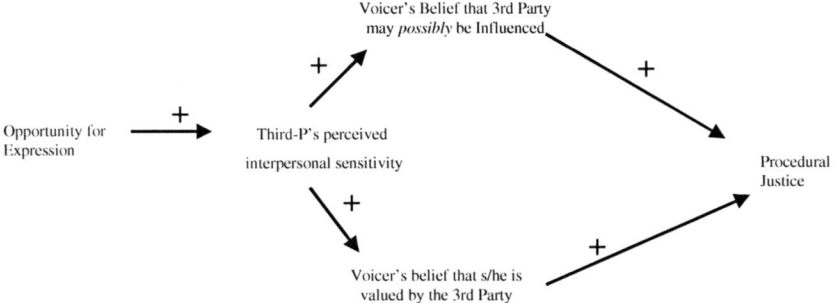

Figure 1. The voice effect, and why.

ence disputants' beliefs about the consequences associated with the expression of grievances.

The Influence of Cultural Values

"Cultural values" refer to the principles people use to guide their lives (Schwartz, 1994). Though technically these values reside in the cognitive structure of individuals, these values are thoroughly culturally constituted (Markus, Kitayama, & Heiman, 1997). As Tinsley and Brett (1999, p.3) explain:

> Since national culture provides a common institutional context and therefore common experiences, and national laws and institutions socialize, sanction, and reward conformity, national culture is one source of an individual's normative mental models.

Since legal, social, and economic structures differ across countries, it is not surprising that the values of country citizens differ, on average, as well (cf. Hofstede, 1980; Kluckhorn & Strodtbeck, 1961; Kirkman & Shapiro, in press). The extent to which disputants value opportunities to express their grievance-related views seems likely to be influenced by three cultural values in particular: (1) a preference for high power distance, (2) a belief in determinism, and (3) a preference for indirect communication.

The Preference for High Power Distance

Power distance refers to a person's ability to accept and, even, expect that others will have more or less authority and status (Hofstede, 1980; Haire, Ghiselli, & Porter, 1966). In high power distance countries such as much of Latin America and Asia (Hofstede, 1980; Schwartz, 1994; Leung, 1997), it is common for a third-party authority figure to unilaterally decide the resolution to a conflict (Leung, 1997; Tinsley, 1997), a method which has advantages such as a speedy resolution (Goldberg, Green, & Sander, 1985) that preserves harmony (Leung, 1997; Tinsley, 1997). It has been theorized and found that this normative practice is generally less acceptable in countries with lower levels of power distance, where participative decision making is more accepted and expected (cf. Brockner et al., in press; Hofstede, 1980). Thus, relative to disputants in low power distance countries, disputants in high power distance countries are more likely to perceive the transfer of process-control from third parties (authorities) to disputants as an *inappropriate* (counter-normative) practice, and therefore an interpersonally uncomfortable and unwanted one (cf. Leung & Ling, 1986; Leung & Wu, 1990). Consistent with this, people in high power distance cultures have been found, even after being insulted, to respond by asking authorities to intervene (cf. Bond, Wan, Leung, & Giacalone, 1985; Tinsley, 1998; in press). The general preference for authorities' intervention held by people in high power distance countries may explain why employees in such countries (who generally expect managers to act authoritatively) tend to negatively evaluate managers who invite employee participation in their decision making (Adler, 1997; Hofstede, 1980; Lind & Earley, 1992; Scandura et al., 1998).

The Influence of Determinism

Determinism, or passivity, refers to people's belief that they are passive reactors or recipients of the events in their world, whereas free will, self-mastery, or activity refers to people's belief that they are active shapers in the events of their world and their future (Schwartz, 1994; Triandis, 1982). Disputants with voice from highly deterministic countries such as the Philippines, China, and Asian countries in general (Schwartz, 1994; Triandis, 1982) are less likely than disputants from active or free-will countries, such as the United States and other North American countries, to believe that their expressed grievances will actually affect their (predetermined) outcomes. That is, deterministic disputants may see less of a connection between their voice and the value to them of the agreement that is reached. Therefore, the opportunity to have voice is likely to be valued less by disputants in deterministic- rather than in free will-oriented countries.

Indeed, deterministic disputants may *resist* the opportunity to express one's views when this opportunity pertains, specifically, to how to resolve the dispute. This is because deterministic thinking (which places responsibility for one's outcome, or fate, in the hands of others) is inconsistent with exercising outcome-control. Indirect support for our prediction is shown by Kirkman and Shapiro's (in press) finding that greater resistance to *self-managing* task assignments was reported by employees of deterministic (rather than free will) countries.

The Influence of Indirect Communication-Preference

"Non-voice strategies," such as ingratiation, impression management, and appeasement (Ohbuchi & Takahashi, 1994), have been referred to as examples of "indirect communication codes" which are generally observed in "high context" cultures, found throughout much of Asia (cf. Gudykunst & Ting-Toomey, 1988; Hall, 1976). Hall explains that in high context cultures members are assumed to share a well-developed basis of understanding so that less information needs to be explicitly communicated. The tendency of members in high context cultures to use indirect communication is due, also, to their tendency to place paramount importance on preserving "face" or positive self-images (Ting-Toomey, 1988; Ting Toomey, Gao, Trubisky, Yang, Kim, Lin, & Nishida,, 1991) which are threatened by expressions of disharmony, or conflict. In contrast, low context communication refers to a preference for overt, direct communication codes and signals (Hall, 1976; Gudykunst & Ting-Toomey, 1988), as exemplified by the more direct influence methods of persuasion, bargaining, and compromise (cf. Brett & Okumura, 1998; Ohbuchi & Takahashi, 1994). These more direct communications are typically found in the U.S. and Germanic cultures (Hall, 1976). Okabe (1983, p. 36) explains:

> [North] Americans' tendency to use explicit words is the most noteworthy characteristic of their communicative style. They prefer to employ categorical words such as "absolutely," "certainly," and "positively" . . . By contrast, the cultural assumptions of interdependence and harmony require that Japanese speakers limit themselves to implicit and even ambiguous use of words. In order to avoid leaving an assertive impression, they like to depend more frequently on qualifiers such as "maybe," "perhaps," "probably," and "somewhat".

Relative to disputants in low context cultures, disputants from high context cultures are thus likely to be less comfortable with direct "voice" concerning the details of a dispute. Consistent with this, Chua and Gudykunst (1987) found that high context Taiwanese were more likely to maintain silence and gloss over differences and ill will, whereas low context U.S. participants were more willing to directly discuss the dispute (see Jehn & Weldon, 1997, for a review).

Cumulatively, the theorizing above leads us to propose the relationships shown in Figure 1b. In this figure, unlike Figure 1a, we show (via the addition of the larger arrows) that people whose cultural values consist of high levels of power distance, determinism, and indirect communication will be *less* likely to associate the opportunity to express one's grievance with: the belief that they may potentially influence their third party, hence their dispute's outcome (illustrated by Arrow F); and feelings of positive affect (e.g., harmony, respect) within one's group or community (illustrated by Arrow G). People living in countries with the cultural values described here are thus not likely to experience the voice-effect (i.e., not likely to value the opportunity to express themselves). As a result, it seems likely that they will prefer third-party interventions that require as little participation from them as possible, hence a procedure (such as inquisition) that

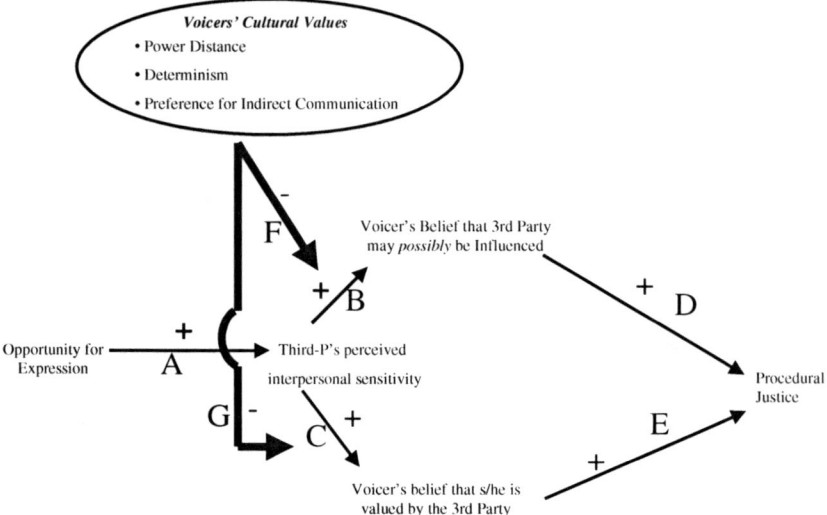

Figure 2. How cultural values may moderate the voice-effect.

gives process- and outcome-control nearly exclusively to the third-party. And the exact opposite prediction would hold for people who have low levels of the three cultural values described here. Thus, we propose:

Proposition 1. Disputants who have higher levels of power distance, determinism, and indirect communication-preferences will prefer third-party interventions that give process- and outcome-control nearly exclusively to the third-party (e.g., inquisition); and

Proposition 2. Disputants who have lower levels of power distance, determinism, and indirect communication-preferences will prefer third-party interventions that give process- and outcome-control nearly exclusively to them (e.g., mediation).

A Third-Party's National (Dis)Similarity With Disputants: Is This "Fair"?

Thus far our discussion has referred to a third-party without giving any personal description of whom this third-party might be. All of the dispute resolution studies (referenced up to this point) had authority figures who shared the same (United States) nationality of their disputants. Would the same findings have obtained if the third party had been nationally-dissimilar? To answer this question, let us reconsider the explanation that some researchers (e.g., Houlden et al., 1978) gave for why disputants preferred the third party (rather than either of the disputing parties) to decide how to settle the dispute: *the third party was perceived as more neutral and unbiased than either of the disputing parties, and thereby had the credibility to suggest a fair settlement.* Since the expectation of how another will behave is called "trust" or "distrust" (when the expectation is that positive versus negative interpersonal responses will occur, respectively; cf. Deutsch, 1965), then we could also say that the disputants in previous studies who preferred giving outcome control to a third party-authority apparently *trusted* the authority more than each other to arrive at a fair outcome. Consistent with this, other studies have found managerial third parties are more likely to give up control over a dispute when they had good, rather than bad, relationships with the disputants (Neale, Pinkley, Brittain, & Northcraft, 1990); and similarly, managers generally delegate decisions to subordinates more (and engage in a control-strategy less) when they trust, rather than distrust, them to make wise decisions (cf.Walton & Hackman, 1986).

In summary, a third-party's trustworthiness may determine how much, if any, value disputants place on expressing facts of a grievance to them and/or leaving the settlement decision completely in the third-party's hands. So, then, will disputants be more likely to trust a nationally-dissimilar or nationally-similar third-party? Because perceptions of interpersonal similarity and feelings of trust are generally positively correlated (Ashforth & Mael, 1989), we believe that as similarity to the third party decreases, there will be a greater preference for outcome as well as process-control. Said differently, a disputant will want as little help as possible from a third-party whom s/he does not trust.

Interestingly, the latter prediction highlights the central role that a third-party's trustworthiness may play in determining the ultimate fairness a disputant will perceive of *any* third-party intervention. The central role of the third-party's trustworthiness is visually shown in Figures 1a and 1b. Figure 1c extends the relationships shown in Figures 1a and 1b by illustrating the possibility that disputants' perceptions of the third party's goodwill, sensitivity (hence trust in the third party) will be greater when they share the same nationality (illustrated by Arrow H). Yet, as we noted in our chapter's beginning, the workplace today is increasingly less likely to allow (at least all) disputants) a nationally-similar third-party. Next, we consider three prototypical cases that are likely to be experienced by disputing employees today. In so doing, we will provide *inter*cultural-related propositions that the relationships we have heretofore proposed (and that are cumulatively shown in Figure 1c) now allow us to make.

The Third Party as Nationally-Different from Both (Nationally-Similar) Disputants

The first case we consider is one where the disputants are from one culture and the third party is from another. In this circumstance, it is likely that the disputants will perceive themselves to be more similar to each

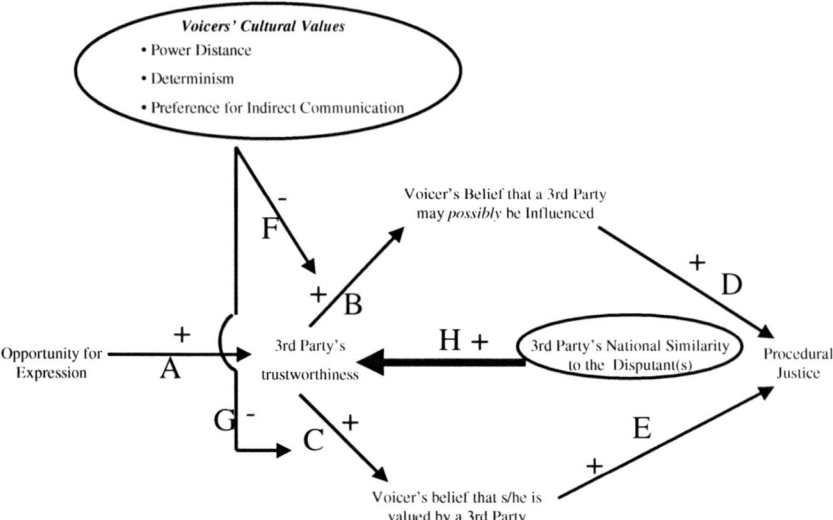

Figure 3. How a third-party's national (dis)similarity to the disputant(s) may influence the voice effect.

other than to the third party; and thus they may see each other as ingroup members and the third party as an outgroup member (Ashforth & Mael, 1989; Thatcher & Jehn, 1998; Turner, Sachdev, & Hogg, 1983). The latter conclusion results from the tendency for people to make ingroup-outgroup distinctions based on visible characteristics (Pelled, Eishenhardt, & Xin, 1999; Tsui, Egan, & O'Reilly, 1992). Subordinate categorization, where a person is classified into increasingly smaller groups, produces more accurate social information about that person than larger, "primary" categorizations. Yet, primary categorizations (based on visible attributes such as race, nationality, gender, or age) are more commonly used by people to make predictions about others (Bruner, 1957; Tajfel & Turner, 1986; Brewer, 1988). Thus, while the disputants and third party may be similar on several other important dimensions (such as personal values and beliefs), demographic attributes and physical characteristics (age, race, nationality) tend to be the most salient (Boucher & Perks, 1971; Boucher & Ohsako, 1977). This implies that while the disputants will acknowledge they have important differences (or they would not be in dispute), they are also likely to perceive a certain similarity with each other and a certain dissimilarity with the third party. Perceived similarity tends to facilitate interpersonal interactions (Evans, 1963) and to increase interpersonal attractiveness, including trust (Ashforth & Mael, 1989). McGuire (1968) explains this is because similar (rather than dissimilar) others are often assumed to share common needs and goals. Conversely, disputants' perceived dissimilarity with the third party will decrease their ability to trust that third party. And therefore, disputants who are nationally-similar to only each other but nationally different from the third party are likely to prefer a dispute resolution procedure that gives the disputants (rather than the third party) outcome control.

Procedures that give, rather than deny, outcome control to the disputants are more likely to enable the disputants to concede a bit on their initial demands, and therefore find an outcome that is better than "one side wins, one side loses"—the latter being a typical outcome of dispute resolution procedures in which third parties (e.g., arbitrators, judges) decide on the settlement (Goldberg, Green, & Sander, 1985). Ingroup members' tendency to behave cooperatively with each other, at least more so than with outgroup members (Brewer, 1979; Earley, 1993), and the greater potential for disputants to engage in mutual cooperation in dispute resolution procedures that leave outcome control in their (rather than the third party's) hands are additional reasons why disputants who see each other as ingroup rather than outgroup members may prefer dispute resolution procedures that encourage them to discuss and settle issues with each other (rather than through a distrusted third party) as much as possible. Said differently, disputants in this situation will probably prefer to have control over the outcome as well as the process. Thus:

Proposition 3. Disputants who share national-similarity with each other but not with the third party will generally see greater procedural justice associated with dispute resolution procedures that give them (rather than the third party) outcome-control as well as process-control (e.g, mediation).

The Third Party as Nationally-Similar to One (or a few) Disputants

The second case we consider is one where one of the disputants is from the same country as the third party and the other disputant is from another. Minimally, in this situation the first disputant will perceive the third party to be more demographically similar to him/herself than will the second disputant; and as a result, the third party's trustworthiness is likely to be greater for the first disputant (Ashforth & Mael, 1989; Tsui et al., 1992). If disputants trust third parties more when they share, rather than lack, national similarity with them, then under these circumstances disputants are likely to be more comfortable giving up outcome control, consistent with others finding that managerial delegation (less control) similarly occurs under high trust circumstances (Walton & Hackman, 1986). And therefore, the disputant who shares national similarity with the third party may be more likely than the disputant who does not to prefer a dispute resolution procedure that gives disputants only process-control (and not also outcome control). Ceding outcome control to the third party also ensures that the other disputant (who is from a different nation) will not have outcome control. The desirability of keeping outcome control out of the hands of the other disputant arises from the likelihood that his/her national dissimilarity, and hence outgroup status (cf. Ashforth & Mael, 1989), breeds greater distrust.

For the same reason, the nationally-dissimilar disputant will probably perceive both the third party as well as the other disputant (with whom s/he is dissimilar) as untrustworthy; and thus probably prefer a dispute resolution procedure that provides neither of them with outcome control. Since the latter characteristic is not practical, then the nationally-dissimilar disputant is likely to see no intervention as fair. Consequently, resolution of the employee dispute under these circumstances is likely to be greatly impeded by the second disputant's real or imagined fears of a biased third party and potential coalition between the first disputant and the third party (Murnighan & Brass, 1991). More optimistically, it is possible that the nationally-dissimilar disputant may accept a dispute resolution procedure that maximizes his/her own feeling of control—hence one that gives the disputants outcome control in addition to process control. The problem with this, however, is that we have suggested above that the other disputant (who shares national similarity with the third party) will prefer a procedure that gives outcome control to the *third party*, not the disputants. In summary, we predict:

Proposition 4. A disputant ("Disputant #1") who is nationally-similar to a third party and nationally-different from the other disputant ("Disputant #2") will prefer a procedure that gives disputants process control but not outcome control (e.g., arbitration); whereas a procedure that gives *both* types of control to disputants will be preferred by Disputant #2 (e.g., mediation).

The Third Party as Nationally-Different from All Parties: "Fairness" Consequences

The last case we consider is one in which the group (of two disputants and a third-party) is completely heterogeneous (with no two people sharing a national identity). Here, there is no basis for perceived similarity and trust. At first glance, this may appear to be the worst case scenario, as all parties' efforts to cooperate may be hindered by their lack of mutual trust. However, this scenario may be easier to resolve than the one above, as the complete heterogeneity here prevents any suggestion of impropriety and coalition formation. Groups with complete heterogeneity have no "faultlines," or places for potential subgroup division that occurs when peoples' multiple demographic attributes co-align with some members and not with others (Lau & Murnighan, 1998).

Lau and Murnighan explain that groups without strong fault lines are less prone to conflict and are more likely to be able to coordinate and integrate. In completely heterogeneous groups (such as when both disputants and the third party come from different cultures) there may be initial struggles to articulate interests and assumptions, which can slow resolution. However, the articulation of interests and assumptions (necessary for coordination among diverse others) would then offer raw material for high quality resolutions. This is the situation where diversity breeds creativity, innovation, and high quality solutions to complex tasks (Watson, Kumar, & Michaelsen, 1993; Michel & Hambrick, 1992). Thus, under complete heterogeneity, the resolution process may be smoother than in the above case of partial heterogeneity; moreover, the outcome reached may be a higher quality solution.

A "smoother" resolution process implies that the parties involved in the dispute are constructively (rather than destructively) communicating their differences. The greater potential of achieving "high quality solutions" in completely, rather than partially, heterogeneous groups described above also implies that the two disputants and third party are sharing information about interests and brainstorming creative suggestions to bridge or trade these interests. This sort of sharing and brainstorming is more likely to occur in a dispute resolution procedure that gives disputants both process control *and* outcome control. Will such a procedure be desired by disputants who see the other disputant and the third party as representatives of two different countries, neither of which are his/her own? Given the degree of uncertainty and distrust that is likely to characterize heterogeneous situations (Evans, 1963; McGuire, 1968), it seems likely that the disputant (say "J.P.") will want to maximize his/her control—and hence have outcome—as well as process control. A caveat, due to our prior theorizing (visually summarized in Figure 1b), is that if J.P. is from a country characterized by high levels of determinism and power distance, and an indirect communication style, then process and outcome control will be *less* important in determining J.P.'s perceptions of fairness. Thus, we predict:

Proposition 5. When the participants of a dispute resolution procedure are each from different countries (the group is completely heterogeneous), then disputants will prefer a procedure that gives them outcome- and process-control; however, this process and outcome-control will be less important to disputants whose country is characterized by high levels of determinism, power distance, and an indirect communication style.

The Third-Party as Authority or Peer: Does this Matter?

It is important to note that the procedural justice studies involving disputants that we have cited in this chapter all involved third-parties who were *authority-figures* to the disputants—that is, police officers or teachers (Tyler, 1987), experimenters (Lind et al., 1990), mediators (Shapiro & Brett, 1993), or arbitrators/judges (Houlden et al., 1978; Shapiro & Brett, 1993; Thibaut & Walker, 1975; see Lind & Tyler, 1988, for a review). Earlier in the chapter we pointed out that the increasingly self-managed workforce of today makes that less and less likely to be the case. How, if at all, would the third-party's status alter the propositions offered above? Because people from high-power distance cultures generally give deference to authorities and prefer authoritative rather than participative decision making (cf. Scandura et al., 1998), and people from higher context cultures prefer to resolve conflict indirectly (e.g., via a superior's intervention, cf. Tinsley, in press), Propositions 2, 3, and 4 would remain unchanged if the third-party were an authority-figure. Importantly, modification to Propositions 2, 3, and 4 would be needed if the third-party were a peer. Specifically:

Proposition 6. Dispute interventions (of any kind) in which the third party is a peer, rather than an authority, will be less acceptable to disputants who come from high power distance and/or high context countries.

Summary

In summary, the theorizing leading to the latter set of propositions all rests on assumptions about when disputants will be more or less likely to trust a third-party to assist them with their grievance. We have theorized that disputants will tend to choose maximum control (both process and outcome control) when they do not trust the third party to make an unbiased settlement decision (or they trust the other disputant more so). Disputants will opt for less control (process control only) when they do trust the third party to make an unbiased settlement decision (or they have even less trust in the other disputant).

How to give a 'fair' dispute intervention experience to nationally-diverse disputants thus seems to rest upon creating trust either in the procedure or in the players involved. Creating trust may be facilitated by understanding parties' expectations for the process and the outcome—and thus their cultural norms for how conflict should be resolved (Tinsley & Brett, 1999). The latter statement suggests that understanding disputants' past (historical, culture-based) norms may be helpful. However, setting, or *developing*, norms, or expectations, with disputants regarding how conflict should be resolved may be helpful as well. We discuss each of these possibilities in the next section.

INTERVENING "FAIRLY" FOR ALL: HOW?

The Importance of Understanding Disputants' Past Norms

Numerous articles and books on negotiation across culture suggest that negotiators' styles should match the norms of the country in which they are negotiating (e.g., Cohen, 1991; Faure & Rubin, 1993). Similarly, cross-cultural researchers have advised managers to implement organizational changes, such as transition to self-managing work teams, in ways that match the cultural values of the host-country in which such changes are occurring (cf. Kirkman & Shapiro, in press). This "when in Rome, do as the Romans do" prescription is consistent with the idea that good things happen when behaviors (of the negotiator) match expectations (of the host country counterpart).

The problem with this prescription is that it assumes two things that could be potentially wrong. First, it assumes that a negotiator can know what the host country representative is expecting, and secondly, it assumes that the negotiator can behave effectively in a way that matches the host country representative's expectations. Thus, the "do as the Romans do" prescription encourages a negotiator to make *unilateral* assumptions that subsequently get expressed in unilateral behavior, which can then potentially create a self-fulfilling prophecy. For example, an American who expects Japanese negotiators to prefer communicating indirectly may, based on this, choose to communicate his or her interests to a Japanese counterpart via a third party; this choice forces the communication to become indirect, when his or her Japanese counterpart may have been quite comfortable communicating directly. Indeed, the Japanese counterpart may have *preferred* to communicate directly, despite the fact that doing so is generally contrary to Japan's cultural norms; and the American's decision to bring in another party (especially if this party is an authority) may have caused the Japanese counterpart to feel a loss of face. When people learn prototypic information about a group first, they are less able to distinguish group variability (Park & Hastie, 1988). Thus, negotiators may anchor on cultural-level stereotypes of their opponent's expectations and fail to adjust for the opponent's expectation-deviations. Ironically, if both negotiators from different countries do this, then they end up adopting culturally-mismatched behaviors—with each behaving in ways that are consistent with the *other* side's culture.

The problems identified above is why a *collaborative* (rather than unilateral) process for understanding a priori norms has been advised by some researchers. For example, Tinsley and Brett (1999) advise negotiators to explicitly discuss their *process*-related expectations *before* negotiating the substantive issues that gave rise to their dispute. Similarly, Jehn (1997) has advised disputing parties to explicitly agree on "process norms" before attempting to resolve task-related conflict. Unspecified, however, is the mechanism by which negotiators should discuss and resolve their process-related expectations. A close exception to this is Janssens and Brett (1997) who advise transnational team members (who are in essence intercultural disputants at times) to engage the latter process, but with only those who have (cultural-based) knowledge that is *relevant* to the issues under dispute. Below we illustrate how process-related concerns might be resolved and show that in discussing and reconciling these expectations, disputants are actually developing new conflict resolution norms, separate from the culture-based, a priori norms they had at the start of the conflict.

DEVELOPING NEW CONFLICT RESOLUTION PROCESS NORMS: A SURER ROUTE TO CULTURAL CONSISTENCY?

One way in which negotiators might discuss and resolve their process expectations is by understanding each side's preferences for process-and outcome-control, and then trading off these preferences so that all parties get what is most important to them. A likely consequence of this trading will be some type of hybrid conflict resolution procedure, such as "med-arb" (Brett & Goldberg, 1983), which gives disputants high outcome-control initially, but then if the disputants cannot derive a resolution after a predetermined amount of time, then they relinquish outcome-control to the third party (Goldberg et al., 1985).

For example, a party (Party A) from a low context, low power distance culture, for whom process- and outcome-control are very important, may suggest to the other disputant (Party B) that the resolution procedure have high process- and outcome-control. Since process- and outcome-control are important in Party A's (low context, low power-distance) culture, obtaining such a conflict resolution procedure would be a win for Party A. In exchange, Party A can promise Party B (who is from a high context, high power distance culture and thus does not value process- and outcome-control but rather values a high-status third party), that Party B will get to choose who the third party mediator will be. Since status and authority are important in Party B's (high context, high power-distance) culture, obtaining a conflict resolution procedure whose third-party has high status and authority (and is of Party B's choosing) would be a win for Party B. Thus, while the resolution may be controlled by the disputants, which is a procedural characteristic that satisfies Party A's most important procedural issue, this resolution will also be blessed by a high status authority figure, which is a characteristic that satisfies Party B's most important procedural issue. As a result, trading one disputant's interest in having process- and outcome-control for another disputant's interest in having a high-status third party involved allows both parties to "win" procedurally. Procedural satisfaction, or procedural justice, is then likely to ease these parties' ability to reach a distributively satisfying outcome—that is, a resolution that both see as fair (see Lind & Tyler, 1988, for a review of evidence showing a generally positive relationship between procedural and distributive justice).

Similarly, it is possible that parties may trade concessions on process issues for wins on content issues. For example, a party from a free-will country (who would typically prefer to retain decision control) may concede to a dispute resolution process where the third party maintains decision control if, in return, the other party concedes on a substantive, content issue from the initial dispute. The point is that if disputants tell each other their preferences regarding process issues, in addition to substantive issues, then it becomes possible for the dispute to be expanded to include both sets of issues; and as a result of this expansion, for concession tradeoffs to be made that allow each side to benefit (cf. Pruitt & Carnevale, 1993)—that is, to find procedural- and, ultimately, distributive-justice.

Another end-result of the latter process is that new norms for resolving the disputants' conflict will be collaboratively created. This process of creating new norms out of parties' differing existing norms is conceptually similar to the process of creating a "third-culture." As Casmir and Asuncion-Lande (1989, p. 290) explain:

> A third culture is a situational subculture wherein temporary behavioral adjustments can be made by the interacting persons as they attempt to reach a mutually agreed upon goal(s). In their efforts to adjust to each other, they build upon a commonality experience that can later serve as a starting point for their renewed interaction.

Thus, what we suggest is that parties make adjustments (concessions) from their a priori, culturally-based dispute resolution norms, to build a common, new set of mutually acceptable conflict resolution processes. Mutual concession-making should, in turn, breed trust (cf. Deutsch, 1958). Earlier, we identified this as critical for determining whether disputants who are given both process- and outcome-control will indeed see procedural justice. In summary, we propose:

Proposition 7. When disputants are from different nations, they will be more likely to perceive procedural justice if the process-norms (procedure) used for resolving the dispute are ones that they explicitly agree on *before* discussing how to resolve the substantive issues giving rise to the dispute.

Proposition 8. Nationally-dissimilar disputants' agreement on process-norms is more likely to occur when they state, rather than do not state, their preferences regarding process- and outcome control; and they use these process preferences, in addition to substantive (resolution) preferences, as issues on which to potentially trade concessions.

Obstacles to Implementing a Collaboratively-Created Dispute Resolution Process

Although the ideas of incorporating and trading these process issues are theoretically compelling, unfortunately the conditionals that accompany these propositions suggest problems in implementing these ideas. First, these ideas require that parties recognize that certain process issues (disputant's control, third party's status) are of high priority. Yet, these priorities may be less conscious choices about dispute process and more unconscious, taken-for-granted assumptions concerning how a conflict should be resolved. That is, these norms may be expectations that parties are not aware of until the expectation is violated (for example, until a third party retains the decision control that a party from a free will country expected the third party to give up).

Once procedural expectations are violated, it may be difficult to rebuild the trust necessary to share information about expectations. Thus, a second problem with the strategy summarized by Propositions 5 and 6 is that parties may be unwilling to work with each other and give up even low priority process issues. If distrust creates rigidity in parties' willingness to give anything away (Kimmel, Pruitt, Magenau, Konar-Goldband, & Carnevale, 1980), then they will not be able to coordinate tradeoffs across priorities.

A third obstacle associated with the collaboratively-created dispute resolution process described above is that this process assumes that disputants will indeed be willing to state their process- or substantive-issue priorities. Possible solutions to these obstacles are offered next, each in turn.

Possible Solutions for International Obstacles in Dispute Resolution

With regard to the first and second obstacles noted above, there are two possible solutions: either parties have to avoid violating each other's process norms or parties have to forgive each other after such a violation is made. To avoid violating each other's norms, parties would have to act consistently with the advice of Proposition 5: discuss process expectations before resolution of the seed dispute begins. Since such expectations may be unconscious, drafting procedural policy for intercultural dispute resolution (that requires the latter discussion) may be required to make parties consciously aware of the need to articulate these.

To enhance parties' willingness to forgive each other after cultural norm-violations occur, the latter policy may benefit from explicitly stating the probability of such errors, and the importance of *not* reacting in ways that escalates the initial conflict. This policy may benefit, further, by mentioning specific behavioral responses that are desirable (de-escalatory) ways to respond to undesirable actions on the part of negotiation-opponents (cf. Brett, Shapiro, & Lytle, 1998), which disputants in essence are. Additional nonpolicy actions that may encourage nationally-dissimilar disputants to forgive each other's process transgressions may include: sensitizing multinational managers that business processes and beliefs are not universal; and in so doing, educating disputants that differing norms and expectations abound, that neither is inherently correct, and that the other party's inevitable process violations simply signals a normative process difference—and an opportunity to use the procedure advocated by Propositions 5 and 6 above.

The third obstacle noted above is that the ideas relating to how to get nationally-dissimilar disputants to collaboratively develop a dispute resolution procedure require that parties be able (and willing) to discuss their process- and substantive-issues with each other, or with the third-party. As we noted earlier in the chapter, such directness is inconsistent with the cultural values of a high context or high-power distance culture. Disputants from high context cultures are less likely to communicate overtly (Ting-Toomey, 1988), and disputants from high-power distance cultures are less likely to discuss differences if any of the parties involved have higher status (Leung, 1997). Here again, perhaps research that elucidated the assumptions about disputant control and third party status, across a variety of cultures, may help. Parties themselves may not have to discuss their individual process priorities because the cultural level information, if accurate, would make these commonly known. Parties can then suggest tradeoff proposals based on their aggregate knowledge of different national culture's process priorities. As one example, parties from low context, free will, low power distance cultures may care more about the *form* of the dispute resolution procedure (who has process control, outcome control), while parties from high context, deterministic, high-power distance cultures may care more about the *people* involved (status of disputants and third party). Proposing this and observing the other's reactions will indirectly give information about the other's process-priorities. If once recognized, these priorities can be traded, then a hybrid resolution process may be created that is acceptable to both parties. As we mentioned previously, basing dispute-resolution behaviors (including proposals) on aggregate-level knowledge risks creating a self-fulfilling prophecy. Thus, caution in doing this needs to be exercised.

CONCLUSION

In closing, we hope that the ideas we have raised in this chapter have accomplished at least one thing: *the need for conflict researchers and procedural justice researchers to question how generalizable current thinking and theory is with regard to managing disputes amongst nationally-different employees.* We recognize that the procedural strategy, its obstacles and the associated solutions that we have identified as possibilities are, in terms of implementation, complicated—and not simple. However, whether it is a question of recognition or discussion of process issues, it does seem that future research detailing the process preferences of disputants from different cultures will help managers and practitioners facing these situations. With accurate knowledge of national culture's process issues and preferences we can perhaps design hybrid dispute resolution procedures to fit the particular intercultural dynamics of a situation, so that all disputants will think the resolution is procedurally just. We suggest this is a suitable goal in the globalized economy of the twentieth century.

NOTES

1. The term process control has been used interchangeably with "voice" in the procedural justice literature (e.g., Folger, 1977; Shapiro, 1993). Importantly, there are variations of process control ranging from procedural marshall, who sets and enforces rules or norms for disputant behavior and the dispute resolution process (Karambayya & Brett, 1989) to motivator, who encourages parties to resolve their disputes, any way they wish, and often provides resources to help grease the wheels (Sheppard, 1994). In this chapter our reference to "voice" refers, simply, to a third-party choosing to solicit (as opposed to not solicit) input from a disputant regarding his/her views and/or feelings relating to the facts or issues leading to the dispute.

2. We highlight that U.S. Americans call the procedures just described to be "mediation" and "arbitration," respectively, because these same procedures may be called by other names in non-U.S. cultures. For example, a third party intervention in community disputes in China is called mediation, but the mediator has decision control (Wall & Blum, 1991). In the United States this is called arbitration. To avoid confusion by a potentially multicultural readership, in this chapter we will focus— not on the names of various dispute resolution procedures, but—on the *behaviors* of the third-party (such as whether s/he gives disputants process-control (a chance to voice their viewpoints) and/or outcome control (a chance to decide on various possible settlements), and the likely reactions that disputing employees from various nations will have to these behaviors.

3. The commonality of voice that is shared by process and outcome control has led Bush (1996, reprinted in Lewicki, Saunders, & Minton, 1999, p.436) to define process control as a term ". . . that includes both the opportunity for meaningful participation in determining the outcome of the procedure (whatever it may ultimately be) and the opportunity for full self-expression."

REFERENCES

Adler, N. (1997). *International dimensions of organizational behavior* (3rd ed.). Boston: PWS-Kent Publishing Company.

Ashforth B.E., & Mael, F. (1989). Social identity theory and the organization. *Academy of Management Review, 14*(3), 20-39.

Barry, B., & Shapiro, D.L. (2000). When will grievants choose voice?: A test of situational, motivational, and attributional explanations. *International Journal of Conflict Management*, *11*(2), 103-134.

Bond, M., Wan, K., Leung, K., & Giacalone, R. (1985). How are responses to verbal insults related to cultural collectivism and power distance? *Journal of Cross-cultural Psychology, 16*, 111-127.

Boucher, S., & Ohsako, T. (1977). Ethnic role salience in racially homogenous and heterogenous societies. *Journal of Cross-Cultural Psychology, 8*, 477-492.

Boucher, S., & Perks, R.W. (1971). National role evocation as a function of cross-cultural interaction. *Journal of Cross-Cultural Psychology, 2*, 157-164.

Brett, J.M. (1986). Commentary on procedural justice papers. In R.J. Lewicki, B.H. Sheppard, & M.H. Bazerman (Eds.), *Research on negotiation in organizations* (Vol. 1, pp. 81-92). Greenwich, CT: JAI Press.

Brett, J.M., Adair, W., Lempereur, A., Okumura, T., Shikhirev, P., Tinsley, C., & Lytle, A. (1998). Culture and joint gains in negotiation. *The Negotiation Journal,* 61-86.

Brett, J.M., & Okumura, T. (1998). Inter- and intra-cultural negotiation: U.S. and Japanese negotiators. *The Academy of Management Journal, 41*(5), 495-510.

Brewer, M.B. (1988). A dual process model of impression formation. *Advances in Social Cognition, 1*, 1-36.

Brockner, J., Ackerman, G., Greenberg, J., Gelfand, M.J., Leung, K., Bierbrauer, G., Gómez, C., Kirkman, B.L., Shapiro, D.L. (in press). Culture and procedural Justice: The moderating influence of power distance on reactions to voice. *Journal of Experimental Social Psychology.*

Bruner, J.S. 1957. On perceptual readiness. *Psychological Review, 64*, 123-152.

Casmir, F.L., & Asuncion-Lande, N.C. (1989) Intercultural communication revisited: Conceptualization, paradigm building, and methodological approaches. *Communication Yearbook, 12*, 278-309.

Chua, E., & Gudykunst, W.B. (1987). Conflict resolution styles in low and high context cultures. *Communcation Research Reports, 4*, 32-37.

Cohen, R. (1991). *Negotiating across culture: Communication obstacles and international diplomacy.* Washington, DC: United States Institute of Peace Press.

De Cieri, H., & Dowling, P.J. (1995). Cross-cultural issues in organizational behavior. In C.L. Cooper & D.M. Rousssseau (Eds.), *Trends in organizational behavior* (Vol. 2, pp. 127-146). New York: John Wiley & Sons.

Deutsch, M. (1958). Trust and suspicion. *The Journal of Conflict Resolution, 2*(4), 265-279.

Earley, P.C. (1993). East meets West meets Mideast: Further explorations of collectivistic and individualistic work groups. *Academy of Management Journal, 36*, 319-348.

Evans, F.B. (1963, May). Selling as a dyadic relationship: A new approach. *American Behavioral Scientist,* 76-79.

Faure, G.O., & Rubin, J. (1993). *Culture and negotiation.* Newbury Park, CA: Sage.

Folger, R. (1977). Distributive and procedural justice: Combined impact of "voice" and improvement on experienced inequity. *Journal of Personality and Social Psychology, 35*, 108-119.

Goldberg, S.B., Green, E.D., & Sander, S.E.A. (1985). *Dispute resolution.* Boston: Little Brown & Company.

Gregersen, H.B. (1992). Commitments to a parent company and a local work unit during repatriation. *Personnel Psychology, 45*(1), 29-54.

Gudykunst, W., & Ting-Toomey, S. (1988). *Culture and interpersonal communication.* Newbury Park, CA: Sage.

Haire, M., Ghiselli, E.E., & Porter, L.W. (1966). *Managerial thinking: An international study.* New York: John Wiley & Sons.

Hall, E.T. (1976). *Beyond culture.* Garden City: Anchor/Doubleday.

Hofstede, G. (1980). *Culture's consequences: International differences in work-related values.* Newbury Park, CA: Sage.

Houlden, P., LaTour, S., Walker, L., & Thibaut, J. (1978). Preference for modes of dispute resolution as a function of process and decision control. *Journal of Experimental Social Psychology, 14,* 13-30.

Jackson, S.E., Stone, V.K., & Alvarez, E.B. (1992). Socialization amidst diversity: The impact of demographics on work team oldtimers and newcomers. In L.L. Cummings & B.M. Staw (Eds.), *Research in organizational behavior* (Vol. 15, pp. 45-109). Greenwich, CT: JAI Press.

Janssens, M., & Brett, J.M. (1997). Meaningful participation in transnational teams. *European Journal of Work and Organizational Psychology, 6*(2), 153-168.

Jehn, K. (1997). A qualitative analysis of conflict types and dimensions in organizational groups. *Administrative Science Quarterly, 42,* 530-557.

Jehn, K.A., & Weldon (1997). Managerial attitudes toward conflict: Cross-cultural differences in resolution styles. *Journal of International Management, 4,* 291-321.

Kanter, R.M., & Corn, R.I. (1994). Do cultural differences make a business difference?: Contextual factors affecting cross-cultural relationship success. *Journal of Management Development, 13*(2), 5-23.

Karambayya, R., & Brett, J.M. (1989). Managers handling disputes: Third party roles and perceptions of fairness. *Academy of Management Journal, 35,* 426-438.

Karambayya, R., Brett, J.M., & Lytle, A.H. (1992). Managerial third parties: The effects of formal authority and experience on third-party roles, outcomes, and perceptions of fairness. *Academy of Management Journal, 35,* 426-438.

Kimmel, M.J., Pruitt, D.G. Magenau, J.M., Konar-Goldband, E., & Carnevale, P.J.D. (1980). Effects of trust, aspirations, and gender on negotiation tactics. *Journal of Personality and Social Psychology, 35,* 9-23.

Kirkman, B.L., & Shapiro, D.L. (in press). The impact of cultural values on employee resistance to teams: A comparative analysis of self-managing work team effectiveness in Belgium, Finland, the Philippines, and the United States. *The Academy of Management Journal.*

Kluckhohn, F.R., & Strodtbeck, F.L. (1961). *Variations in value orientations.* Evanston, IL: Row, Peterson & Company.

Kolb, D. (1986). Who are organizational third parties and what do they do? In R.J. Lewicki, B. Sheppard, & M. Bazerman (Eds.), *Research on negotiation in organizations* (Vol. 1, pp. 207-278). Greenwich, CT: JAI Press.

Kolb, D.M., & Glidden, P. (1986). Getting to know your conflict options. *Personnel Administrator, 31*(6), 77-90.

Kolb, D.M., & Sheppard, B.H. (1985, Oct.) Do managers mediate, or even arbitrate? *Negotiation Journal,* 379-388.

Lau, D.C., & Murnighan, J.K. (1998). Demographic diversity and faultlines: The compositional dynamics of organziational groups. *Academy of Management Review, 23,* 325-340.

Leung, K. (1997). Negotiation and reward allocations across cultures. In P.C. Earley & M. Erez (Eds.), *New perspectives on I/O psychology* (pp. 640-675). San Francisco: Jossey-Bass.

Leung, K., & Ling, E.A. (1986). Procedural justice and culture: Effects of culture, gender, and investigator status on procedural preferences. *Journal of Personality and Social Psychology, 50,* 1134-1140.

Leung, K., & Wu, P.G. (1990). Dispute processing: A cross-cultural analysis. In R.W. Brislin (Ed.), *Applied cross-cultural psychology* (pp.209-231). Thousand Oaks, CA: Sage.

Lewicki, R.J., Saunders, D.M., & Minton, J.W. (1999). *Negotiation: Readings, exercises, and cases.* Boston: Irwin/McGraw-Hill.

Lewicki, R.J., & Sheppard, B.H. (1985). Choosing how to intervene: Factors affecting the use of process and outcome control in third party dispute resolution. *Journal of Occupational Behavior, 6,* 49-64.

Lind, E.A., & Earley, C. (1992). Procedural justice and culture. *International Journal of Psychology, 27,* 227-242.

Lind, E.A., Kanfer, R., & Earley, P.C. (1990). Voice, control, and procedural justice: Instrumental and non-instrumental concerns in fairness judgments. *Journal of Personality and Social Psychology, 59,* 952-959.

Lind, E.A., & Tyler, T.R. (1988). *The social psychology of procedural justice.* New York: Plenum Press.

Manz, C.C., & Sims, H.P., Jr. (1993). *Business without bosses: How self-managing teams are building high performance companies.* New York: Wiley.

Markus, H.R., Kitayama, S., & Heiman, R. (1997). Culture and 'basic' psychological principles. In E.T. Higgins, & A.W. Kruglanski (Eds.), *Social psychology: Handbook of basic principles.* New York: Guilford Press.

McGuire, W.J. (1968). The nature of attitudes and attitude change. In L. Gardner & G. Aronson (Eds.), *The handbook of social psychology.* Reading, MA: Addison-Wesley Publishing.

Michel, J., & Hambrick, D. (1992). Diversification posture and the characteristics of the top management team. *Academy of Management Journal, 35,* 9-37.

Mintzberg, H.R. (1975, July/August). The manager_s job: Folklore and fact. *Harvard Business Review,* 49-61.

Murnighan, J.K., & Brass, D.J. (1991). Intraorganizational coalitions. In M. Bazerman, R. Lewicki, & B. Sheppard (Eds.), *The handbook of negotiation research* (pp. 283-306). Greenwich, CT: JAI Press.

Neale, M.A., Pinkley, R.L, Brittain, J.W., & Northcraft, G.B. (1990). *Managerial third-party dispute resolution.* Final report, Dispute Resolution Research Center, Northwestern University, Evanston, IL.

Ohbuchi, K., & Takahashi, Y. (1994). Cultural styles of conflict management in Japanese and Americans: Passivity, covertness, and effectiveness of strategies. *Journal of Applied Social Psychology, 24,* 1345-1366.

Okabe, R. (1983). Cultural assumptions of East and West: Japan and the United States. In W. Gudykunst (Ed.), *Intercultural communication theory.* Beverly Hills, CA: Sage.

Park, B., & Hastie, R. (1987). Perception of variability in category development: Instance versus Abstraction-based stereotypes. *Journal of Personality and Social Psychology, 53,* 621-635.

Pelled, L.H., Eisenhardt, K.M., & Xin, K.R. (1999). Exploring the black box: An analysis of work group diversity, conflict, and performance. *Administrative Science Quarterly, 44,* 1-28.

Peterson, R.S. (1999). Can you have too much of a good thing?: The limits of voice for improving satisfaction with leaders. *Personality and Social Psychology Bulletin, 25,* 313-324.

Pruitt, D.M., & Carnevale, P. (1993). *Negotiation in social conflict.* Pacific Grove, CA: Brooks/Cole.

Sander, F.E.A., & Goldberg, S. B. (1993, March 27-28). *Fitting the forum to the fuss: Some guidelines for a taxonomy of dispute resolution procedures.* Paper presented at the workshop sponsored by Standing Committee on Dispute Resolution of the American Bar Association.

Scandura, T., Von Glinow, M.A., & Lowe, K. (1998). Effects of leader behavior on job satisfaction and leadership effectiveness in the U.S. and the Middle East. In Mobley (Ed.), *Advances in global leadership.* Greenwich, CT: JAI Press.

Schwartz, S. (1994). Beyond individualism/collectivism: New cultural dimensions of values. In K. Uichol, H. Triandis, & H. Hakhoe (Eds.), *Individualism and collectivism: Theory, methods, and applications* (pp. 85-119). Thousand Oaks, CA: Sage.

Shapiro, D.L. (1993). Reconciling theoretical differences among procedural justice researchers by re-evaluating what it means to have one's views "*considered*:" Implications for third-party managers. In R. Cropanzano (Ed.), *Justice in the workplace: Approaching fairness in human resource management* (pp.51-78). Hillsdale, NJ: Lawrence-Erlbaum Publishers.

Shapiro, D.L., & Brett, J.M. (1993). Comparing three processes underlying judgments of procedural justice: A field study of mediation and arbitration. *Journal of Personality and Social Psychology, 65*(6), 1167-1177.

Shapiro, D.L., & Rosen, B. (1994). An investigation of managerial intervention in employee disputes. *Employee Responsibilities and Rights Journal, 7*(1), 37-51.

Shapiro, D.L., & Von Glinow, M.A. (1999). Negotiation in multicultural teams: New world, old theories? In R.J. Bies, R.J. Lewicki, & B.H. Sheppard (Eds.), *Research on negotiation in organizations* (Vol.7). Greenwich, CT: JAI Press.

Sheppard, B.H. (1984). Third party conflict intervention: A procedural framework. In B.M. Staw & L.L. Cummings (Eds.), *Research in organizational behavior* (Vol. 6, pp. 141-189). Greenwich, CT: JAI Press.

Sheppard, B.H. (1983). Managers as inquisitors: Some lesson from the law. In M. Bazerman, R. Lewicki, & B. Sheppard (Eds.), *Negotiating in organizations.* Beverly Hills Sage.

Sheppard, B.H., Saunders, D.M., & Minton, J.W. (1988). Procedural justice from the third party perspective. *Journal of Personality and Social Psychology, 54*(4), 629-637.

Tajfel, H., & Turner, J.C. (1986). The social identity theory of intergroup behavior. In S. Worchel & W.G. Austin (Eds.), *Psychology of intergroup relations.* Chicago: Nelson-Hall.

Thatcher, S., & Jehn, K. (1998). A model of group diversity profiles and categorization processes in bicultural organizational teams. In M. Neale, E. Mannix, D.

Gruenfeld (Eds.), *Research on managing groups and teams* (Vol. 1, pp. 1-20). Greenwich, CT: JAI Press.

Thibaut, J.W., & Walker, L. (1975). *Procedural justice: A psychological analysis.* Hillsdale, NJ: Erlbaum.

Ting-Toomey, S. (1988). A face-negotiation theory. In Y.Kim & W.Gudykunst (Eds.), *Theory in intercultural communication.* Newbury Park, CA: Sage.

Ting Toomey, S., Gao, G., Trubisky, P., Yang, Z., Kim, H., Lin, S-L., & Nishida, T. (1991). Culture, face maintenance, and styles of handling interpersonal conflict: A study in five cultures. *The International Journal of Conflict Management, 2,* 275-296.

Tinsley, C. (in press). How we get to yes: Predicting the constellation of strategies used across cultures to negotiate conflict. *Journal of Applied Psychology.*

Tinsley, C.H. (1997). Understanding conflict in a Chinese cultural context. In R.J. Bies, R. Lewicki, & B. Sheppard (Eds.), *Research on negotiations in organizations* (Vol. 6, pp. 209-225). Greenwich, CT: JAI Press.

Tinsley, C.H. (1998). Models of conflict resolution in Japanese, German, and American cultures. *Journal of Applied Psychology, 83*(2), 316-323.

Tinsley, C.H., & Brett, J.M. (in press). Managing workplace conflict in the United States and Hong Kong. *Organizational Behavior and Human Decision Processes.*

Tinsley, C.H., & Pillutla, M. (1999). The influence of culture on business negotiations in the United States and Hong Kong. *Journal of International Business Studies.*

Triandis, H.C. (1982). Dimensions of cultural variations as parameters of organizational theories. *International Studies of Management and Organization, 12*(4), 139-169.

Tsui, A.S., Egan, T.D., & O'Reilly III., C.A. (1992). Being different: Relational demography and organizational attachment. *Administrative Science Quarterly, 37,* 549-579.

Turner, J.C., Sachdev, I., & Hogg, M.A. (1983). Social categorization, interpersonal attraction and group formation. *British Journal of Social Psychology, 22,* 227-239.

Tyler, T.R. (1987). Conditions leading to value expressive effects in judgments of procedural justice: A test of four models. *Journal of Personality and Social Psychology, 52,* 333-344.

Wall, J.A., Jr., & Blum, M.E. (1991). Negotiation. *Journal of Management, 17,* 273-303.

Walton, R.E., & Hackman, J.R. (1986). Groups under contrasting management strategies. In P.S. Goodman et al. (Eds.), *Designing effective work groups* (pp. 168-201). San Francisco: Jossey-Bass.

Watson, W.E., Kumar, K., & Michaelsen, L. (1993). Cultural diversity's impact on interaction processes and performance: Comparing homogeneous and diverse task groups. *Academy of Management Journal, 36,* 590-602.

Wellins, R.S., Wilson, R., Katz, A.J., Laughlin, P., Day, C.R., Jr., & Price, D. (1990). *Self-directed teams: A study of current practice.* Pittsburgh, PA: DDI.

PART III

COMMENTARY

CHAPTER 9

DOING JUSTICE TO ORGANIZATIONAL JUSTICE:
Forming and Applying Fairness Judgments

Jason A. Colquitt and Jerald Greenberg

ABSTRACT

The chapters in this volume examine two themes. Five chapters (Folger; Ambrose & Kulik; van den Bos; Bobocel & Holmvall; Steiner) consider why and how individuals form justice judgments. The remaining chapters (Gilliland & Gilliland; Leung, Su, & Morris; Shapiro & Tinsley) concern how justice theories can be applied to diversity management. We integrate these contributions by combining the authors' major ideas into an integrative model of the justice judgment process. We then apply this model to diversity management to examine the practical insights our framework offers. In so doing, we ask: Does the additional complexity inherent in the theoretical chapters improve our ability to apply organizational justice to organizational issues? Simply put, do the authors' ideas "do justice to organizational justice?" After addressing this question, we close by offering suggestions for managing the complexity-applicability tradeoff in the literature.

INTRODUCTION

In the previous decade, observers commenting on the state of the science in organizational behavior have painted wildly contrasting pictures of some of its most prominent sub-fields. Consider, for example, the following statements regarding the topics of leadership and goal setting.

> The field of leadership is presently in a state of ferment and confusion. Most of the theories are beset with conceptual weaknesses and lack strong empirical support. Empirical studies have been conducted on leadership effectiveness, but many of the results are contradictory or inconclusive. The confused state of the field can be attributed in large part to the disparity of approaches, the narrow focus of most researchers, and the absence of broad theories to integrate findings from the different approaches. (Yukl & Van Fleet, 1992, p. 149)

> Locke and Latham report on hundreds of studies, performed in many countries and in the laboratory as well as in the work environment. They offer us a theory and guidelines for conducting goal setting studies. And they suggest that goal setting does not apply just to work—it applies to life! They have achieved a great deal, and goal-setting theory indeed offers us much in the way of theory and application. Not the least, Locke and Latham have offered us a model against which we can consider what has been left out and what remains to be understood. (Pervin, 1992, p. 164)

Although the leadership literature was launched on the simple premise that a few leader behaviors explained most of the variance in subordinates' satisfaction and performance, it is now criticized for its complexity. Indeed, most contemporary leadership theories contain several different independent variables (e.g., autocratic style, charisma) as well as a wide variety of mediators (e.g., goal clarity, motivation) and moderators (e.g., task structure, follower maturity) (Yukl, 1997). These theories, often represented by complex diagrams or decision trees, likely would seem overwhelming to managers who dared look to them for practical guidance.

Likewise, the goal setting literature also began with a simple idea—namely, that difficult and specific goals boost motivation and performance more than "do your best" goals (Locke & Latham, 1990). Over time, goal setting theory has grown more complex, adding a few mediators (e.g., self-efficacy, task strategies) and moderators (e.g., task difficulty, goal commitment) (Klein, Wesson, Hollenbeck, & Alge, 1999; Locke & Latham, 1990). Unlike the leadership literature, however, the goal setting literature has retained a good deal of its simplicity. As a result, goal setting principles are applied routinely by managers as part of their performance management and compensation strategies (Hale & Whitlam, 1999).

As in the case of these more venerable literatures, the organizational justice literature was initially quite simple. By adhering to certain rules (e.g., equitable outcomes, consistent procedures, providing voice), managers could improve employee satisfaction, commitment, and compliance with decisions (Greenberg, 1987). Few studies examined mediators; fewer still examined moderators. Recent years, however, have signaled a growth spurt in the justice literature. The field has moved beyond the "intellectual adolescence" that characterized its development a decade ago (Greenberg, 1993). Indeed, conceptualizations of justice have become more complex (e.g., Bies 2001; Colquitt, in press), theories of justice have become more intricate (e.g., Folger & Cropanzano, 1998, 2001; Lind, 2001), and increasing attention is being paid to moderator variables (e.g., Skarlicki, Folger, & Tesluk, 1999; Sweeney & McFarlin, 1997).

Many of the chapters in this volume continue this trend toward complexity. At a general level, five of the chapters (specifically, those by: Folger, Ambrose & Kulik, van den Bos, Bobocel & Holmvall, and Steiner) concern why and how individuals form justice judgments. The authors draw on literatures from cognitive psychology, culture, and ethics to present a much more thorough examination of the formation of justice judgments than heretofore available. Given our observations about the turns taken by the literatures in leadership and goal setting, we wonder if this increased complexity is justified. Is it good for the literature as a whole, adding needed richness, or does it lead us down the path toward inappropriate complexity? Put differently, which literature do we most want to resemble—leadership or goal setting? Our take on this question is straightforward. We contend that the increased complexity is justified *if* it helps us apply justice theories to real organizational problems. To the extent that it does, then promoting such complexity is effectively "doing justice to organizational justice"—not coincidently, the title of this chapter—by enhancing both its predictive validity and its potential for application.

With this in mind, we will attempt to integrate the chapters in this volume by examining the extent to which the visions of justice judgment formation articulated in the five aforementioned chapters shed light on the practical problems of diversity and multicultural relations addressed in the three remaining chapters (by Gilliland & Gilliland; Leung, Su, & Morris; and Shapiro & Tinsley). To that end, we have divided this chapter into three major sections. First, we will synthesize the ideas about justice judgment formation presented in this book by proposing an integrative model. This model combines the major characteristics of the authors' formulations, along with a few ideas of our own. Second, we will consider the insights provided by this model for practical applications in the areas of diversity training, multicultural relations, and multicultural disputes. Our focal key question is: What practical insights do the ideas about justice judgment formation offer in these three contexts? Finally, in closing we will offer more general observations about how to manage the complexity-applicability tradeoff in the justice literature.

WHY AND HOW DO INDIVIDUALS FORM JUSTICE JUDGMENTS?

Five of the chapters in this volume examine why and how individuals form justice judgments. For example, Folger examines the motives behind justice and concerns about justice. Ambrose and Kulik peer inside the "black box" of justice judgment formation. van den Bos examines how individuals combine and prioritize available information in arriving at justice judgments. Bobocel and Holmvall examine the validity of the distinctions separating some types of justice information from others. Finally, Steiner looks at the role of culture in justice judgment formation.

Each of the authors tackles a related but distinct facet of the justice judgment process. By way of integrating these authors' ideas, we have combined many of their arguments into the model shown in Figure 1. Our intention is not to propose yet another approach to the justice judgment

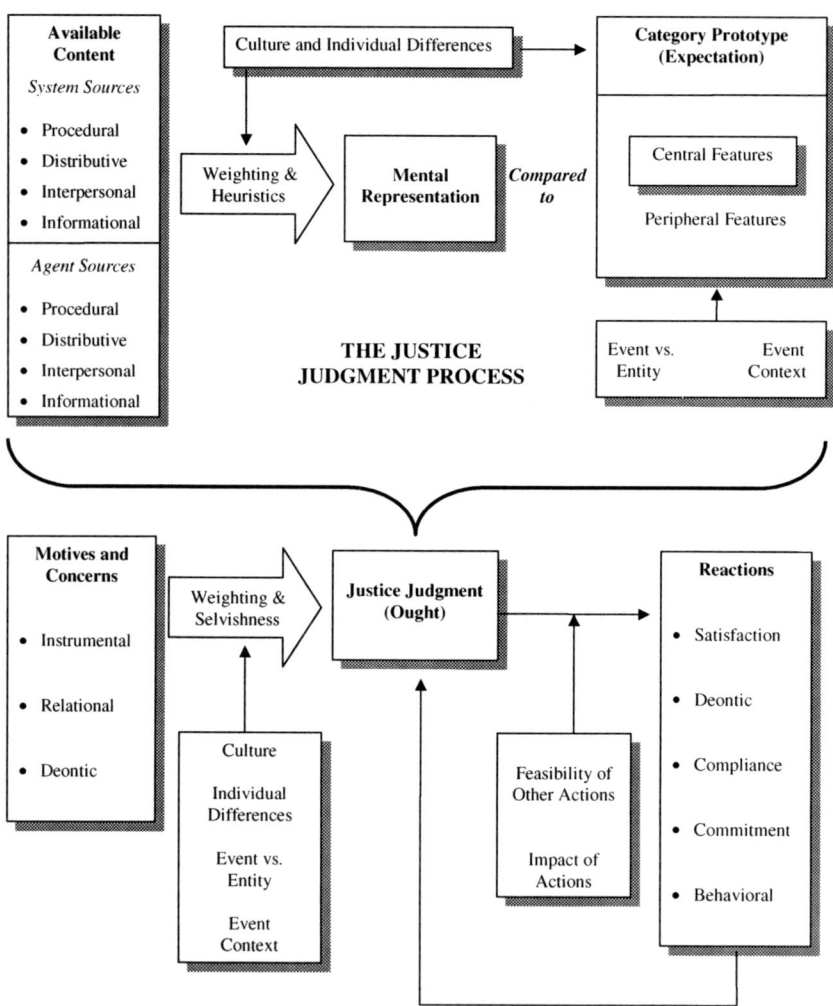

Figure 1. An integrative model of why and how people form justice judgments.

process, but to integrate the authors' complementary views into a single formulation. We could not resist the temptation, however, to expand their ideas by interjecting several additional sub-processes that either are implicit in the authors' discussions, or that seem a natural outgrowth of them. We caution the reader that Figure 1 does not capture the authors' ideas in their entirety, but integrates what we believe are some of their most important points. After explaining the model, we will consider the insights it provides into the applied areas of diversity training, promoting multicultural relations, and managing multicultural disputes.

Justice Motives: Why Do People Care About Justice?

Our model begins where this volume begins, by asking, "why do individuals care about justice?" Three major answers predominate. First, the instrumental model of justice contends that people attend to fairness insofar as it allows them to gauge the degree to which their long-term economic interests are enhanced or protected (Lind & Tyler, 1988; Thibaut & Walker, 1975). In other words, justice is valued because it creates a "level playing field" that protects one's self-interest. Second, the relational model of justice contends that people care about fairness insofar as it allows them to gauge the degree to which they are valued by the collectives to which they belong (Lind & Tyler, 1988; Tyler & Lind, 1992). That is, justice is valued because it reaffirms an individual's sense of self-worth and value to the collective.

Folger argues that these approaches fail to acknowledge the possibility that justice is an "ought," an end in itself. That is, people value justice simply because it is moral—a third major motive. In Folger's terminology, justice is "deontic," that is, it is an obligation or duty (in keeping with his moral virtues model of justice; Folger, 1998). In support of his deontic view, Folger reviews circumstances in which justice is valued even when economic and collective esteem-based outcomes do not appear to exist, such as when an individual acting behind a veil of anonymity still behaves fairly toward a stranger.

Greenberg (in press) has noted that all three reasons could be subsumed under the motive of self-interest, from both reactive and proactive perspectives (on the proactive-reactive distinction, see Greenberg & Wiethoff, 2000). Reactively, instrumental concerns express self-interest regarding economic outcomes whereas relational concerns express self-interest regarding interpersonal outcomes (e.g., social approval). Proactively, instrumental and relational motives may promote compliance with decisions. As for deontic motives, decision makers may follow moral duties so as to protect their self-images or to avoid feelings of guilt. Similarly, the subjects of decisions may attend to deontic concerns to ensure that they belong to virtuous collectives, thereby reaffirming their own moral philosophies.

Putting this counterargument aside, given that each of these motives are reflected by the contributions to this book, our model recognizes instrumental, relational, and deontic reasons for attending to justice issues. If viewed from a proactive perspective, where the individual is a decision maker concerned with promoting fairness, the three reasons comprise motives to create and foster justice. If viewed from a reactive perspective, where the individual is subject to a decision-making process, the three reasons comprise concerns that activate justice evaluations.

Weighting of Justice Motives

A key contribution of Folger's chapter is the introduction of the concept of pluralism, or "selvishness." Folger argues that people care about justice for different reasons based on multiple selves, and that these selves come together to examine justice questions. Figure 1 represents this concept using the "weighting and selvishness" arrow linking motives and concerns with justice judgments.

Implicit in Folger's selvishness argument is the idea that individuals hold different "motive primacies"—that is, implicit beliefs in the relative importance of various motives. For example, Person A's justice examinations may be based 50% on instrumental concerns, 25% on relational concerns, and 25% on deontic concerns. Person B's examinations may be based 10% on instrumental concerns, 40% on relational concerns, and 50% on deontic concerns. What could explain such variation? As suggested by Steiner's contribution to this volume, one potential factor is culture. For example, following Hofstede's (1980) typology, people from collective or low power distance cultures may weigh relational and deontic motives more heavily than instrumental ones (Brockner, Ackerman, Greenberg, Gelfand, Francesco, Chen, Leung, Bierbrauer, Gomez, Kirkman, & Shapiro, in press). Likewise, members of cultures high in uncertainty avoidance or achievement may give primacy to instrumental motives (Miles & Greenberg, 1993).

Some of the individual differences discussed by Ambrose and Kulik also may have similar effects. For example, consistent with their tendency to attend to distributive issues (Brockner & Adsit, 1986; Sweeney & McFarlin, 1997) men may weigh instrumental motives more heavily than women. Indeed, research has shown that men are more likely to divide resources in proportion to people's relative contributions (i.e., equitably) whereas women are more inclined to ignore these differences, favoring equal allocations (Major & Deaux, 1982).

Two additional factors may affect the weighting of justice motives or concerns. The first is whether an individual is concerned about the fairness of a specific decision event (e.g., a performance appraisal evaluation, a pay raise) or the fairness of the organization as a whole—what Cropanzano, Byrne, Bobocel, and Rupp (in press) refer to as the distinction between "event" and "entity." Individuals may weigh instrumental concerns and motives more heavily when examining entity issues, so as to protect long-term economic viability. However, someone concerned about the fairness of a specific decision event will likely be more highly concerned with the context of the event. In keeping with Ambrose and Kulik, certain decision contexts may increase the importance of specific motives or concerns. For example, deontic motives may take primacy in selection decisions, given the moral and ethical ideals that underlie equal employment opportunity.

Regardless of how the three motives or concerns are weighted, they trigger people's examination of justice issues. If the situation is proactive, decision makers examine the justice of their own conduct (real or potential). If the situation is reactive, however, subjects of the decision assess the justice of their own treatment. Either way, the process of arriving at a justice judgment begins. The justice judgment process, as we have described it here, is represented in the upper portion of Figure 1.

Justice-Relevant Information

As noted by van den Bos, the justice judgment process almost always begins with incomplete information. For example, in judging outcome fairness, people do not always know the input and outcome components of Adams's (1965) equity theory equation. Lacking such information, they fall back on whatever information they do possess, which often consists of procedural justice criteria. In the parlance of fairness heuristic theory (Lind, 2001; van den Bos, Lind, & Wilke, in press), people use heuristics, or shortcuts, to arrive at justice judgments quickly. They then use these judgments to assess whether or not to cooperate with a potentially untrustworthy party.

We acknowledge in Figure 1 that the justice judgment process begins with incomplete procedural content, distributive content, interpersonal content, and informational content. Whatever information may be available is subjected to a weighting and heuristic usage process of the type discussed by van den Bos. If lacking distributive content for a distributive judgment, then procedural information may be weighed and used as a heuristic. If lacking procedural content for a procedural judgment, distributive information may be weighed and used as a heuristic. Thus, when examining how people form justice judgments, it is necessary to consider the content they have readily available (Lind, 2001; van den Bos et al., in press).

The reader will note that Figure 1 characterizes procedural, distributive, interpersonal, and informational content as inputs into the justice judgment process. At this point, however, fairness heuristic theory has not been tested using the full menu of justice information. As reviewed by van den Bos, tests of the theory have focused primarily on voice as a heuristic for equity or trust information. Less clear is the heuristic value of Leventhal's (1980) less control-based justice criteria, such as consistency, bias suppression, or correctability. Also unclear is the heuristic value of interpersonal and informational content. Because these types of information are often related to qualities of replaceable decision making agents, rather than more permanent formalized systems, they may be poor proxies for trust. At the same time, however, people are often able to evaluate dignity and respect more quickly than other procedural characteristics.

In keeping with Bobocel and Holmvall's chapter, we also note that Figure 1 distinguishes between procedural content and interpersonal and informational content. These authors review theoretical, operational, and empirical evidence supporting a distinction between procedural justice and interactional justice. Specifically, they argue that the two constructs differ in terms of the way they signal an agent's intentions, as well as in their connection to various outcome variables. Although Bobocel and Holmvall do not distinguish between the interpersonal and informational facets of interactional justice, we maintain this distinction in Figure 1 insofar as it is in keeping with recent factor-analytic and meta-analytic evidence (Colquitt, in press; Colquitt, Conlon, Wesson, Porter, & Ng, in press; Thurston, 2000).

Bobocel and Holmvall also distinguish between justice content and justice source, noting that operationalizations of procedural justice and interactional justice typically vary with respect to both content (i.e., voice, consistency vs. respect and explanations) and source (i.e., human agent vs. formalized policy systems). This key distinction also is reflected in Figure 1. Procedural justice can be a function of either formalized systems or human agents, as can interpersonal and informational justice (Blader & Tyler, 2000; Byrne & Cropanzano, 2000; Colquitt, in press; Colquitt et al., in press; Masterson, Bartol, & Moye, 2000). For example, companies may mandate that key information be made readily available to employees through the use of message board postings. Doing so promotes informational justice through formalized policies. Fortunately, recent research is beginning to examine Bobocel and Holmvall's distinction by crossing justice content with justice source to examine their joint effects (Blader & Tyler, 2000; Byrne & Cropanzano, 2000; Masterson et al., 2000).

The Justice Category Prototype

In Figure 1 we suggest that procedural, distributive, interpersonal, and informational content, whether from system or agent sources, are subjected to weighting and heuristic usage to form mental representations of one's own treatment. Following Ambrose and Kulik, that representation is then compared to a justice category prototype. This prototype possesses central features that are very typical of the "just" or "fair" category, as well as peripheral features that do not always fit these categories.

Category prototypes may be affected by several factors. For example, Steiner reviews several potential relationships between 13 cultural characteristics and "justice expectations"—a concept similar to, if not identical to, the concept of justice prototypes. Specifically, drawing on Lytle, Brett, Barsness, Tinsley, and Janssens (1995), individuals from achievement-oriented cultures may have justice prototypes in which voice is a central feature. By contrast, individuals from ascription-oriented cultures may consider voice to be a peripheral category feature. People from idealistic cultures may have prototypes with ethicality as a central feature, whereas those from pragmatic cultures will see ethicality as a peripheral feature. Although not directly suggested by Steiner, it also may be the case that culture affects the weighting of the information used to create the mental representation in the first place. For example, people from low context cultures may weigh informational content more heavily in creating their mental representations than their counterparts from high context cultures.

Ambrose and Kulik review research linking additional individual differences to category prototypes. For example, people who have developed expertise in decision making (possibly due to having considerable tenure as a manager) may have prototypes composed of many central features. Women, for example, may possess justice prototypes in which interpersonal content is central, whereas men may possess prototypes in which interpersonal content is peripheral. As with culture, such individual differences also may affect the weighting of information used to create the mental representation. For example, whereas experts may weigh procedural and informational content most heavily, novices may weigh distributive and interpersonal content most heavily.

Two additional factors may affect the composition of the justice category prototype. The first is the "event vs. entity" distinction noted earlier (Cropanzano et al., in press). When creating prototypes for "fair organizations," individuals may look to procedural content as a central feature given its longer-lasting nature. More episodic content, like distributive or interpersonal justice, may play a central role in event prototypes. Entity prototypes also are likely to possess a larger number of central features, as noted by Ambrose and Kulik in their discussion of superordinate-level prototypes. If forming category prototypes for an event, the specific event context likely will affect which features are central and which are peripheral. For example, the prototype for pay plan decisions may rely on distributive content (e.g., merit) as a central feature, whereas the prototype for drug test decisions may emphasize procedural content (e.g., accuracy).

Figure 1 shows that an individual's mental representation of a decision-making event is compared to a category prototype, and that comparison results in a justice judgment. Whenever individuals' mental representations do not possess the same features as the prototype, they decide they have been treated unfairly. Cast in terms of Folger and Cropanzano's (1998, 2001) fairness theory, the decision maker should have acted differently. From Folger's deontic perspective, by acting in an unjust manner, the decision maker has failed to uphold an "ought."

Once the justice judgment process is complete, the individual's judgment affects his or her reactions. We list several such reactions in Figure 1, although admittedly, our list is far from exhaustive. As discussed by Folger, justice judgments have strong effects on satisfaction reactions and deontic reactions. The latter consist of morally based reactions, such as righteous indignation. Also shown in Figure 1 are compliance, commitment, and behavioral reactions, several forms of which have been meta-analytically linked to justice judgments (Colquitt et al., in press). Consistent with fairness theory, these relationships become stronger as the perceived impact of the decision maker's actions becomes stronger (Folger & Cropanzano, 1998, 2001). The relationships also become stronger if the decision maker could have acted in a different manner (i.e., he or she had other feasible courses of action available).

Finally, we include a feedback loop in Figure 1, linking reactions back to justice judgments. In so doing, we acknowledge that the justice judgment process appears to be ongoing and continuous. Indeed, insofar as people are constantly updating the information they have available to them, and as they react to new events or changes in the work environment, the need to examine justice perceptions may be renewed (e.g., Lind, 2001).

APPLYING THE MODEL TO PRACTICAL ISSUES

Now that we have integrated various perspectives regarding how and why people make justice judgments (see Figure 1), the stage is set to examine the extent to which the complexities we have revealed facilitate our capacity to offer practical insight into real organizational issues. With this objective in mind, we will apply the integrative model to the three applications represented in this book to see if it enhances our understanding of organizational justice in those settings—diversity training (Gilliland & Gilliland), multicultural relations (Leung, Su, & Morris), and multicultural disputes (Shapiro & Tinsley).

We find it intriguing that these chapters deal with race, ethnicity, and culture because, although matters of justice are commonly voiced when addressing disparate treatment with respect to these variables, the organizational justice literature has widely ignored such matters (for an exception, see Greenberg & McCarty, 1990). Accordingly, we believe that these three chapters represent a long overdue application of justice concepts.

Justice and Diversity Training

In articulating their reasons for applying justice theories to diversity training, Gilliland and Gilliland ask, "Why is it that some diversity training initiatives can provide a competitive advantage, whereas others can result in lost morale and, in extreme cases, lawsuits?" Can the model in Figure 1 provide potential answers to this question? To examine this issue, let us begin by examining what might cause participants in diversity training programs to attend to justice issues. Specifically, participants may ask three justice-related questions: (1) Is the diversity training process helping me attain important outcomes? (2) Does the training suggest that I am a valued member of this organization? and (3) Does participating in this training meet a moral obligation on my part? Administrators of diversity training programs who fail to address these concerns will find themselves unprepared to address questions that may arise about the fairness of their training efforts.

Ironically, the only matter anticipated by most program administrators tends to be the matter of morality—Folger's deontic concern—despite the fact that it is the least visible in the justice literature. Administrators mistakenly may believe that employees will not question training fairness assuming that "diversity training is the right thing to do." However, Folger shows us that individuals rarely, if ever, consider justice for a single reason, suggesting instead that their "multiple selves" care about justice for a variety of different reasons. To be effective, diversity trainers should anticipate justice examinations by all participants, despite the fact that these may be prompted by different reasons.

If diversity trainers anticipate justice questions, how can they manage the justice judgment process? One way is to anticipate what content is available to participants for judging justice. In their Table 2, Gilliland and Gilliland review procedural, distributive, interpersonal, and informational content important in diversity training. Fairness heuristic theory suggests that individuals make hurried justice judgments, using whatever information is available at the time (van den Bos; Lind, 2001). With this in mind, some of the information in Gilliland and Gilliland's Table 2 may not be known to training participants unless trainers make it a point to provide that information. For example, participants may not know all the specific groups targeted for training, and as a result, they may not be able to judge whether the equality, equity, or need norm has been followed.

Lacking that information, van den Bos would suggest that participants will rely on procedural content (e.g., use of a diversity council, unbiased criteria) as a heuristic for distributive content. However, this information may be lacking as well. All that may be left is to judge the reasonableness of managers' explanations or the sensitivity of their communication (fairness heuristic theory is only just beginning to examine the role of interpersonal and informational justice; Lind, Greenberg, Scott, & Welchans, 2000). The fairness of the entire training assignment decision may rest on one person's words—a person who may not be adequately trained for the task at hand. Thus, when presiding over a legitimately fair training program, managers should take steps to ensure that trainees have information available that illustrates that fairness, reinforcing it in their minds, so as to avoid the tendency for participants to rely on potentially damaging heuristics. This is in keeping with Greenberg's (1990) arguments about the importance of taking proactive steps to promote impressions of organizational justice in other settings.

Extending the question of what information is available is the question of what information will be used. Extrapolating ideas from Ambrose and Kulik, and from Steiner, we suggested that culture and other individual differences affect how available information is weighed in forming a mental representation of a decision event. Because participants in diversity training sessions are likely to come from diverse groups, they may be expected to focus on different content when forming their personal heuristics. As a result, promoting justice in such groups may be affected by the "weakest link in the chain." In other words, one individual's expressions of unfairness may adversely influence other participants' social constructions of fairness (Lind, Kray, & Thompson, 1998), potentially "poisoning" the entire group.

Regardless of the information used, diversity training participants will create mental representations of training justice, which in turn will be compared to their own category prototypes for diversity training. These prototypes may be created to represent the entire diversity training experience as a whole or only specific facets of it (e.g., training assignment, delivery of content, evaluation). Regardless of the level of specificity, the category prototype will depend on culture and other individual differences (Ambrose & Kulik; Steiner). Again, justice judgments may be dependent on the weakest link in the fairness chain, insofar as different participants may focus on different central features. For example, although the training assignment and content delivery may be considered fair according to nine of the twelve criteria in Steiner's Table 3, individuals who look to the other three as central features still may arrive at negative justice judgments. Likewise, participants who have been more involved in training throughout their careers may be expected to have developed more central features and fewer peripheral features than those who are less experienced.

How can managers in charge of diversity training cope with these potential differences? One strategy is to ensure that all phases of training comply with all justice criteria. This solution will not be feasible, however, whenever the central features of different people's category prototypes conflict with one another. For example, Gilliland and Gilliland suggest that an equality distribution norm should be observed in diversity training sessions insofar as everyone within an organization is assigned to the program. However, they also suggest that a need-based distribution norm is appropriate for some forms of training, as only those most need training participate.

What happens when the central features of some participants conflict with those of others? In such cases, trainers may need to spend more time on the person analysis phase of the training needs assessment, which provides trainers with important information needed to design the training environment (e.g., Colquitt, LePine, & Noe, 2000; Goldstein, 1991; Noe & Colquitt, in press). Perhaps the simplest way to assess differences in trainees' justice prototypes is to collect information on their expectations, much as trainers may gather information on trainees' motivation and readiness for training. If it proves impossible to supply certain central justice features, then part of the training could involve convincing participants about what features make diversity training fair. For example, trainers could emphasize the centrality of features on which most participants agree, such as relevant content, lack of bias, and the use of extensive information.

In summary, the chapters on why and how individuals form justice judgments do, in fact, provide valuable insight into Gilliland and Gilliland's question regarding why some diversity training programs succeed while others fail. Specifically, our analysis suggests that such programs may fail because they pay little, if any, attention to why people attend to justice, what information they use to assess justice, what expectations they hold regarding justice content, and how much these factors can vary from trainee to trainee. There can be no doubt that the theoretical questions raised by our integrative model currently outpace our empirical answers. Still, the chapters in this volume provide a useful framework for understanding the complexities of justice as they are experienced in organizational settings such as diversity training.

Justice and Multicultural Relations

As Gilliland and Gilliland acknowledge, diversity training is only a part of most organizations' larger diversity management efforts. Also important is the day-to-day management of multicultural interactions—the type discussed by Leung, Su, and Morris. Can our integrative model shed light on improving such multicultural relations?

To answer this question, we begin by again asking what might cause individuals to examine justice issues in multicultural contexts. Leung et al. identify both instrumental and relational concerns. Interestingly, they argue that the concerns weighed most heavily depend on culture (and identification with one's culture) and to event context. People working in multicultural settings therefore may examine justice for a variety of reasons.

Leung et al. also suggest that, when examining justice, people in multicultural settings may weigh available justice content differently. Specifically, they suggest that some cultures are more concerned with respectful and sincere treatment than with any particular distributive or procedural content (for example, as Kidder & Muller, 1991, reveal, this is the case in Japan). Individuals from such cultures may value interpersonal content for its heuristic value, using it as a proxy for trust rather than voice or other procedural content (Lind, 2001; van den Bos et al., in press). Even if individuals do attend to the same type of content, however, they may focus on different types of data. For example, Leung et al. argue that people in some cultures judge equity using job performance as an input, whereas people in other cultures judge equity using relationships or seniority as inputs.

Moreover, even if people from different cultures attend to similar distributive and procedural content, they may compare that content to different category prototypes. Leung et al. discuss two contrasting diversity strategies: treat everyone the same, regardless of culture, or treat people differently according to culture. These two strategies subsume a variety of conflicting justice features. Whereas the former appeals to equality distribution norms and consistency and bias suppression procedural norms, the latter appeals to equity or need distribution norms and representativeness procedural norms. The problems created by these strategies, discussed by Leung et al., can be explained by differences in central and peripheral prototype features.

As suggested by Ambrose and Kulik, central and peripheral prototype features also differ as a function of context. Indeed, as Leung et al. note, "the impact of each approach differs depending upon context and domain." They then review several different event contexts, including conflict resolutions, reward allocations, and disciplinary actions, noting that even within cultures, what is considered fair in one context often is not considered fair in another. For example, people from Asian cultures tend to view disciplinary actions from the perspective of collective responsibility. In such cases, the equality norm tends to be followed although it often results in having innocent parties bear some of the responsibility for others' wrongdoings. By contrast, these same cultures also may favor an equity norm for allocating various interpersonal rewards. Clearly, the view that certain norms prevail across all settings within cultures is overly simplistic, and may well be responsible for the failure to find consistent culture-based predictions of justice behavior (Miles & Greenberg, 1993).

Thus far, we have analyzed the justice judgment process across individuals in a multicultural context. However, Leung et al. also discuss differences in reactions to justice judgments. Specifically, they review research on the universalistic attribution bias and the cultural attribution bias. The latter involves overemphasizing culture as a cause of behavior. Interestingly, whereas this bias can have many adverse effects (e.g., stereotypic confirmation, ingroup favoritism), it also may lessen the effects of negative justice judgments. For example, people possessing a cultural attribution bias may attribute an individual's unjust behavior to culture: "I find that unfair, but then again, he's doing exactly what his culture teaches him to do."

In summary, many elements of our integrative model are relevant to Leung et al.'s analysis of multicultural relations. However, as is the case with diversity training, the theoretical basis for our model lies beyond existing empirical support. This state of affairs leaves it unclear how to tailor decision-making processes to cultural groups, or how to react to attributional or ingroup biases. What is clear, however, are the challenges that multicultural contexts place on the informational aspect of justice. To the extent that decision makers are attempting to tailor decision processes to cultural values (for example, using seniority as an input into equity decisions), they need to explain themselves completely, reasonably, and honestly. After all, it is precisely when individuals lack knowledge of intentions that they are most likely to resort to potentially damaging heuristics.

Justice and Multicultural Disputes

By applying justice theories to multicultural disputes, Shapiro and Tinsley's contribution complements the work of Gilliland and Gilliland, and of Leung et al. In particular, Shapiro and Tinsley examine how culture impacts the effectiveness of various dispute resolution procedures. Does our integrative model provide a useful framework for examining these types of issues? We believe it does.

To begin, let us examine why people involved in disputes care about justice. An especially salient concern is the protection of valued economic outcomes, making instrumental concerns a likely trigger of justice examinations. However, Shapiro and Tinsley also review the potential importance of relational motives. Folger's deontic motives, which are likely so crucial in diversity training contexts, may be less critical in dispute-resolution cases.

Shapiro and Tinsley explain that trust is a critical factor in dispute resolution, although, as van den Bos notes, trust information is usually lacking in such situations. Accordingly, people will use available information as a proxy for trust. And, the most readily available types of information, according to Shapiro and Tinsley, are process control and decision control. Although bias suppression is another important procedural quality, it is far more difficult to observe, and therefore, less likely to be used.

The need to substitute procedural factors as a heuristic for trust may be especially important when the parties called upon to help resolve a dispute are peers, although as Shapiro and Tinsley note, their trustworthiness is likely to be unknown. These authors also note that the strength of this effect depends on the cultural characteristics of the individuals involved. For example, they argue that people from high-power distance cultures may be uncomfortable using peers to help resolve conflicts. To the extent that those individuals weigh procedural factors heavily, as proxies for trust, the linkage between culture and heuristic usage we specify in Figure 1 is supported.

In terms of our model, after disputants weigh process control and decision control to create mental representations of the dispute event, they will compare that representation to a category prototype. Here, Shapiro and Tinsley draw on research similar to that used by Steiner and by Ambrose and Kulik. Whereas process control and decision control are likely to be central features of most individuals' dispute resolution prototypes, culture affects both. Specifically, Shapiro and Tinsley suggest that process control and decision control will be peripheral features for individuals from cultures with high power distance, high determinism, and strong preferences for indirect communication.

Interestingly, Shapiro and Tinsley suggest that the reason why process control is a central feature in many dispute prototypes is its effect on interpersonal sensitivity. The idea that one piece of justice content can have a causal effect on another piece is an idea not often explored in the justice literature. At the least, it supports some of Bobocel and Holmvall's arguments for separating structural and interactional components of procedural justice. Without subscribing to a multicomponent model of justice, it is impossible to examine potential causal effects among justice types. Although Shapiro and Tinsley do not review cultural effects on the centrality of interpersonal sensitivity, Steiner suggests that dimensions such as power distance and masculinity-femininity could exert such effects.

After comparing their category prototypes to their mental representations, participants in a dispute will form a justice judgment. There are reasons to suspect that this judgment will have especially strong effects, even relative to some of the decision contexts discussed in other chapters. In dispute contexts, the third party in charge of resolving the dispute often has two courses of action: rule in favor of one party or rule in favor of the other (assuming a win-win compromise is not possible). Thus there exists a clear alternative action. Moreover, most disputes center around important disagreements, the resolution to which has a great impact on the parties involved. Fairness theory suggests that the feasibility of alternative actions, and the impact of decision maker actions, enhance the relationship between justice judgments and attitudinal and behavioral reactions (Folger & Cropanzano, 1998, 2001). Thus, to the extent that cultural differences lead to justice judgment differences, culture may have particularly strong effects in a dispute context.

In summary, several elements of our integrative model help inform the examination of multicultural disputes. However, as we acknowledged in the context of applications on diversity training and multicultural relations, our model exceeds existing empirical support. Importantly, however, Shapiro and Tinsley review several relevant studies and present a set of testable hypotheses bearing on many of the processes we described. These, we believe, will guide research that promises to clarify the role of justice in multicultural disputes.

Summary: Does the Integrative Model Inform Application?

Thus far, we have discussed the extent to which the conceptual ideas presented in this chapter, as summarized in our integrative model (see Figure 1), improve our ability to apply justice theories in the contexts of diversity training, multicultural relations, and multicultural disputes. Does, in fact, understanding why and how individuals form justice judgments help apply justice theories to these practical problems? At this point, our answer would have to be "yes and no." Not surprisingly, applying the model to the analyses of Gilliland and Gilliland, Leung et al., and Shapiro and Tinsley resulted in our raising more questions than we answered.

However, the model does provide a useful framework for understanding the complexities suggested in these authors' arguments. Notably, our analysis underscores a point that is critical to the organizational justice literature—namely, that being "fair" does not mean the same thing to all people all the time. The model also suggests several important directions for future research. But, perhaps the most important contribution of the model is that it asks the kinds of questions needed to solve the problems raised in the three diversity-related chapters. Specifically, the model acknowledges the complexity of justice in organizations marked by multiple cultures, multiple event contexts, multiple justice types and sources, and multiple concerns and motives.

FUTURE DIRECTIONS: MANAGING COMPLEXITY IN THE JUSTICE LITERATURE

That said, we may ask: Is the model in Figure 1 *too* complex? Although it provides a broad and integrative view of previously segmented approaches, does it also bring us closer to the types of decision-tree theories that have made the leadership literature impenetrable to practitioners (and new graduate students)? Or, does it supply, as Pervin (1992) put it, "a model against which we can consider what has been left out and what remains to be understood?" At the least, the ideas embedded in Figure 1 signal the continuation of a "growth spurt"—an end to the intellectual adolescence of organizational justice (Greenberg, 1993), and a step toward adulthood.

Thus, as the literature enters its next stage of existence, it may be worthwhile to recommend some ground rules for managing the increases in complexity represented in this volume. Some of these ground rules come in the form of suggestions for future research, whereas others are pleas against conducting unnecessary research. Still others are methodological suggestions that may clarify potential inconsistencies. We offer these suggestions in the hope that following our advice will improve the predictive validity of justice theories while simultaneously enhancing their applied potential.

Literature Inconsistencies: Moderators or Sampling Error?

Many of the ideas expressed in this volume were inspired by the authors' awareness of inconsistencies in justice findings. For example, Ambrose and Kulik noted that the voice effect was significant in performance appraisal and grievance procedures (Greenberg, 1986; Fryxell & Gordon, 1989), but not relocation contexts (Daly & Geyer, 1994). Bobocel and Holmvall noted that supervisor-related citizenship behaviors were related to interactional justice, but not procedural or distributive justice (Moorman, 1991). Steiner noted that job satisfaction was related to distributive and procedural justice, but not to interactional justice, among Chinese employees (Leung, Smith, Wang, & Sun, 1996).

These results may be a function of moderators related to decision context, culture, individual differences, or other factors. However, such results also may be a function of sampling error. Colquitt et al. (in press) conducted a meta-analysis of the organizational justice literature, including many of the relationships cited above. For the voice effect, the uncorrected meta-analytic correlation between voice (or process control) and procedural fairness perceptions was .41, based on 46 studies with a combined sample size of 8,736. Most important to this discussion, 14% of the variance in the correlations from the 46 studies was a function of artifacts like sampling error. That the remaining 86% cannot be explained by sampling error suggests that moderators clearly exist in the voice effect.

In contrast, the uncorrected meta-analytic correlation between voice and organizational commitment was .22, and over 50% of the variance in study correlations was a function of artifacts like sampling error. Other relationships were even less indicative of moderators. For example, 15 studies examined the relationship between procedural justice and both individual and organization-referenced citizenship behaviors (i.e., OCBI and OCBO). Virtually all of the variance in OCBI correlations was explained by artifacts like sampling error; and 79% of the variance in

OCBO correlations. Thus, moderators do not appear to influence relationships with citizenship behaviors.

Of course, Colquitt et al. (in press) did not identify specific moderators in their review, except for the operationalization of the justice variable (e.g., fairness perceptions, Leventhal's criteria). Identifying moderators would involve, for example, creating a database with all 46 of the voice-procedural fairness perception correlations, then dummy coding them according to event context (e.g., performance appraisal, dispute resolution, relocation), culture (e.g., high vs. low power distance, individualism vs. collectivism), event vs. entity, or some other moderator. If the dummy codes are significantly related to the study correlations, then moderators are supported.

Unfortunately, such tests require a larger number of studies than are currently present in the justice literature. They also require a better representation of all levels of certain moderator variables. This point is particularly important with respect to culture. Meaningful tests of the ideas presented by Leung et al., Steiner, and Shapiro and Tinsley require that we conduct many more justice studies in other cultures. Likewise, to test the event context predictions of Ambrose and Kulik, we must conduct many more justice studies in the field, across a wider variety of event contexts.

To summarize, it may be too soon to tell if inconsistencies in the justice literature represent true moderators or simply the effects of sampling error. Although most of the relationships in Colquitt et al.'s review support the existence of moderators, some key relationships do not. Moreover, the composition of justice studies, in terms of both cultures and contexts, remains too homogeneous to test moderators meta-analytically. Thus, besides building moderators into justice theories, it is critical to continue testing current conceptualizations of justice in different cultures and different contexts, in order to build more data on potential moderators.

Type of Moderator: Strength vs. Direction

Assuming that future research can verify the existence of the moderators discussed in this volume, another critical issue is: What type of moderation is occurring? Consider the moderating role of individual differences, such as gender, on the relationship between voice and procedural fairness perceptions. Three general types of moderation effects are possible. First, the voice effect could be significant and positive for both genders, but more positive for one. Second, the voice effect could be significant and positive for one gender, but not significant for the other. Third, the voice effect could be significant and positive for one gender, but significant and negative for the other (i.e., a crossed interaction).

Sweeney and McFarlin (1997) examined gender as a moderator of the relationships between procedural and distributive justice and intention to stay. Their results suggested that procedural justice was significantly and positively related to intention to stay for both genders, albeit more positively for females. Their results also suggested that distributive justice was significantly and positively related to intention to stay for both genders, but in this case, more positively for males. This type of moderation does not warrant altering practical prescriptions insofar as either way, intentions to stay benefit from promoting both procedural justice and distributive justice.

Very few of the moderators proposed in this volume predict fully-crossed interactions. For example, most of the cultural effects proposed by Steiner alter only the strength of the effect, not the direction. This is true of the procedural justice relationships, although less so for distributive justice relationships. Indeed, one could envision a case in which the effects of an equity allocation norm are positive in individualist countries but negative in collectivist countries (e.g., Miles & Greenberg, 1993). This is a key point insofar as many of the more complex contingency theories of leadership were a reaction to leadership behaviors that were beneficial in some cases but detrimental in others. For example, Fiedler's (1967) well-known contingency theory suggested that relationship-oriented leadership was detrimental in highly favorable conditions (i.e., when there were good leader-follower relations, when task structure was high, and when the leader's power was high), but beneficial in moderately favorable conditions (Peters, Hartke, & Pohlmann, 1985).

Without crossed interactions, it may not be necessary to complicate the relatively simple practical implications of justice theories. Consider, for example, cases in which leaders are trained to act in a procedurally just manner, as in the study by Skarlicki and Latham (1997). As justice scholars, we could recommend that leaders be trained to act in accordance with all six of Leventhal's (1980) procedural justice rules. Would our advice change if a few studies indicated positive, but nonsignificant effects, for representativeness or correctability in the specific culture or event context in question? We believe, probably not.

Another worthwhile pursuit would be to arrive at a consensus on the most "universal" justice rules. In their discussion of justice category prototypes, Ambrose and Kulik distinguished between central and peripheral justice features. When judging entities, perhaps justice rules that always have positive effects, regardless of moderators, could be classified as central features whereas those that may have either positive or negative effects, depending on the moderators, could be classified as peripheral features. As our knowledge of "universalness" or "central vs. peripheral" progressed, we would be able to focus our practical applications on using the universal justice rules. Practicing managers, we suspect, would find these unqualified recommendations of greater use than the more typical "it depends" answers that moderators force us to use. Although some may argue that this may be an unwise move toward parsimony, we counter that it would be unwise only to the extent that universal justice features cannot be identified. And, in the absence of efforts to find such principles, we discourage readers from discounting this possibility.

Locating Moderators: Measurement Prescriptions

To the extent that organizational justice researchers focus on separating consistent, substantive moderator effects from those driven by study artifacts, improved measurement will be critical. Lind and Tyler (1988) distinguished between two general types of measures. Direct measures simply ask "how fair" something is; indirect measures ask about justice rules, such as voice or Leventhal's (1980) criteria. Colquitt et al.'s (in press) meta-analysis showed that indirect measures correlated more highly with most outcome measures than direct measures. Indirect measurement is particularly critical if cultural and contextual moderators are going to be examined. For example, assume that Leventhal's (1980) correctability rule is more critical in dispute resolution contexts than in compensation contexts. If the researcher simply asks, "how fair were the decision making procedures?" such differences will be missed. If an indirect measure had been used, however, then the researcher would have data on correctability (along with Leventhal's (1980) other rules).

If we agree that indirect measurement is needed, it becomes incumbent upon us to examine precisely what type of indirect items to use. Bobocel and Holmvall persuasively argue that procedural and interactional concepts should be separated. Specifically, they argue that the two concepts are theoretically distinct, can be measured separately, and have different antecedents and consequences. This is consistent with meta-analytic evidence showing that procedural, distributive, interpersonal, and informational justice are distinguishable from one another (Colquitt et al., in press). Recently, Colquitt (in press) has validated a measure of organizational justice that uses indirect measurement to assess all four justice dimensions, and his measure is also convertible to multiple event contexts. Using this type of standardized measure in different contexts and cultures would help ensure that differences across studies were a function of context instead of measurement.

Other measurement prescriptions also follow from Bobocel and Holmvall's chapter. For example, they note that justice content (procedural, distributive, interpersonal, or informational) must be distinguished from justice source (agent vs. system-originating). We can envision a situation in which one study would examine agent-originating voice in a performance appraisal context, while a second would examine system-originating voice in a compensation context. Without holding justice source constant across studies, it would be impossible to attribute differences in results to event contexts. Similar problems would arise, for example, if an event-based measure was used in one culture, and an entity-based measure was used in another. Differences across studies could be attributed either to culture or to measurement referent. With this in mind, we encourage future researchers to design their studies systematically, in a manner that enhances comparability between them.

Ending Unnecessary Distinctions

In their recent review, Cropanzano et al. (in press) noted, "Identifying moderator variables has become something of a growth industry in the organizational justice literature." Clearly, the chapters in this volume have continued this trend. One way to manage the increasing complexity created by contingency approaches is to eliminate distinctions that are unnecessary. Cropanzano and Ambrose (in press) discuss such unnecessary distinctions in their monistic perspective of organizational justice. These authors reviewed many differences in how justice scholars study procedural and distributive justice. For example, procedural justice is normally studied using adherence to normative rules, whereas distributive justice is normally studied using social comparisons. However, we know that procedural justice is affected by social comparisons in much the same manner as distributive justice (Grienberger, Rutte, & van Knippenberg, 1997; Lind et al., 1998).

Cropanzano and Ambrose (in press) have argued that the means vs. end distinction between procedural and distributive justice has created artificial differences in how these constructs are treated. Having theories of distributive justice, such as equity theory, and theories of procedural justice, such as the relational model, causes unnecessary segmentation in the literature. One way of limiting complexity in the literature is to build integrative justice theories, which are able to explain the effects of all four justice types: procedural, distributive, interpersonal, and informational. Fortunately, theories recently introduced in the literature accomplish this goal. Fairness theory, for example, considers all types of justice in predicting reactions to decision making events (Folger & Cropanzano, 1998, 2001). Fairness heuristic theory also has mechanisms for including all justice dimensions (Lind, 2001; van den Bos et al., in press).

CONCLUSION

The tension between complexity and parsimony—or predictive validity and applied potential—exists in all scientific literatures. Illustrating this, we opened this chapter by juxtaposing the leadership literature and the goal setting literature. Over the years, researchers in both fields reacted to inconsistencies in their literatures by introducing increasingly complex models that incorporated new mediating and moderating variables. However, whereas the goal setting literature retained a good deal of its simplicity and applied potential over time, the leadership literature became impenetrably intricate.

Which of these literatures do organizational justice researchers most want to resemble? If the answer is the goal setting literature—as we hope—then the challenge for future researchers will be to incorporate necessary complexities like multiple motives, cognitive heuristics, culture, individual differences, and event context without making our theories needlessly complex. How will we know when our models have become too complicated? A useful litmus test will be our ability to design field interventions around our justice theories. Greenberg and Lind (2000) have argued that the applied potential of the justice literature has yet to be realized. If the chapters in this volume improve our ability to increase satisfaction, commitment, citizenship, and performance in organizations, then the authors will have contributed worthwhile complexities. Put another way, their ideas will have "done justice to organizational justice."

REFERENCES

Adams, J.S. (1965). Inequity in social exchange. In L Berkowitz (Ed.), *Advances in experimental social psychology* (Vol.2, pp. 267-299). New York: Academic Press.

Blader, S.L., & Tyler, T.R. (2000, August). *A four-component model of procedural justice: What makes a process fair in work settings?* Paper presented at the meeting of the Academy of Management, Toronto, Canada.

Bies, R.J. (2001). Interactional (in)justice: The sacred and the profane. In J. Greenberg & R. Cropanzano (Eds.), *Advances in organizational justice.* Stanford, CA: Stanford University Press.

Brockner, J., Ackerman, G., Greenberg, J., Gelfand, M.J., Francesco, A.M., Chen, Z.X., Leung, K., Bierbrauer, G., Gomez, C., Kirkman, B.L., & Shapiro, D. (in press). Culture and procedural justice: The influence of power distance on reactions to voice. *Journal of Experimental Social Psychology.*

Brockner, J., & Adsit, L. (1986). The moderating impact of sex on the equity-satisfaction relationship: A field study. *Journal of Applied Psychology, 71,* 585-590.

Byrne, Z.S., & Cropanzano, R.S. (2000, April). *To which source do I attribute this fairness? Differential effects of multi-foci justice on organizational work behaviors.* Paper presented at the meeting of the Society for Industrial & Organizational Psychology. New Orleans, LA.

Colquitt, J.A. (in press). On the dimensionality of organizational justice: A construct validation of a measure. *Journal of Applied Psychology.*

Colquitt, J.A., Conlon, D.E., Wesson, M.J., Porter, C.O.L.H., & Ng, K.Y. (in press). Justice at the millennium: A meta-analytic review of 25 years of organizational justice research. *Journal of Applied Psychology.*

Colquitt, J.A., LePine, J.A., & Noe, R.A. (2000). Toward an integrative theory of training motivation: A meta-analytic path analysis of 20 years of research. *Journal of Applied Psychology, 85,* 678-707.

Cropanzano, R., & Ambrose, M.L. (in press). Procedural and distributive justice are more similar than you think: A monistic view and a research agenda. In J. Greenberg & R. Cropanzano (Eds.), *Advances in organizational justice.* Lexington, MA: New Lexington Press.

Cropanzano, R., Byrne, Z.S., Bobocel, D.R., & Rupp, D.E. (in press). Moral virtues, fairness heuristics, social entities, and other denizens of organizational justice. *Journal of Vocational Behavior.*

Daly, J.P., & Geyer, P.D. (1994). The role of fairness in implementing large-scale change: Employee evaluations of process and outcome in seven facility relocations. *Journal of Organizational Behavior, 15,* 623-638.

Fiedler, F.E. (1967). *A theory of leadership effectiveness.* New York: McGraw-Hill.

Folger, R. (1998). Fairness as a moral virtue. In M. Schminke (Ed.), *Managerial ethics: Moral management of people and processes* (pp. 13-34). Mahwah, NJ: Erlbaum.

Folger, R., & Cropanzano, R. (1998). *Organizational justice and human resource management.* Thousand Oaks, CA: Sage.

Folger, R., & Cropanzano, R. (2001). Fairness theory. In J. Greenberg & R. Cropanzano (Eds.), *Advances in organizational justice.* Stanford, CA: Stanford University Press.

Fryxell, G.E., & Gordon, M.T. (1989). Workplace justice and job satisfaction as predictors of satisfaction with union and management. *Academy of Management Journal, 32,* 851-866.

Goldstein, I.L. (1991). Training in work organizations. In M.D. Dunnette & L.M. Hough (Eds.), *Handbook of industrial and organizational psychology* (Vol. 2, pp. 507-620). Palo Alto, CA: Consulting Psychologists Press.

Greenberg, J. (1986). Determinants of perceived fairness of performance evaluations. *Journal of Applied Psychology, 71,* 340-342.

Greenberg, J. (1987). A taxonomy of organizational justice theories. *Academy of Management Review, 12,* 9-22.

Greenberg, J. (1990). Looking fair vs. being fair: Managing impressions of organizational justice. In B.M. Staw & L.L. Cummings (Eds.), *Research in organizational behavior* (Vol. 12, pp. 111-157). Greenwich, CT: JAI Press.

Greenberg, J. (1993). The intellectual adolescence of organizational justice: You've come a long way, maybe. *Social Justice Research, 6,* 135-148.

Greenberg, J. (in press). Setting the justice agenda: Unanswered questions about what? why? and how? *Journal of Vocational Behavior.*

Greenberg, J., & Lind, E.A. (2000). The pursuit of organizational justice: From conceptualization to implication to application. In C.L. Cooper & E.A. Locke (Eds.), *I/O psychology: What we know about theory and practice* (pp. 72-105). Oxford: Blackwell.

Greenberg, J., & McCarty, C. (1990). Comparable worth: A matter of justice. In G.R. Ferris & K.M. Rowland (Eds.), *Research in personnel and human resources management* (Vol. 8, pp. 265-301). Greenwich, CT: JAI Press.

Greenberg, J. & Wiethoff, C. (2000). Organizational justice as proaction and reaction: Implications for research and application. In R. Cropanzano (Ed.), *Justice in the workplace, Vol. 2: From theory to practice* (pp. 271-301). Mahwah, NJ: Lawrence Erlbaum Associates.

Grienberger, I.V., Rutte, C.G., & van Knippenberg, A.F.M. (1997). Influence of social comparisons of outcomes and procedures on fairness judgments. *Journal of Applied Psychology, 82,* 913-919.

Hale, R., & Whitlam, P. (1999). *Target setting and goal achievement: A practical guide for managers.* London: Kogan Page.

Hofstede, G. (1980). *Culture's consequences.* London: Sage.

Kidder, L.H., & Muller, S. (1991). What is "fair" in Japan? In H. Steensma & R. Vermunt (Eds.), *Social justice in human relations, Vol. 2: Societal and psychological consequences of justice and injustice* (pp. 139-154). New York: Plenum.

Klein, H.J., Wesson, M.J., Hollenbeck, J.R., & Alge, B.J. (1999). Goal commitment and the goal-setting process: Conceptual clarification and empirical synthesis. *Journal of Applied Psychology, 84,* 885-896.

Leung, K., Smith, P.B., Wang, Z., & Sun, H. (1996). Job satisfaction in joint venture hotels in China: An organizational justice analysis. *Journal of International Business Studies, 27,* 947-962.

Leventhal, G.S. (1980). What should be done with equity theory? In K.J. Gergen, M.S. Greenberg, & R.H. Willis (Eds.), *Social exchange: advances in theory and research* (pp. 27-55). New York: Plenum Press.

Lind. E.A. (2001). Fairness heuristic theory: Justice judgments as pivotal cognitions in organizational relations. In J. Greenberg & R. Cropanzano (Eds.), *Advances in organizational justice.* Stanford, CA: Stanford University Press.

Lind, E.A., Greenberg, J., Scott, K.S., & Welchans, T.D. (2000). The winding road from employee to complainant: Situational and psychological determinants of wrongful-termination claims. *Administrative Science Quarterly, 45,* 557-590.

Lind, E.A., Kray, L., & Thompson, L. (1998). The social construction of injustice: Fairness judgments in response to own and others' unfair treatment by authorities. *Organizational Behavior and Human Decision Processes, 75,* 1-22.

Lind, E.A., & Tyler, T.R. (1988). *The social psychology of procedural justice.* New York: Plenum Press.

Locke, E.A., & Latham, G.P. (1990). *A theory of goal setting and task performance.* Englewood Cliffs, NJ: Prentice Hall.

Lytle, A.L., Brett, J.M., Barsness, Z.I., Tinsley, C.H., & Janssens, M. (1995). A paradigm for cross-cultural research in organizational behavior. In L.L. Cummings & B.M. Staw (Eds.), *Research in organizational behavior* (Vol. 17, pp. 167-214). Greenwich, CT: JAI Press.

Major, B., & Deaux, K. (1982). Individual differences in justice behavior. In J. Greenberg & R. L. Cohen (Eds.), *Equity and justice in social behavior* (pp. 42-76). New York: Academic Press.

Masterson, S.S., Bartol, K.M., & Moye, N. (2000, April). *Interactional and procedural justice: Type versus source of fairness.* Paper presented at the meeting of the Society for Industrial & Organizational Psychology, New Orleans, LA.

Miles, J., & Greenberg, J. (1993). Cross-national differences in preferences for distributive justice norms: The challenge of establishing fair resource allocations in the European community. In J.B. Shaw, P.S. Kirkbride, & K.M. Rowland (Eds.), *Research in personnel and human resources management* (Supplement 3, pp. 133-156). Greenwich, CT: JAI Press.

Moorman, R.H. (1991). Relationship between organizational justice and organizational citizenship behavior: Do fairness perceptions influence employee citizenship. *Journal of Applied Psychology, 78,* 845-855.

Noe, R.A., & Colquitt, J.A. (in press). Planning for training impact: Principles of training effectiveness. In K. Kraiger (Ed.), *Creating, implementing, and managing effective training and development.* San Francisco: Jossey-Bass.

Pervin, L.A. (1992). The rational mind and the problem of volition. *Psychological Science, 3*, 162-164.

Peters, L.H., Hartke, D.D., & Pohlmann, J.T. (1985). Fiedler's contingency theory of leadership: An application of the meta-analysis procedures of Schmidt and Hunter. *Psychological Bulletin, 97*, 274-285.

Skarlicki, D.P., Folger, R., & Tesluk, P. (1999). Personality as a moderator in the relationship between fairness and retaliation. *Academy of Management Journal, 42*, 100-108.

Skarlicki, D.P., & Latham, G.P. (1997). Leadership training in organizational justice to increase citizenship behavior within a labor union: A replication. *Personnel Psychology, 50*, 617-633.

Sweeney, P.D., & McFarlin, D.B. (1997). Process and outcome: Gender differences in the assessment of justice. *Journal of Organizational Behavior, 18*, 83-98.

Thibaut, J., & Walker, L. (1975). *Procedural justice: A psychological analysis.* Hillsdale, NJ: Erlbaum.

Thurston, P. (2000, April). *Clarifying the structure of justice using perceptions of performance appraisal processes.* Paper presented at the meeting of the Society for Industrial & Organizational Psychology, New Orleans, LA.

Tyler, T.R., & Lind, E.A. (1992). A relational model of authority in groups. In M. Zanna (Ed.), *Advances in experimental social psychology* (Vol. 25, pp. 115-191). San Diego, CA: Academic Press.

van den Bos, K., Lind, E.A., & Wilke, H. (in press). The psychology of procedural justice and distributive justice viewed from the perspective of fairness heuristic theory. In R. Cropanzano (Ed.), *Justice in the workplace, Vol. 2: From theory to practice.* Hillsdale, NJ: Lawrence Erlbaum Associates.

Yukl, G. (1997). *Leadership in organizations* (4th ed.). Upper Saddle River, NJ: Prentice-Hall.

Yukl, G., & Van Fleet, D.D. (1992). Theory and research on leadership in organizations. In M.D. Dunnette, & L.M. Hough (Eds.), *Handbook of industrial and organizational psychology* (Vol. 3, pp. 147-197). Palo Alto, CA: Consulting Psychologists Press.

INFORMATION ON CONTRIBUTING AUTHORS

Maureen L. Ambrose is Professor of Management in the College of Business at the University of Central Florida. She received her Ph.D. in 1986 from the University of Illinois at Urbana-Champaign. Her research interests include organizational fairness, cognitive processes, and ethics. Her work has appeared in the *Academy of Management Review, Journal of Applied Psychology, Academy of Management Journal, Journal of Management, Organizational Behavior and Human Decision Processes* and *Administrative Sciences Quarterly*.

Ramona Bobocel is Associate Professor in the Department of Psychology at the University of Waterloo. Dr. Bobocel obtained her Ph.D. degree in Psychology at the University of Western Ontario in 1992. Her research focuses on the study of justice in work organizations and seeks to understand the basis of people's perceptions of fairness and unfairness. She has published her research in leading journals, including the *Journal of Applied Psychology, Journal of Personality and Social Psychology, Journal of Personality,* and *Journal of Management*. Dr. Bobocel currently serves on the editorial board of the *Journal of Organizational Behavior* and is Chair-elect of the Canadian Society of Industrial and Organizational Psychology, a division of the Canadian Psychological Association.

Jason A. Colquitt is Assistant Professor of Management at the University of Florida's Warrington College of Business. He received his Ph.D. in Organizational Behavior from Michigan State University. His research interests include organizational justice, team effectiveness, and personality influences on learning and task performance. He has published several articles on these and other topics in the *Academy of Management Journal, Journal of Applied Psychology,* and *Personnel Psychology*.

Robert Folger is Freeman Professor of Doctoral Studies and Research in the A. B. Freeman School of Business at Tulane University. He received his Ph.D. from the University of North Carolina, Chapel Hill, and was previously on Southern Methodist University's faculty. His research interests include behavioral ethics and decision-making, fairness, and motivation. His articles on such issues appear in the *Academy of Management Journal, Academy of Management Review, Journal of Applied Psychology,* and *Organizational Behavior and Human Decision Processes.* He is currently on the editorial boards of the *Academy of Management Review* and the *Journal of Organizational Behavior* and previously served on the board of the *Journal of Management.* His co-authored book with Cropanzano, *Organizational Justice and Human Resource Management,* was named 1998s best book by the International Association for Conflict Management. He has also won best-paper and new-concept awards from the Academy of Management's Organizational Behavior Division.

Cindi Gilliland received her doctorate in social psychology at Michigan State University in 1992. She is a Lecturer in the Management and Policy Department of the Eller College of Business and Public Administration at the University of Arizona, and is President of Gilliland Consulting, a management consulting firm in Tucson, Arizona. Clients of the company include Tucson Unified School District, Sargent Controls and Aerospace, Farmer's Investment Company, and the University of Phoenix. Dr. Gilliland's areas of specialty are communication, teambuilding, strategic planning, and diversity management. She has published numerous articles, both popular and scholarly, on topics ranging from decision making to diversity management. She is a member of the Society for Human Resource Management of Greater Tucson and the Southern Arizona Diversity Association.

Stephen Gilliland is Associate Professor and the FINOVA Fellow of Management and Policy in the Eller College of Business and Public Administration at the University of Arizona. He received his Ph.D. from Michigan State University and was previously on the faculty at Louisiana State University. Stephen's research interests include organizational justice, individual decision making, and the application of these areas to human resource policies and procedures. He has published numerous articles on these issues in the *Academy of Management Review, Journal of Applied Psychology, Personnel Psychology, Organizational Behavior and Human Decision Processes,* and *Journal of Management.* He is currently on the editorial boards of the *Journal of Applied Psychology* and *Personnel Psychology* and previously served on the board of the *Academy of Management Journal.* Stephen was the 1997 recipient of the Ernest J. McCormick Award for Early Career Contributions from the Society for Industrial and Organizational Psychology.

Jerald Greenberg (Ph.D., Industrial/Organizational Psychology, Wayne State University, 1975) is Abramowitz Professor of Business Ethics and Professor of Management and Organizational Behavior at the Ohio State University. Dr. Greenberg has authored over 130 publications, specializing in the topic of organizational justice. He has lectured extensively on this topic, with over 100 national and international professional presentations to his credit. Among Dr. Greenberg's publications are fifteen books, including *Advances in Organizational Justice* (with Cropanzano), *The Quest for Justice on the Job*, *Justice in Social Relations* (with Bierhoff and Cohen), and *Equity and Justice in Social Behavior* (with Cohen). He is a Fellow of both the American Psychological Association and the American Psychological Society. Among his professional honors are: a Fulbright Senior Research Fellowship (1980), the *New Concept Award* from the Organizational Behavior Division of the Academy of Management (1986), and the Best Paper Award from the Organizational Behavior Division of the Academy of Management (1998).

Camilla Holmvall is a Ph.D. student in the Department of Psychology at the University of Waterloo. Her research interests lie in the study of organizational justice. For her doctoral dissertation, she is investigating how people form judgments of fairness and unfairness.

Carol T. Kulik is Professor of Management in the College of Business at Arizona State University. She received her Ph.D. in 1987 from the University of Illinois at Urbana-Champaign. Her research interests include demographic diversity, organizational fairness, and cognitive processes in organizations. She serves on the editorial boards of the *Journal of Organizational Behavior* and the *Journal of Management*, and her work has been published in the *Academy of Management Review, Journal of Applied Psychology, Journal of Management, Journal of Organizational Behavior* and *Administrative Sciences Quarterly*.

Kwok Leung received his Ph.D. in Psychology from University of Illinois, Urbana-Champaign. He is a Professor of Management at the City University of Hong Kong. His research interests include justice, conflict resolution, social beliefs, and cross-cultural research methodology. He has co-authored *Methods and data analysis for cross-cultural research* (Sage) and co-edited *Conflict Management in Asia Pacific Rim* (Wiley), *Progress in Asian Social Psychology, Vol. 1* (Wiley), and *Innovations in cross-cultural psychology* (Swets & Zeitlinger). He is the Editor of *Asian Journal of Social Psychology*, and is on the editorial board of several journals, including *Journal of Cross-Cultural Psychology, Applied Psychology: An international Review*, and *Acta Psychologica Sinica*.

Michael W. Morris received his Ph.D. in Psychology from the University of Michigan. He is an Associate Professor of Organizational Behavior at the Graduate School of Business at Stanford University. His research focuses on social cognition, decision-making, and cross-cultural psychology.

Debra L. Shapiro (Ph.D., Northwestern University) is the Willard Graham Distinguished Professor of Management and Associate Dean for Ph.D. Programs at the Kenan-Flagler Business School at The University of North Carolina at Chapel Hill. Debra is a Past Chair of the Conflict Management Division of the National Academy of Management (where she won Best Paper Awards in 1991, 1992, and 1996). Debra's research focuses on how to manage conflict (e.g., change-resistance, perceived injustice/mistreatment, negotiations) in organizations—especially in cross-cultural and team-contexts. Debra's publications are in numerous journals and books including *The Administrative Science Quarterly, The Academy of Management Journal, The Academy of Management Review, Organizational Behavior and Human Decision Processes, Journal of Applied Psychology, Journal of Personality and Social Psychology, Journal of Experimental Social Psychology, International Journal of Conflict Management, The Negotiation Journal, Organizational Dynamics, Research on Negotiation in Organizations* (Vol. 7), *Advances in Organizational Justice, Research on Managing Groups and Teams* (Vol. 4), and others.

Daniel P. Skarlicki is an Associate Professor at the Faculty of Commerce, University of British Columbia, in Vancouver, Canada. He received his Ph.D. from the University of Toronto. He has taught at the University of Toronto, Tulane University in New Orleans, and the University of Calgary. Dr. Skarlicki has also provided training to corporate executives in Canada, the United States, Mexico, Chile, and Taiwan. Dr. Skarlicki's research focuses on organizational justice in the workplace. His work has been published in *Academy of Management Journal, Administrative Science Quarterly, Journal of Applied Psychology, Personnel Psychology,* and *Applied Psychology: An International Review.* He serves on the editorial board of the *Journal of Organizational Behavior.* In 2000, he received the Ascendant Scholar Award for the Western Academy of Management.

Dirk D. Steiner is Professor of Psychology at the Université de Nice-Sophia Antipolis in Nice, France where he is affiliated with the Laboratoire de Psychologie Expérimentale et Quantitative. He earned his Ph.D. in Industrial/Organizational Psychology at the Pennsylvania State University and began his academic career at Louisiana State University before moving to France. He has published research in both English and French on topics such as job satisfaction, organizational justice in personnel selection, and performance appraisal in journals such as *Journal of Applied Psychology, Journal of Occupational and Organizational Psychology,* and *Human Relations.* Currently, he is conducting research on cognitive processing of organizational justice information, attitudes toward personnel selection in France, and on individual differences in time orientation. He is an associate editor of the journal, *Revue Internationale de Psychologie Sociale/International Review of Social Psychology*.

Steven K. Su received his Ph.D. in Business from Stanford University. He is an Assistant Professor of Organizational Behavior at INSEAD, in Fontainebleau, France. Prior to entering academics, he worked in both the investment banking and management consulting industries. His research focuses on issues of conflict management and decision-making.

Catherine H. Tinsley is as Assistant Professor at the McDonough School of Business at Georgetown University. She received her Masters and PhD from Northwestern University. She is on the editorial board of *The Academy of Management Journal* and *International Negotiations: A Journal of Theory and Practice*. She studies how factors such as culture, reputations, and mobility influence how people negotiate and how they manage conflict. She has published in *Journal of Applied Psychology, Organization Behavior and Human Decision Processes, American Sociological Review, Research in Organizational Behavior, Journal of International Business Studies, Research on Negotiations in Organizations, Negotiation Journal, and International Negotiation*.

Kees van den Bos got his PhD in 1996 with high honors (*cum laude*) at Leiden University, the Netherlands. He is a consulting editor of the *Interpersonal Relations and Group Processes* of the *Journal of Personality and Social Psychology*. His research interests focus on the psychology of fairness judgments and how people react to events they consider fair or unfair. To explore these interests, he used and expanded insights of theories like fairness heuristic theory, the group-value and relational models, referent cognitions theory, and terror management theory. Other research interests include human decision-making, social cognition, and organizational behavior. He won a dissertation award of the Association of Dutch Social Psychologists and obtained a fellowship from the Royal Netherlands Academy of Arts and Sciences. Currently he is an assistant professor at the Department of Social Psychology at the Free University in Amsterdam, the Netherlands.

HD
6971.3
.T474
2001